QUILTMAKING TIPS and TECHNIQUES

QUILTMAKING TIPS and TECHNIQUES

*Over 1,000 Creative Ideas
to Make Your Quiltmaking
Quicker, Easier
and a Lot More Fun*

From 60 Top-Notch Quilters and the Editors of
Quilter's Newsletter Magazine

Written by Jane Townswick
Edited by Suzanne Nelson

Rodale Press, Emmaus, Pennsylvania

OUR PURPOSE

*"We inspire and enable people to improve
their lives and the world around them."*

Printed in the United States of America on acid-free ∞ ,
recycled ♻ paper

Editor: Suzanne Nelson
Interior Designer: Denise Shade
Cover Designer: Patricia Field
Cover Photographer: Mitch Mandel
Cover Photo Stylist: Marianne Grape Laubach
Copy Editor: Patricia A. Sinnott
Illustrators: Barbara Field, Janet Bohn, and
    Kathleen M. Geosits
Manufacturing Coordinator: Patrick T. Smith
Indexer: Nanette Bendyna
Administrative Assistant: Susan L. Nickol
Editorial Assistance: Deborah Weisel

Rodale Home and Garden Books
Vice President and Editorial Director:
    Margaret J. Lydic
Managing Editor, Quilt Books: Suzanne Nelson
Associate Art Director: Patricia Field
Studio Manager: Leslie M. Keefe
Copy Director: Dolores Plikaitis
Book Manufacturing Director: Helen Clogston
Office Manager: Karen Earl-Braymer

About the Cover: The quilt blocks were created by
Suzanne Nelson, Karen Soltys, and Tanya L. Lipinski.
The rotary cutter was provided by Olfa; the rotary ruler,
by Omnigrid, Inc.; and the appliqué scissors, by Dovo.

We're happy to hear from you.

For questions or comments concerning the
editorial content of this book, please write to:
    Rodale Press, Inc.
    Book Readers' Service
    33 East Minor Street
    Emmaus, PA 18098

Visit our World Wide Web site at
http://www.quilters.com, the best source for
quiltmaking news you can use.

ISBN 0–87596–958–5 paperback

**The Library of Congress has cataloged the
hardcover edition as follows:**

Townswick, Jane
    Quiltmaking tips and techniques: over 1,000
    creative ideas to make your quiltmaking quicker,
    easier, and a lot more fun: from 60 top-notch quilters
    and the editors of *Quilter's Newsletter Magazine* /
    written by Jane Townswick; edited by Suzanne Nelson
        p.   cm.
    Includes index.
    ISBN 0–87596–588–1 hardcover
    1. Patchwork 2. Appliqué. 3. Quilting. I. Nelson,
Suzanne. II. Quilter's newsletter magazine.
III. Title.
TT835.T69   1994
746.9'7—dc20   93–29301

Distributed in the book trade by St. Martin's Press

2 4 6 8 10 9 7 5 3 1   paperback
   4 6 8 10 9 7 5 3   hardcover

Contents

Foreword

Don't you love it when someone shares a clever idea with you that immediately solves some prickly problem you're having? You are likely to say to yourself, "Of course! Now why didn't I think of that?" You just wish you had known about it sooner. This book is full of those kinds of bright ideas. Not only will they solve quiltmaking problems for you, but they also will prevent your having problems as you make your next quilt, whether it is your first quilt or your twentieth.

The reason the tips and techniques in this book are so valuable is that they come from dozens of quiltmaking "experts." My definition of a quiltmaking expert is a person who has had substantial experience actually making quilts and who has learned, through trying and mastering a variety of procedures, what works most successfully. This book is rich in hundreds of years of accumulated experience of the greatest number of quilting experts ever assembled between two book covers.

Who are these experts and how were their ideas gathered? Among them are practicing quiltmakers—both staff and readers—who have contributed to *Quilter's Newsletter Magazine*. More than 250 back issues of the magazine were mined for those nuggets of information that can enhance some portion of the quiltmaking process by making it easier, quicker, or more productive.

The editors and artists at *QNM* have been learning from the experience of the magazine's readers for a quarter of a century. Since the magazine was started in the late 1960s, its editors and readers have had an energetic dialogue going about tips and techniques for making quilts. In response to invitations to contribute their best suggestions for quiltmaking strategies and methods, readers have sent their ideas about ways to plan, design, and sew quilts. Those of us who have been with *QNM* over the past 25 years have tried those suggestions, chosen the best of them, and included them in the pages of the magazine. Other readers have put them into practice, improved on them and expanded them, and shared the results of their experience. These good ideas from the many experienced quiltmakers who have contributed tips, techniques, and treasures to *QNM* have been included in this book.

During the past quarter century, the ongoing and growing *QNM* staff also has been making quilts, discovering their own tricks and tips for making them more easily. Recently, we calculated that our combined quiltmaking and designing experience totals quite a bit more than 200 years. And these years of practice have resulted in some recognized successes that indicate quality experience. Several members of our staff have had their quilts accepted into juried exhibits and have won prizes in various competitions over time. Of course, we have written about what we have learned, and many of our most helpful ideas have been collected for this book. Often, they have been updated and enhanced with new information and recent innovations.

But there are still more experts represented in this book. Thirty well-known, highly regarded professionals from the quilt world—teachers, authors, editors, and quilt-shop owners—were interviewed and asked for their most helpful and up-to-date tips and hints on how to save time, money, and energy in the making of quilts. They were generous in sharing favorite ideas they have discovered.

The result of collecting so much wisdom from the accumulated experience of so many people is an informative and entertaining book of exceptionally wide scope. It is the kind of book that at first you will want to read page by page to savor the full import of its content, then you will leaf through periodically to find good ideas and inspiration; and it is the book you will want to keep handy to look up immediate solutions to specific problems. *Quiltmaking Tips and Techniques* is sure to make you exclaim again and again, "Why didn't I think of that before!"

Bonnie Leman

Bonnie Leman, Editor-in-Chief
Quilter's Newsletter Magazine

Introduction

At the heart of this book is the considerable quiltmaking expertise of the staff and contributing editors of America's foremost quilt publication, *Quilter's Newsletter Magazine* (referred to as *QNM* throughout this book). Combined with this is a treasure trove of timely and topical tips, hints, and innovative ideas from 30 of today's most successful and gifted quiltmakers. Each of these experts very graciously shared his or her know-how and experience in quiltmaking over the course of an hour-long telephone interview, giving specific and useful ideas and tips that help make quilting quicker, easier, more creative, and just plain fun. Having this book by your sewing table is the next best thing to spending a day in a workshop with each of these very talented and respected quiltmakers.

The tips and techniques are organized according to the steps involved in making a quilt, so use the Contents to easily locate a chapter on the general topic you want to read about. Once you've turned to a chapter, use the different levels of headings to help you pinpoint more specific information on the subject that interests you. This book has been designed to make it easy to browse through the pages, although there's so much exciting new and helpful information that you may find you want to take your time and read every tip.

Some very special features are included, written to be both fun and informative for quiltmakers. Each chapter has a "Shopping Savvy" box, pointing out some unusual or overlooked sources that carry first-rate quiltmaking tools and supplies. (Did you ever consider the supermarket or a hardware store as a haven for quiltmakers? You will now!) Also in every chapter, look for the light bulb—the logo for the "Creative Flash" box. There, you'll find clever and creative ideas that will motivate and inspire your quiltmaking endeavors.

The motivation behind putting all these tips and techniques together in one book is to give you the very best and very latest information on every aspect of quiltmaking in short, useful, fun-to-read segments. This book will have succeeded if it makes you pause and think, "I didn't know that!" followed by, "I can't wait to try that!"

Because quilters are always eager for an opportunity to learn more about the art of quilting, we thank all of the experts who contributed to this book for their willingness to share their trials, failures, successes, and most of all, their ongoing passion for making quilts.

Jane Townswick

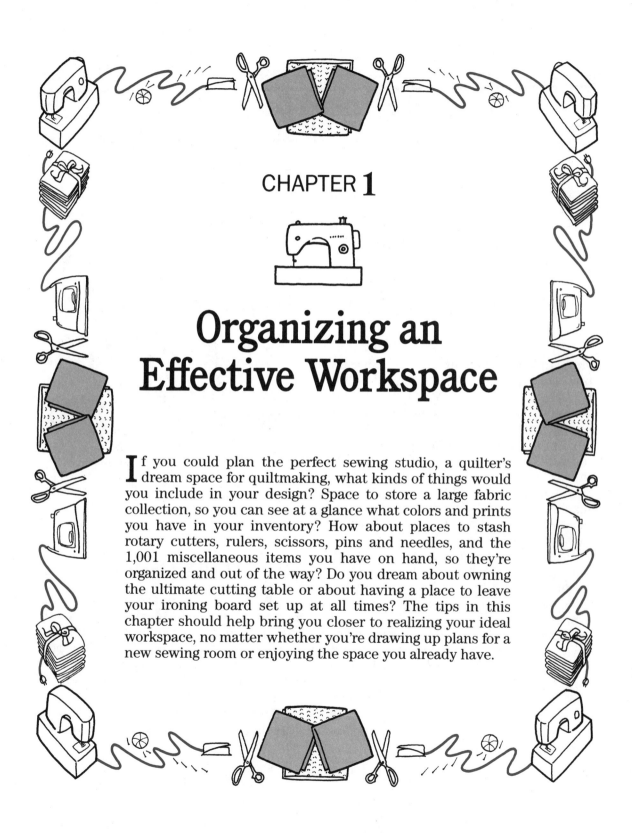

CHAPTER 1

Organizing an Effective Workspace

If you could plan the perfect sewing studio, a quilter's dream space for quiltmaking, what kinds of things would you include in your design? Space to store a large fabric collection, so you can see at a glance what colors and prints you have in your inventory? How about places to stash rotary cutters, rulers, scissors, pins and needles, and the 1,001 miscellaneous items you have on hand, so they're organized and out of the way? Do you dream about owning the ultimate cutting table or about having a place to leave your ironing board set up at all times? The tips in this chapter should help bring you closer to realizing your ideal workspace, no matter whether you're drawing up plans for a new sewing room or enjoying the space you already have.

The Well-Stocked Sewing Space

Choosing, Using, and Maintaining a Sewing Machine

❖ Go for a Test Drive! ❖

There are many superb sewing machines available now, and each one has its own strengths and weaknesses. I think it's best to shop for a sewing machine the way you would shop for a new car. Allow enough time to become familiar with a sewing machine—sit right down at the machine in the dealer's showroom and take it for a test drive! Knowing ahead of time which features you want in a sewing machine is helpful. For example, a built-in or attachable walking foot and a darning foot are good features to have for machine quilting, and if you like garment sewing, your machine should be able to make an attractive buttonhole with ease. When you shop for a machine, take along some of the fabrics you like to work with, as well as specialty threads (like nylon or metallic) if you use them. Machine quilters should take along a small portion of a layered quilt to practice on. The best advice I can give is to take whatever amount of time you need to satisfy yourself that the machine you buy will do all the kinds of sewing you want it to do.

Anne Colvin

❖ Sewing with Class ❖

When you purchase a new sewing machine, it's a good idea to take instructional classes from the dealer. And if you can arrange to take classes with other people, their questions will probably help you learn more than if you had taken individual instructions. And owner's manuals are worth reading—they are often helpful in learning the things your sewing machine can do.

Anne Colvin

❖ Fail-Safe Footfeed ❖

If your sewing machine foot control tends to slide away as you sew, try placing a strip of self-adhesive Velcro (the loop part, not the hook, which can snag carpet) on the bottom of it. If your studio has wood or tile flooring, you can purchase a carpet sample to put underneath the foot control and attach Velcro, as before. If the carpet sample seems slippery as well, place a small piece of rubber padding underneath it.

QNM Editors

❖ A Breath of Fresh Air ❖

It's a good idea to clean out the lint from your sewing machine each time you change the bobbin. Lint can build up very quickly in most machines, especially when you machine quilt on cotton battings. Keep a can of condensed air on hand and use it often, but sparingly, to clean out lint buildup from your machine. You can find cans of condensed air at local camera shops.

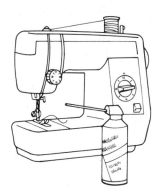

Anne Colvin

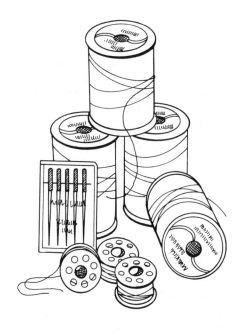

❖ Stress-Free ❖ Tension Adjustments

On most sewing machines, you can usually make all the tension changes you need by adjusting the top thread. Be cautious about making any changes to the bobbin tension. When you check for proper thread tension, start by threading your machine with the same brand and weight of thread on the top and bottom, but in two different colors (white for the top and red for the bottom, for example). That way, you can sew a seam and see whether the white thread is being pulled through to the wrong side of your fabric. If that's the case, your top tension is too loose. If the red thread is being pulled to the right side of the fabric, your top tension is too tight. I like to write down the number at which the tension was set before making any adjustments. That way, it's easy to go back to that original setting if you like.

Here's a checklist that may help you solve tension problems at home and avoid taking your machine in to the shop for major adjustments or repairs:

♦ The very first thing to try is to take the top and bobbin threads out of your machine and completely rethread it. If something has gotten stuck in one of the little tension disks, you may be able to dislodge it by simply pulling the thread out and threading the machine again.

♦ Make sure you're using the same brand and weight of thread on the top and in the bobbin.

♦ Make sure the bobbin and its case are inserted correctly.

♦ Put in a new needle.

♦ Oil the machine.

Liz Porter

machine. If you can't find a self-stick ruler, make your own with a regular ruler and two-sided tape.

QNM Editors

❖ Sound Advice ❖

To lessen the noise of a sewing machine and keep the machine from moving around on a table, try placing it on the kind of thick plastic mat typically used under typewriters, which you can find at an office supply store.

QNM Editors

❖ Inch by Inch, It's a Cinch ❖

For quick and easy measuring, place a self-stick ruler at the front edge of the mat or table underneath your sewing

❖ Patchwork in the Fast Lane ❖

If you're interested in speedy stitching, it's easy to fall in love with the quilter's "lean and mean sewing machine"! An overlock machine, or a serger, trims, stitches, and overcasts a seam in a single step. It works at a rate of up to 1,700 stitches per minute, or about twice the speed of a conventional sewing machine. If you're thinking about expanding on the tools and equipment in your sewing room, spend a moment reading about the features of sergers and the pros and cons of overlocked seams to help you decide whether a serger is right for you and your quiltmaking projects:

◆ There are several different types of sergers, but the basic mechanism is the same in each machine. A serger forms stitches over a metal stitch "finger" that prevents the edges of the fabric from drawing up. "Loopers" replace the bobbin of a regular sewing machine; looper stitches go over and under the edges of the fabric.

◆ Two-thread sergers have one needle and one looper that form a two-thread overedge stitch that finishes a seam allowance. This type of serger doesn't actually sew a seam, so it's not useful in making quilts.

Two-thread serger seam

◆ Three-thread overlock machines have one needle and an upper and a lower looper. The loopers go over and under the fabric and are caught by the needle thread. You can sew seams with this kind of serger, but it doesn't make any additional stitches to reinforce seams. It can be helpful for making small quilts that won't receive a lot of wear and tear.

Three-thread serger seam

◆ A three/four-thread overlock machine is basically a three-thread machine that makes an extra stitch down the middle using two needles and two loopers. The extra stitching adds strength and durability to a seam.

Three/four-thread serger seam

◆ A four-thread serger has two needles and an upper and a lower looper. It forms a two-thread chain stitch from the left needle and the lower looper, and the two remaining threads, threaded through the upper looper, form an overedge stitch. The combination of four threads forms a very strong seam, with a wide enough seam allowance to press easily to one side in a quilt.

Four-thread serger seam

◆ A five-thread overlock machine has two needles and three loopers, and it sews a two-thread chain stitch with a three-thread overlock stitch for added durability. This is a wonderful machine for sewing quilts with cotton fabrics.

Five-thread serger seam

- Because there are no bobbins in a serger, you won't spend time winding bobbin threads to match the colors of the thread you use in a quilt. You can thread a serger with a neutral shade of thread and sew for months without rethreading.

- Overcast seams lie neat and flat. The knife edge of a serger cuts off all sloppy, straying threads and trims seam allowances evenly.

- Pressing seam allowances to one side is easy when the seams are overlocked.

- Serged seams are very strong and they do not come apart, which can be a wonderful feature for frequently laundered children's quilts.

- Sergers feed two layers of fabric evenly, which is super for strip piecers, and a fabric guide attachment will allow you to produce perfect ¼-inch seams.

- When you use a serger, lifting a presser foot is unnecessary, which makes chain piecing easier on a serger than on a sewing machine. A serger doesn't jam when you operate it without fabric under the foot.

- Although the most daunting thing about a serger is threading it, most machines now come with color-coded thread guides and charts that help to simplify the process. And owner's manuals show you how to rethread the machine by tying new threads onto the tails of the old threads and pulling them gently through the machine.

- Because there is a lot of thread in an overcast seam, the seam allowances are usually bulkier than those sewn on a regular sewing machine. Sergers are not meant to replace sewing machines, but to be used in addition to regular machines to make finishing seams easier and quicker.

Eleanor Burns

Effective Lighting

❖ Highlight Your Stitches ❖

Fluorescent light is a more advanced alternative to "hot" incandescent lighting. Besides being energy effient, compact, and cool to work under, fluorescent lamps can help in accurate color perception. Some lamps have magnifying lenses and are also adjustable, so that you can rotate them directly over your work to highlight the area you're stitching.

QNM Editors

❖ The Light from Above ❖

Even the best lighting can sometimes be inadequate if the angle is wrong. The best solution is to eliminate, or at least reduce, shadows on your work. In general, light from an overhead source works well enough for most machine sewing, but a light source from the left is usually better. For hand sewing, the light source should be directed from the left for right-handed people and from the right for left-handed stitchers.

QNM Editors

❖ The Traveling Quilter ❖

To make it easier to sew when you're on the go, use a battery-powered portable light that hangs around your neck. Some of these lights can also be plugged into electrical wall outlets—or even into car lighters! This type of light isn't a substitute for a floor or table lamp with a high-watt bulb, but it can make it possible to sew while traveling, so you don't have to leave your projects at home.

QNM Editors

❖ Always Travel Light ❖

When you go on vacation or to an out-of-town quilt show, tuck a 100-watt light bulb in your suitcase for stitching in hotel rooms. Or for the ultimate in portable light sources, take along a tiny high-intensity lamp—the kind made for reading at night.

QNM Editors

Furnishings

❖ It's High Time ❖

To reduce back strain, why not try raising your sewing machine 4 to 6 inches above average table height? And if you have an adjustable chair, lower it. The closer your eyes are to the throat plate on the machine, the less likely you will be to lean over and strain your back.

QNM Editors

❖ Big Wheel ❖

An office chair that has wheels, swivels, and is adjustable for height is perfect for quilting at a floor frame. The wheels will roll easily around the frame or across a floor. The swivel feature enables you to find your most comfortable position, and the adjustable height allows you to raise or lower the seat to a comfortable level.

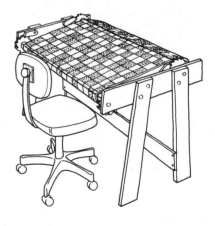

QNM Editors

❖ Cutting in Stereo ❖

One of the things I like and use most in my sewing area is a stereo cabinet that I bought inexpensively at a wooden furniture store. It's exactly kitchen counter height and is ½ inch larger on all sides than my rotary-cutting mat. It has doors on the front and adjustable shelves inside, which are great for storing templates, fabric, and rotary-cutting equipment.

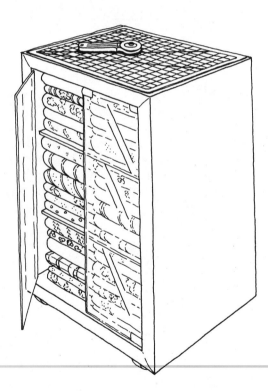

Sharyn Squier Craig

A SPACE TO CALL YOUR OWN

Many of us have very limited space to devote solely to our sewing, but I really think it's important to have some small area that you can call your very own. For many quilters, time spent stitching is an escape, a creative outlet, a way to relax and unwind. All of those important reasons call for a space of your own. For years, my only sewing area was in a closet, where I gathered equipment and tools and created a usable workroom. An extension cord gave me easy access to electrical power for my sewing machine. I hung an inexpensive under-the-shelf lamp beneath the closet shelf so that I could see to sew. I put pegboard on the back wall, with hooks on it for little shelves to hold my scissors, threads, and other sewing notions. It might not have been spacious, but it was functional, self-contained, and wonderful.

❖ Sharyn Squier Craig

❖ Wonderful Worktables ❖

To design a worktable for your sewing room, think about the features that will be helpful for your own style of working, as well as the space you have available. Here are a few ideas for inexpensive, easy-to-make worktables. See if any of these suit your needs, or add features that will make them perfect for you and your quilt-making activities.

♦ You can make a great plywood table that folds down from wooden storage shelves. Start by cutting slots that will accommodate bent metal fittings in a board, and fasten the board to the front of the shelves. Then attach the plywood to the board and attach hinged legs to the opposite side of the plywood. This table will fold up and hide the shelves when you're not using it.

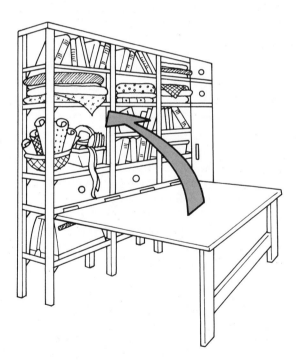

♦ Make a quilter's version of a gateleg table by putting two hinged sheets of plywood onto a base cabinet. Then attach a hinged piece of plywood at each end of the cabinet. These swing-out ends will support the top when it's unfolded.

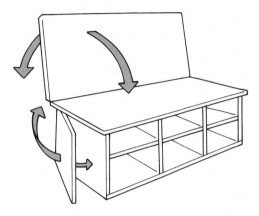

♦ Install shelf fronts on a bookcase that will open out to create table legs, and add a door that folds down to create a tabletop. You can attach magnetic fasteners or hooks to hold the door when you want it closed.

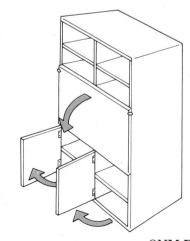

QNM Editors

Equipment and Accessories

❖ That's Easel for You to Say ❖

I often use a small, portable flannel design board when I'm piecing. I like to lay out all the pieces for one block on the board to keep them organized as I stitch the block together. I find that by keeping a block laid out on my board at all times, I can use free minutes here and there to sew. You can make a flannel design board like mine from an 18×24-inch piece of pegboard, corrugated cardboard, foam core board, or any other kind of sturdy board. Wrap flannel or batting around the front and tape it in place on the back.

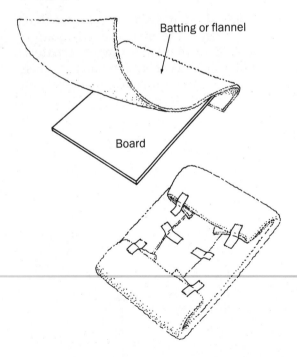

Batting or flannel

Board

Sharyn Squier Craig

THERE'S A REASON THEY CALL IT A "SUPER" MARKET!

Don't overlook your neighborhood grocery store as a great source of handy tools and supplies for your quiltmaking projects. Next time you go grocery shopping, take along this list of "have-to-have" supplies for quilting:

✳ Freezer paper, the absolute staple of many appliqué techniques

✳ Graph paper, for pattern drafting and designing quilts

✳ Shelf paper, for drawing sections of quilting and appliqué border designs

✳ Children's coloring books, for appliqué designs

✳ Index cards, for English paper piecing

✳ Permanent markers, for writing and drawing lines on template plastic

✳ A spoon, for catching the tip of a basting needle when you baste the layers of a quilt together

✳ Toothpicks, for needle-turn appliqué

❖ Jane Townswick

❖ Berry Interesting! ❖

Nearly everyone has seen the little strawberry emery on a tomato pincushion, and most people know that it is very handy for sharpening needles, pins, and safety pins. What's not so well known is that there's a trick to using it. Just stick a needle or pin straight into the emery and then pull back on the sides of the fabric with your fingers, compacting the crystals. Then move the pin gently in a circular motion, and the crystals will grate against the point, sharpening it quickly and easily.

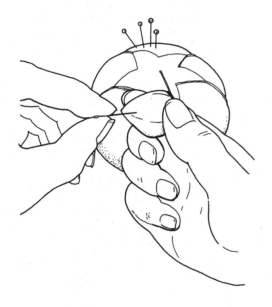

Debra Wagner

❖ No More Ironing Bored ❖

For quick and convenient pressing, set up a low ironing board or padded surface at a right angle to your sewing machine. Add to this arrangement a chair that swivels, and there's no need to get up every time you want to press a seam.

QNM Editors

❖ Choose Cotton Covers ❖

I avoid putting a reflective cover, like the ones covered with silver Teflon, on an ironing board because these covers were made to use with synthetic fabrics. They reflect heat, which means you can set your iron at a lower temperature and still get good pressing results on synthetics. But when you're a quilter working with cottons and the higher iron temperatures they require, you can sometimes burn fabrics this way. To be on the safe side, I like to use a cotton covering for my ironing board.

Doreen Speckmann

❖ Keep a Travel Iron at Home ❖

I recommend having a travel iron at your sewing table for pressing patchwork blocks. This type of iron works much better than the kind of large, heavy iron used for pressing garments, because it doesn't distort fabric as much (and it's also kinder on your hands and wrists because it's easier to lift and maneuver). I lower my ironing board so that the point fits under my sewing table. The travel iron is right there, ready for me to use, and the rest of the ironing board surface is a handy place to lay out blocks.

Carol Doak

❖ Mark This Down! ❖

I like to store my blue water-soluble markers in self-sealing plastic bags to keep them from evaporating quickly. In addition,

I place them in a tall tin container, in a vertical position with the tips down, so the ink will flow easily whenever I want to use a marker.

Debra Wagner

❖ Dental Assistance ❖

For an unusual and lovely accent to your sewing room, look for an old-fashioned wooden dentist's cabinet. The many small drawers have porcelain dividers that can provide storage for your small quilting tools and accessories, making the cabinet a practical, as well as a beautiful, addition to your workspace.

QNM Editors

❖ Doing Two Things at Once ❖

Make the most of the time you have for quiltmaking—put a speakerphone in your sewing room! This will allow you to continue working while you talk. Or, if you have a regular telephone, try using a shoulder phone-rest to cradle the receiver between your ear and your shoulder while you continue to sew or quilt.

QNM Editors

- ◆ An electric mug warmer will keep your coffee or tea at the perfect sipping temperature while you sew.
- ◆ An audiocassette player will let you stitch to the sound of your favorite symphony or enjoy a current best-seller.
- ◆ A TV with a VCR will let you weep over the good-bye scene in the movie *Casablanca* or watch a quilt program on your local Public Broadcasting Station—from the comfort of your own sewing room.

QNM Editors

❖ You Deserve It! ❖

A cozy and comfortable workspace with all the amenities can make your quiltmaking time pure ecstasy. Try some of these little treats to help you relax and get your creative juices flowing:

❖ Kid-Friendly Sewing Space ❖

Since I spend a lot of time in my sewing room, my two little girls naturally gravitate there. I've found that with the right things around for them to play with, I can manage to spend an hour or two at a time blissfully sewing, surrounded by my two favorite little people. Here are some of the sewing room strategies I've used to keep them happy and occupied while I work on my quilts:

◆ Scrap bags bursting with bits of fabric are a never-ending source of entertainment. My girls sort the pieces by color, make giant mosaics on the floor, or use fabric squares and strips to make togas for Troll dolls (held in place by rubber bands).

◆ Spools of thread make great sewing room substitutes for building blocks.

◆ A stash of sewing room toys has come in very handy. These are toys that they play with only when they're in the room with me. The novelty factor ensures that they'll be interested in playing with them for a good stretch of time.

◆ A portable tape player is a must. The three of us have spent many afternoons absorbed in various kids' books on tape or even tapes of children's music.

◆ Promoting my older daughter, who is six, to sewing assistant has made her much more interested in watching me sew. She sits next to me, in charge of pins or stacks of patches, and hands them to me as I need them. The best benefit of this is that she is picking up pointers on quiltmaking without my actually having to "teach" her.

Suzanne Nelson

Storing Fabric, Tools, and Equipment

Creative Storage Ideas for Fabric and Batting

❖ Getting Things ❖ Out in the Open

I like to store my fabrics on shelves, where I can look at them as I work. Fabric and color are stimulating, and I often get inspiration from looking at them. If you store your fabrics folded up and out of sight, you tend to forget exactly what you have, which can stifle your creativity. Storing fabrics in a light-filled room can cause them to fade, however, so you should have some way to darken the room if you display your fabrics on open shelves. For example, you could keep your fabrics in a cupboard with doors that can be closed when you're not working.

Mary Mashuta

❖ Fabulous Fabric Files ❖

All of my fabrics are neatly tucked away in file cabinets. I prefer to keep my fabrics out of sight because I find that looking at all that color at the same time can sometimes be too stimulating and overwhelming. I do like to be able to locate my fabrics easily when I need them, however, so I organize them by color families, fold them, and put them into drawers so that each fabric is visible when the drawer is open.

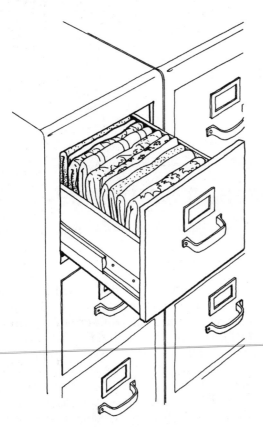

Sharyn Squier Craig

❖ Putting Prints in Plastic ❖

My favorite fabric storage place is clear plastic boxes that let me see the colors and prints. I organize and sort fabrics by color, so that if I need reds, I can just reach for the right box and go through my red shades. Since my fabric collection is of long standing, it's difficult to organize so many differently shaped pieces neatly. Keeping fabrics in plastic boxes is a practical way to store them, no matter what shape they are.

Marsha McCloskey

❖ Fabrics at Your Fingertips ❖

I like to use plastic-lidded tubs, like the ones made by Rubbermaid, for fabric storage. I fold the fabrics and place them upright in each tub, so when I take the lid off, each fabric is visible. I label the ends of the tubs and store them on shelves above my file cabinets. I've found that this is a great way to keep my fabrics easily accessible whenever I need them.

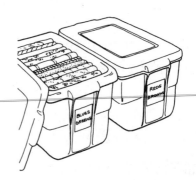

Sharyn Squier Craig

❖ "Planned-Overs" ❖ instead of Leftovers!

When I'm cutting strips, squares, rectangles, and triangles for one project, I'll cut some extra ones on purpose for my "planned-over" bins. I have a whole set of lidded plastic storage boxes labeled first by color, then by size of strips, and I keep "feeding" this inventory with every project I cut. I also collect the extra squares, rectangles, and triangles in plastic boxes according to shape and size. This gives me a ready-made collection of precut fabrics that will be perfect for some project someday!

Sharyn Squier Craig

❖ Shade Your Bookcase ❖

If you store your fabric collection in a bookcase or on shelves where it might be exposed to sunlight, you can protect it by covering the bookcase or shelves with inexpensive window shades. You can have shades cut to whatever size you need. For example, if you have shelves that are 6 feet wide, you could use three 2-foot-wide shades to cover them.

Sharyn Squier Craig

❖ Closet Organizers ❖

If you don't have one specific closet, room, or space in which you can store your fabric collection, consider these ideas for organizing your treasures and keeping them within easy reach:

◆ Install a few shelves in a spare closet and use them to store your fabrics.

◆ Go through the closet in your bedroom and get rid of anything you haven't used in the past year. Then invest in a closet organizer system and make the most of this new space for fabric.

storage systems to discover new and different storage possibilities.

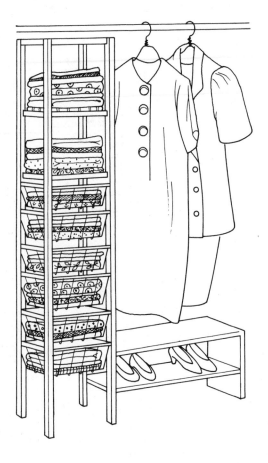

♦ Use baskets, antique furniture, or stacks of pretty hatboxes to store and display a profusion of colorful prints.

♦ Corrugated boxes, steel shelves, and unfinished furniture may not be especially elegant, but they are perfectly functional places to stash your fabrics.

♦ Put a coatrack in your foyer and use the hall closet for storing your fabrics out of direct sunlight.

♦ Explore dime stores, mail-order catalogs, kitchen shops, office supply stores, and shops that specialize in

QNM Editors

❖ Clever Fabric Hideaways ❖

Many quiltmakers share this dilemma: Where do you hide fabric from anyone who doesn't understand why you need it all? Creative storage saves the day! Here are some of the suggestions and ideas I've heard from customers in my quilt shop:

◆ Store your newest fabric treasures in the attic.

◆ Tuck your purchases into a box labeled "Christmas ornaments" or "baby clothes."

◆ Stash stripes, prints, and solids in the freezer, wrapped in butcher paper and labeled "meat loaf."

◆ Go fabric hunting with a friend, trade shopping bags before you go home, and then proclaim, "This fabric isn't mine—I'm just holding it for a friend."

◆ The trunk of a car keeps fabrics safely stored away from direct sunlight and prying eyes.

◆ A wire coat hanger will usually support up to 2 yards of fabric, with a dress or blouse covering it.

◆ You can hide your fabrics in plain sight—on an open shelf, neatly folded and color-coordinated to your room decor.

Kay Steinmetz

❖ Batts in the Belfry ❖

Rather than use valuable sewing room space for batting, store it in unexpected places, such as under beds, in linen closets, or in empty suitcases. Just keep it rolled and wrapped in plastic so that it stays dust-free and ready to use.

QNM Editors

❖ Taming the Wild Batts ❖

Batting is one of the most difficult things to store because it's bulky, lightweight, and the plastic bag it comes in is usually slippery. One of my students stores her batts in a small closet and keeps them in place by putting up a tension curtain rod in front of them. That way, her batts are contained, and she can pull one out and still keep the others in place.

Sharyn Squier Craig

Storing Tools and Equipment

❖ A New Slant ❖

On the wall of my sewing room, I have slanted office files that I use for storing things that don't have holes in them for hanging on a pegboard. These files are great for keeping rotary rulers within easy reach, and you can add more files as you collect more things to store in them.

and even to keep rotary cutters accessible yet safely out of reach of small children. You can also put cup hooks inside a closet door and use them to store stencils vertically and organized by border and block designs.

Sharyn Squier Craig

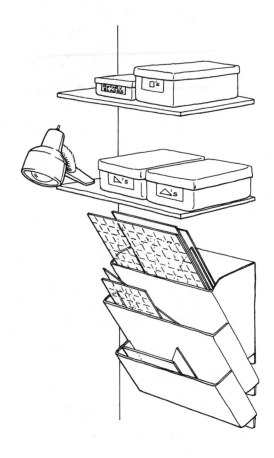

Sharyn Squier Craig

❖ Creative Hooking ❖

I like to hang cup hooks underneath my shelves to hold templates and rulers

❖ That's a Cool Idea ❖

To keep your glue sticks fresh and avoid having them dry out or turn moldy, keep them in the refrigerator!

Sharyn Squier Craig

❖ Dear Diary ❖

To keep project directions clean and neat, slip pattern instruction sheets into a clear plastic page protector. After completing a quilt, add scraps of the fabrics used, make a note of the date you finished the project, and include any other pertinent information (such as the number of hours or months you spent on the quilt). Put the plastic page in a binder as a record of your quiltmaking. You'll enjoy reminiscing about past projects, and future family members will thank you.

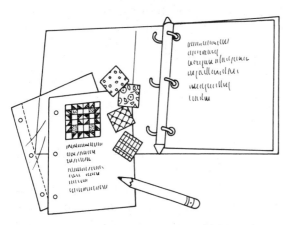

QNM Editors

❖ Start a Block Box ❖

When I start a project, I like to get a box large enough to hold and organize all of the cut pieces. I may spend an entire morning just cutting pieces for this project, and I store everything in that box, including my templates.

Sharyn Squier Craig

❖ Keep an Idea File ❖

Whenever you find quilting designs you like, trace them on artist's tracing paper and keep the designs together in a manila file folder. The next time you need a quilting design, you'll be able to find the perfect motif quickly and easily, without having to go through your entire library of quilt books.

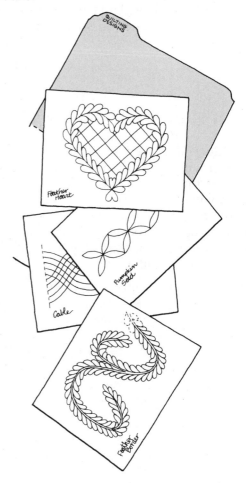

QNM Editors

❖ Material Matters ❖

If you are packing for a move, you can save time and space and make unpacking and organizing your new sewing room a joy by using your fabric collection as packing material for your tools and equipment. Folded fabric makes a great cushion for fragile treasures, and scraps of batting tuck easily into box corners to create extra padding for breakables. And whole batts make ideal supports for lamp shades or other large items.

QNM Editors

❖ The Earth-Friendly Quilter ❖

Recycling is a way of life today, which ties in with the quiltmaking tradition of "use it up, wear it out, or make do." To help you carry on that proud tradition, here are some suggestions for creatively organizing and storing your quilting paraphernalia and reusing common household castoffs at the same time:

◆ Diaper wipe containers are terrific for storing lots of small notions: marking pens and pencils; small plastic templates; rotary cutters and spare blades; buttons, beads, and other embellishments; and spools of thread.
◆ Small cream cheese and margarine containers with tight-fitting lids make perfect traveling containers for pins. They'll also hold rotary blades, thimbles, extra bobbins, and premade bias stems.
◆ Laundry detergent boxes are perfect for storing magazines upright while allowing you to see the covers. When you've shaken out the last granules of detergent, cover the outside of the box with wrapping paper or some wallpaper remnants, and you'll have a handy shelf organizer for back issues of your favorite quilt magazine.
◆ Foam meat trays are lightweight, lap-size, and make handy, portable work surfaces. Use them to collect scraps and snips of thread, to arrange patches for your next quilt block, and to hold pins and needles.

Suzanne Nelson

❖ Storage all ❖ around the House

You can find lots of places to store quilts and quilt-related items around the house, some of them surprisingly unexpected and useful. The table on the opposite page lists some ideas for creative storage options. Once you read through this listing, you may be able to add some ideas of your own.

QNM Editors

Innovative Storage Ideas

Item	Where to Store
Finished quilts	Armoires, blanket chests, cedar chests, clothes racks, dressers, large covered baskets, linen closets, open shelves, quilt racks
Works-in-progress	Baskets, rolling carts, sweater boxes, tote bags
Fabrics	Armoires, bookcases, closets, cupboards, dressers, étagères, open shelves, pie safes, stacking bins
Scraps	Baskets, buckets, canvas bags from quilt shows, laundry sorters, lingerie bags, pails, produce crates, rolling carts, stacking bins, sweater boxes
Batting	Closets, deep shelves, underneath worktable
Sewing notions	Antique spool chests, baskets, desk drawers, multidrawer organizers, pegboards, stacking bins, tool chests
Large tools	Broom closets, deep shelves, hooks, inside closet doors, map chests, pegboards, underneath worktables
Drafting tools (rulers, etc.)	Baskets, desk drawers, hatboxes, rolling carts, sewing cabinets, shaker boxes, spool chests, stacking bins
Sewing machine	Tabletop, covered when not in use
Ironing board	Set up at all times

CHAPTER 2

Color and Fabric

What quilter hasn't at some time felt an almost physical pull toward a kaleidoscopic array of bright-hued fabric bolts lined up on a quilt-shop shelf? We all have our own unique sense of color, a personal palette of hues, shades, and intensities that call out to us, practically demanding to take their places in our quilts. Are you drawn to a luxuriant rainbow of solids? Or does the deep, dark jewel-toned spectrum invite you to stitch? Whatever you like, when you've chosen the fabrics for a quilt you want to make, the most important question still remains: How much will be enough? To make sure you can answer that question easily, handy yardage-figuring charts are provided so you'll be sure to get enough of the colors you love.

Shopping for Quilt Fabrics

Helpful Hints When You're Looking at Fabrics

❖ That's Child's Play ❖

When you're coordinating fabrics for your next quilt project, try looking at them through a child's kaleidoscope—the kind that is a tube of cardboard with a clear marble at one end. Turn it this way and that, and the fabrics will seem to dance in colorful configurations. If you like the way the colors and prints look together when you see them through the kaleidoscope, chances are they will also please you in a quilt.

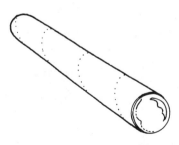

Eleanor Burns

❖ Binoculars ❖ in a Fabric Store?

In choosing colors for a quilt, the name of the game is the way color values (or their degree of lightness or darkness) move across the design. When you reach the point where you can go to a fabric store and look at any piece of fabric and think of it immediately as a dark, medium, light, or medium-light, you'll have made a quantum leap in putting fabrics together effectively. To help you see color values more easily, take a pair of binoculars with you the next time you go shopping. Look at fabrics through the "wrong" end, and you'll see value more, color less.

Margaret Miller

❖ It's All a Blur . . . ❖ But That's Good

If you wear glasses for nearsightedness, try taking your glasses off when you study color combinations in a fabric store. The figures and prints of each fabric will be blurry, and you'll get a whole new perspective on colors, scale differences, and contrast levels.

QNM Editors

❖ A Portable Palette ❖

Collect paint samples, fabric swatches, and scraps of carpeting for each room in your house. Place each set of samples in a self-sealing plastic bag, labeled on the outside with the name of the room. Then you can carry the "room" with you whenever you go shopping for fabrics.

QNM Editors

❖ A Pretty Packet of Prints ❖

If you've already decided on some of the fabrics for your next project and you want to shop for others to go with them, clip off a corner of each fabric you have and put the pieces into a plastic page protector. Pop it into a three-ring binder and take the binder along with you whenever you go fabric shopping. You can include some graph paper and some blank paper for figuring yardages, and if your three-ring binder has a pocket on the inside, slip in a small pocket calculator to help with any figuring you might need to do.

QNM Editors

THROUGH THE LOOKING GLASS

A quilter's reducing glass is a very helpful tool to use when you are coordinating fabrics. You can buy one of these lenses at most quilt shops. The tool looks like a regular magnifying glass, but it gives just the opposite effect, making things seem smaller and farther away. By looking at fabrics through this kind of lens, you'll see them as though at a distance, which can be very helpful in evaluating levels of color contrast. You'll notice the actual values of the fabrics rather than the prints.

❖ Roberta Horton

Helpful Hints on Buying Fabrics

❖ Feed Your Fabric Collection ❖

One way to shop for fabrics is to think in terms of "feeding your collection" when it is low on certain colors. Thinking about your fabric collection in this way can also help you learn to purchase even those shades you might not particularly like. I like to think that just as a gardener feeds the soil, not the plants, so a quilter needs to feed her fabric collection and not necessarily buy fabrics for a particular quilt only.

Marsha McCloskey

❖ Fabric to Dye For ❖

Dye lots can sometimes be dramatically different from one bolt of fabric to another, so if possible, make sure to buy enough from one bolt to cut all the patches of that print that you'll need for your quilt. If that isn't possible and you need to buy from a second bolt, try to separate the patches that you've cut from each bolt so that they don't occur right next to each other in your quilt. The closer they are, the more noticeable the difference in color will be.

QNM Editors

❖ Fabric Marriages ❖

For a more versatile fabric collection, try to buy a variety of print scales and fabric types. Look for geometric prints, florals, stripes, plaids, and checks, as well as solids. If you tend to buy the same kinds of fabrics and color families again and again, consider "marrying" your fabric collection to that of a quilting friend whose collection tends to differ from yours. If you know you're usually drawn to only jewel tones and brights, large-scale prints, and bold geometrics, consider trading several fabrics with a friend who loves grayed tones, pastels, smaller-scale prints, or florals. Both of your collections will be enriched by this fabric "marriage."

Sharyn Squier Craig

Personal Fabric Buying Guide

Hue	Solid	Print	Value			Intensity	
			Light	Medium	Dark	Bright	Dull
Red							
Red-orange							
Orange							
Yellow-orange							
Yellow							
Yellow-green							
Green							
Blue-green							
Blue							
Blue-violet							
Violet							
Red-violet							
Neutral							
Total							

SOURCE: **Personal Buying Guide, workbook pages 46 and 47, first published in *Color and Cloth*, by Mary Coyne Penders, The Quilt Digest Press, 1989.**

Hue	Scale					Layout		Visual Texture	
	Very Small	Small	Medium	Large	Very Large	Random	Repeat	Describe	Describe
Red									
Red-orange									
Orange									
Yellow-orange									
Yellow									
Yellow-green									
Green									
Blue-green									
Blue									
Blue-violet									
Violet									
Red-violet									
Neutral									
Total									

❖ Fantastic Fat Quarters ❖

Consider increasing the number of colors you buy for your fabric collection by starting with small amounts of many different hues. Try to purchase the ones you need, as well as the ones you already like. If you know that you don't like orange and will probably never want to use a lot of it in a quilt, it is easier and less expensive to buy it for your collection by purchasing just small amounts. Most fabric shops will cut ¼-yard lengths, but fat quarters (18 inches × 22 inches) are a more workable size. Then when you make glued fabric mock-ups of your quilt blocks, you'll be able to pull the right color from your fabric collection. If you're pleased with the color combination, you can then go ahead and purchase the amount needed to complete the project. I think it would be ideal to buy small amounts of fabrics in all 12 colors as represented on the color wheel, in all of the values, from the palest pale to the deepest dark and from the brightest to the dullest intensities.

Mary Coyne Penders

❖ Quilter's Hanky-Panky ❖

Vacations and travels of any kind offer a perfect chance to stock up on unusual additions to your fabric collection. I love to visit quilt shops whenever I travel, but it isn't always easy to fit a shopping trip into a tight tour schedule or into days filled with teaching or taking workshops and classes. Even on the busiest of days, though, it's still possible to find beautiful cotton fabrics for your collection by making a point of looking in airport or hotel gift shops for cotton handkerchiefs! I like to find colorful hankies made of high-quality cotton fabrics suitable for quilt-making. They're wonderful reminders of other cities and foreign countries, and they can become unique accents in your quilts.

Nancy J. Martin

❖ Take Stock of Your Stash ❖

Whether you want to catalog your current collection of colors or add new shades to your fabric library, an inventory list can be helpful. You can draw up an inventory sheet of your own, or you may photocopy the "Personal Fabric Buying Guide" on pages 26 and 27. Use it to record the colors, styles, and intensities of the fabrics you already have and those you need to purchase. Keep the sheet up-to-date and take it along whenever you go fabric hunting.

Mary Coyne Penders

Creative Color Use for Quilters

Understanding Color

❖ Hue and I Are Harmonious ❖

You can develop color schemes by looking at quilt pictures in books and magazines, but it is much more fun and surprisingly easy to devise your own combinations of color. Begin by looking at how the colors progress in even steps around the color wheel, from reds through oranges to yellows and from greens to blues to violets and back to reds. (To find a color wheel, check your local art store or find a book in your library that deals with color theory.) Here are a few general guidelines to follow when using a color wheel to work out color schemes for your quilts:

♦ Color complements are opposite each other on the color wheel. Each completes the other by providing what the other lacks of the full color spectrum. Combining color complements creates a harmonious color scheme.

♦ Good color schemes can be made from two colors that flank another and the complement of the middle color.

♦ Any two neighboring colors will go together.

♦ To keep a color scheme lively and brilliant, use a variety of values to create a good level of contrast. Include lights, mediums, darks, and very darks.

Judy Martin

❖ Shades of Prominence ❖

One of the most helpful things to know about color is that in any design, warm, dark, and pure colors will advance, while cool, light, and dull colors will recede. Warm colors are the colors of fire and the sun; cool colors are those of the sky and the sea and the grass. And pure colors are those of the color wheel in their most intense and saturated form—the reddest red and the bluest blue, for example. One thing you can do that will really show how color advances and recedes in a quilt block is to select an easy pattern like Ohio Star or Monkey Wrench and make it up using one warm and two cool fabrics, such as orange (warm), blue (cool), and green (cool). Then make a second block with the same fabrics, but place each color in a different position within the block. You'll be able to see immediately that the warm colors take over, because in each block, the areas that are orange will appear more prominent than the blue and green areas.

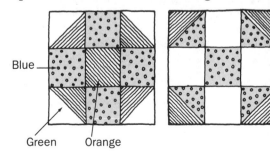

Susan McKelvey

29

LISTEN TO YOUR INNER VOICE

In working with color, it's important to pay attention to the feelings you have inside of you. Many of us are familiar with the concept that different parts of the brain are responsible for different thought patterns. The right brain is creative, intuitive, and nonverbal, whereas the left brain is the verbal part that can decide rules. Try to learn to listen to your right brain by paying attention to your inner feelings. These can take the form of an insistent feeling that you can't ignore, one that comes back to you again and again. Or it may seem as if a light bulb suddenly goes on in your mind. One of the best ways to hear the intuitive part of you is to pin your work up on a wall. Just leave it there for a while, and periodically take a look at it. Your right brain will be working on it, even when you are not consciously aware of the process. Then, suddenly, some wonderful ideas may pop into your mind out of nowhere, and that will be something creative coming from inside of you.

❖ Mary Mashuta

❖ Back to Nature ❖

One great way to "collect" color combinations is to observe nature. The next time you go for a walk or take a ride in a car, take along a pencil and paper. Write down all of the colors you notice at one of your favorite spots, or record what your eye sees in an especially pretty sunset or a wonderfully misty morning fog. When you make this list, try to analyze which colors predominate—the ones that really stand out from the rest because they're rich and deep or because they occupy a large part of the scene. If you look at the trees in a forest, you'll see hundreds of shades of green; if you are out on the plains, an expanse of blues in the sky. Write down which colors add an unexpected dash of sparkle—just small amounts of color that really stand out. Perhaps you'll find bright red tulips on a stony gray ledge, or twinkling, sunny yellow highlights on deep blue water. Look hard to see which colors recede and move into the background. Those will probably be the cool colors of blue, green, and purple, especially darker shades of each. Which colors seem to come forward or be closest to you? Usually, they will be the warm colors—red, orange, and yellow—or the lighter shades of any color. You can build a wonderful color combination from observing the myriad colors that "go together" in a natural setting.

QNM Editors

❖ Pick a Color Bouquet ❖

One fun way to work with colors is to play with the fabrics in your collection and create your own "fabric bouquets."

Whenever you buy a new piece of fabric, take it home and pull out a bunch of other fabrics from your collection. Make little piles of fabric. You can put cool colors and warm colors together. Take a multicolored print and find a variety of greens to go with it, from very light to medium to dark. If there is a red in your print, try playing with different tones of red—fuchsia, cherry, cardinal—even purple! You can have a lot of fun arranging the fabrics into little color bouquets, and in the end, they'll probably be so attractive that you'll want to roll them up and display them in a basket.

Doreen Speckmann

❖ Span a ❖
Spectrum of Shades

I think that color value is the most important part of a quilt. I believe that you'll get a nice color scheme every time if you select the colors you want to work with and then use whatever shades you need to shade those colors together. There is not one specific way of shading two colors together. A quilter should have a palette of colored fabrics, just as an artist needs many paints. One method of shading fabrics is to go darker and darker with each color until they become almost black, and then place the darks of each group next to each other. Another idea is to go lighter and lighter with each color until they become almost white, and then the colors can be linked through a neutral beige or gray. Ten people can try this and each will do it in a different manner and come up with a nice color scheme.

Jinny Beyer

❖ Have You Got the Blues? ❖

There's a very simple but effective way to boost the color impact of your quilts. Try using many different shades of a particular color in your quilts rather than a single shade or even a couple of shades. I like to say, never use 2 fabrics when you can use 20! If there are 20 blues in your quilt, the eye will blend all of those values together. By joining together those varied fabrics, you create a different value and richness than if you had used any one of those fabrics alone. It's just like an artist mixing paints. By piecing strips of color together, a quilter can join 2, 3, or 4 fabrics that together seem to create a different value and richness than any one of them alone.

Margaret Miller

❖ All Colors Great and Small ❖

I tell my students that contrary to their preconceived notions, colors do not have to "match." All colors go with all colors; they just create different kinds of color statements. It is a good idea to work with values and intensities to find the colors you like. Say, for instance, that you don't care for the combination of blue and orange, which are complementary on the color wheel. Try thinking in terms of adding white or black to each color. If you look for lighter or darker tones of orange, you may end up with a shade you really like, such as peach, and the same thing can happen with blue.

Sharyn Squier Craig

❖ Scene from Afar ❖

To see the effects of color and the importance color has in quiltmaking, place one of your blocks on a flannel design board in a place where you will have to come around a corner to look at it. Then wait a few days before taking another look at your block. Coming around a corner will give you a new perspective, and it will show you that what the eye sees first are colors, rather than the shapes of the block or the prints of the fabrics. Certain colors will seem to almost shoot out at you, and others will recede.

Susan McKelvey

❖ Polaroids of Value ❖

When you want to determine color values of a group of fabrics, try taking an instant film snapshot of the group. Polaroid cameras do not take pictures that accurately represent color, but they're good working tools for determining what the fabrics will look like from a distance. And you can continue making new combinations of fabrics, taking Polaroids, and comparing them with each other. If you can get the amount of darkness and lightness and the contrast right in your quilt, then the actual color selection naturally follows. When you find that you're disappointed in a quilt, it often means that the colors were too similar in value.

Judy Mathieson

❖ Let Your Lights Shine ❖

Pictorial quilts are "paintings" you create from a palette of fabrics. In these kinds of quilts, you can imitate the beauty of nature by creating the illusions of luminosity, luster, and depth. Consider the following definitions and ideas when you are trying to bring these effects into a quilt that portrays a natural setting:

♦ *Luminosity* is the relative brightness of something, the illusion that it glows with light. If you want to create this kind of radiant energy in a quilt, any area you want to appear luminous must be comparatively small in relation to the entire piece. If it is too large, the impact of the luminosity will be diminished. It doesn't have to be an especially bright color to appear luminous, either, as long as you follow this rule: An area that is to appear radiant, or luminous, must be purer in color (closer to the color on the color wheel) than the other colors in the area surrounding it.

♦ *Luster* is an effect created when light reflects evenly, without glitter or sparkle. Pearls and opals have a lustrous quality, giving off a glossy sheen. You can achieve the same effect in your quilts, with the proper choice of cotton fabrics. Any portion of a quilt that you want to appear lustrous should be a small area, and it should also be a pure hue, one that's close to the color as it appears on the color wheel. Then you can make the area around the lustrous part appear dim, dark, or shadowed in comparison, by going from the pure-colored, lustrous area to a dark, rich shade in several steps. This will result in the illusion that the pure color is bright and lustrous, even fluorescent.

♦ *Depth* has to do with the direct linear measurement from the point of view-ing to the back of something. To understand how the illusion of depth is created, study nature. Gaze toward a horizon and notice what happens to colors in the distance. Distant hills are grayer and lighter in color, making them appear misty or hazy. Closer hills and mountains look darker at the base, gradually lightening in color as they rise. To incorporate the illusion of depth in your pictorial quilts, use many gradations of your colors and place darker, more intense shades in foregrounds and lighter, grayer tones in backgrounds.

Joen Wolfrom

"Cooking" with Color

❖ Mix All ❖ Ingredients Together Well

When you're making a quilt that has a repeated block design, glued fabric mock-ups are a great way to experiment with different color combinations. First, draw your block design on a piece of 8½ × 11-inch graph paper and make six or eight photocopies of it. Then select some fabrics in colors you want to work with, cut out the pieces, and glue them in position on the graph paper block.

It can be very helpful to make up several versions of the block with the same fabrics in different places. Then you can continue to make more fabric mock-ups and work with the complements of each color, as well as different values. For instance, if you like blue, try making mock-ups with different tones of orange, peach, or rust as its complement. When you've created six or eight different mock-ups, put them up on a wall. Look at them periodically for a few days and think about them. In the end, you'll discover the things you like about the various combinations. It's a process that's a lot like cooking—you can make changes, combine two color harmonies, or add a spicy dash of an unexpected color, altering the ingredients until they dissolve into a color recipe that's uniquely your own.

Mary Coyne Penders

❖ Add a Touch of Burgundy ❖

If you're working on a repetitive-block quilt, you can make each block look a bit different from the others and create interest by following a color recipe for each block. Decide on the color families and accent colors you want to use, and choose a variety of them in different values. Maybe you'll want to use beiges and a variety of navies with accents of burgundy. If you use the lights for the backgrounds, position the navies in the same places (for example, at the tips of stars), and use the reds as the centers, each block will be similar to, but not exactly like, the others. The basic colors will create repetition, which is a valuable element in quiltmaking. Working with this kind of color recipe can take the boredom out of making a single block over and over again, allow you to integrate new prints into the quilt, and help you use up your scraps at the same time.

Nancy J. Martin

Pretreating Fabrics

❖ To Treat or ❖
Not to Treat, That's the Question

The new look and crisp feel of just-off-the-bolt fabrics can be exciting and can inspire you to want to use the fabrics in a quilt. Today's fabrics are treated with protectants against the ultraviolet light in stores with fluorescent lighting. When those protectants are washed off, fabrics fade progressively, even in home storage. To keep the brand-new finish of your fabrics, consider waiting to wash them until you are actually ready to use them. Before washing, test them for colorfastness. If your fabrics are truly colorfast, you can decide to pretreat them or not, as you like. And if they aren't colorfast, you'll need to decide whether you want to use them in your quilt at all.

Harriet Hargrave

❖ Vinegar to the Rescue ❖

You can often set color in a fabric by soaking the fabric in a sink filled with warm water and a cup of white vinegar. If the color does not stop running, try a second solution of vinegar and water or use straight vinegar. If the color continues to run after a second or third try, however, you may be better off not using that particular fabric in your quilt or using it only for something like a wall quilt that you know you will not launder.

QNM Editors

❖ Help! ❖
The Fabric's Bleeding!

Try this quick test for colorfastness, especially for dark reds, greens, and blues. Cut a small piece from the fabric you wish to test. Place it in a sink filled with hot water and add a little bit of liquid soap or detergent to the water if you like. Let the fabric soak for a few minutes and check the water to see if it's discolored. If it is, then test the fabric for color migration, or "bleeding." Place the wet fabric on a white paper towel. If the color seeps into the towel, try rinsing the fabric until no color remains.

QNM Editors

❖ Retayne in Water ❖

You can set color in fabric by using a liquid fixative called Retayne. It actually "locks" dye molecules onto the surface of the fabric, making the fabric permanently colorfast. To use it, mix 1 teaspoon of Retayne and 2 gallons of 120 degree to 140 degree water *per yard* of fabric. Soak the fabric in this solution for 15 to 20 minutes in a washing machine and then rinse it lightly with cool water and dry it at once. Set the color in only one fabric at a time to avoid mixing colors. If you don't have a source for this product in your area, you can contact ProChem, P.O. Box 14, Somerset, MA 02726; 1-800-2BUY DYE.

Jane Townswick

❖ Finding the Fade Factor ❖

To check your fabrics for fading, cut a small piece of each new fabric you buy and tape the pieces in a sunny window. After one week, check the cut pieces against the original pieces of fabric to get an idea of how easily or quickly those fabrics might fade in that kind of light.

QNM Editors

❖ Shrinking Violets (or Reds, ❖ Blues, Greens, or Yellows)

When you pretreat your fabrics for a quilt, keep these helpful hints in mind:

◆ You can shrink small pieces of fabric at the same time that you test them for colorfastness, by soaking them in hot water. Then allow them to air dry, and press them.

◆ Large pieces of fabric can go through a hot-water wash cycle in your washing machine.

◆ Cutting or pulling off any raveled or tangled threads between wash and dry cycles will help to avoid wrinkling.

◆ Washing small pieces of fabric in a mesh lingerie bag will reduce raveled and tangled threads.

◆ Remove fabric from the dryer while it is still damp. If you can't press it then, smooth it out flat and allow it to dry thoroughly to avoid mildew. The most important thing for keeping fabric smooth and easy to work with is to avoid letting it dry in a wrinkled or twisted position.

◆ If you prefer to pretreat some fabrics and not others, it can later be difficult to look at your fabric collection and tell which pieces have been washed and which ones haven't. For a quick way to distinguish between the two, develop the habit of snipping the corners off any piece of fabric you pretreat.

◆ Because selvages are densely woven and difficult to sew through, they should be removed after you pretreat the fabric and before you use it. If the fabric is 100 percent cotton, you can remove a selvage by clipping the fabric ½ inch in from the edge and tearing it along the lengthwise grain.

You can also cut the selvages off with shears or a rotary cutter.

QNM Editors

Figuring Yardages

❖ Make a Quilt Map ❖

When you plan a quilt of your own, making correct yardage calculations can save you time and money and ensure you'll have enough of each fabric to complete your project. The first step in planning a quilt is to do a drawing that shows the blocks, borders, templates, and all of the important measurements. (See the diagram on the right for an example.) Then make a list of the patches you'll need, including the total number of each and in which fabrics, and draft the full-size templates, including seam allowances.

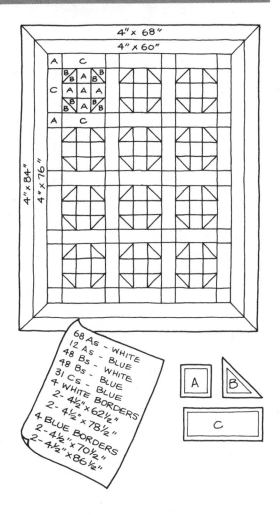

When you begin to figure yardages, it's very helpful to make a cutting layout on graph paper for each fabric you will use in the quilt. Or you can draw a freehand sketch of each fabric and write in the measurements. (The Sample Cutting Layout on page 38 gives you an idea of what this would look like.) When you do this kind of cutting layout, remember these guidelines:

1. It's often a good idea to have seamless borders, so draw the borders on your cutting layout first. Adding an extra 2 inches to the length of each border can also be good insurance.

Sample Cutting Layout

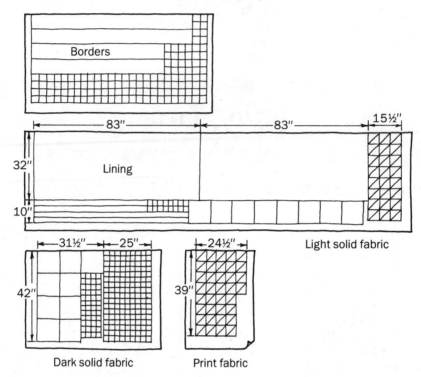

2. After you have drawn in the larger pieces on your cutting layout, fit the smaller patches in the remaining areas.

3. To figure how many patches of a particular shape and size can be cut across the width of the fabric, measure the width of the patch and divide that number into 42 inches.

4. Divide this number into the total number needed of this type of patch to see how many rows of patches you'll need.

5. Multiply this number of rows by the length measurement of the patch to see how much actual yardage you'll need.

6. After you have measured and calculated the yardage for a particular piece of fabric, it is still a good idea to add a little bit extra to allow for shrinkage and a margin of error.

QNM Editors

___

❖ **Space-Saving Layouts** ❖

Whatever the shapes of the pieces in your quilt, you'll save fabric by arranging them efficiently for cutting. Because your fabric purchases will be based on your drawn cutting layout and your yardage calculations, remember to actually cut the pieces this way, too, or you might not have enough fabric. Each row in the Space-Saving Layout on the opposite page shows a differently shaped template and the way to cut it most efficiently across the width of the fabric.

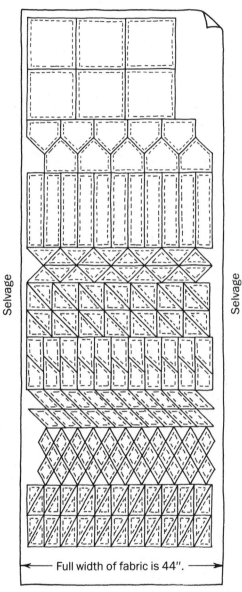

Selvage

Selvage

← Full width of fabric is 44". →

Space-Saving Layout

❖ Now Cut That Out! ❖

When you have determined the size, shape, and number of patches you'll need to cut from each fabric, you can use the charts beginning on page 40 for calculating yardages for squares, rectangles, and isosceles right triangles. The charts can also come in handy when you are shopping and want to quickly estimate how much fabric you'll need for your project. These yardage listings are based on 44- to 45-inch fabric widths, and they allow for 2 percent shrinkage and for trimmed selvages. If you plan to cut your patches with the grain aligned in a way other than shown in the diagrams that accompany the charts, be sure to allow extra yardage. Use these charts for each fabric individually. If you plan to cut several different kinds of patches from the same fabric, find the yardage for each shape and add them together to get the total yardage. For the fabric from which you plan to cut borders, sashing, or lining, use a graph paper cutting layout.

QNM Editors

Squares

Number of Squares
That Can Be Cut from Various Yardages

Finished Size (inches)	Yardage (44-inch fabric)									
	¼	½	¾	1	1¼	1½	1¾	2	2¼	2½
1	140	308	476	644	812	980	1148	1316	1456	1624
1½	84	168	273	357	462	546	630	735	819	924
2	48	112	160	224	272	336	384	448	496	560
2½	28	70	112	154	196	238	280	322	364	406
3	24	60	84	120	144	180	204	240	264	300
3½	20	40	60	80	110	130	150	170	190	220
4	9	27	45	63	81	99	117	135	153	171
4½	8	24	40	56	64	80	96	112	120	136
5	7	21	28	42	56	63	77	84	98	112
5½	7	14	28	35	49	56	70	77	91	98
6	6	12	24	30	36	48	54	60	72	78
6½	6	12	18	30	36	42	48	60	66	72
7	5	10	15	20	25	35	40	45	50	55
7½	5	10	15	20	25	30	35	40	45	55
8	4	8	12	16	20	24	28	32	36	40
8½		4	8	12	16	20	24	28	32	36
9		4	8	12	16	20	24	28	32	36
9½		4	8	12	16	20	24	28	28	32
10		4	8	12	16	20	20	24	28	32
10½		3	6	9	12	12	15	18	21	24
11		3	6	9	9	12	15	18	18	21
11½		3	6	6	9	12	15	15	18	21
12		3	6	6	9	12	12	15	18	21
12½		3	6	6	9	12	12	15	18	18
13		3	3	6	9	9	12	15	15	18
13½		3	3	6	9	9	12	15	15	18
14		2	2	4	6	6	8	8	10	12
14½		2	2	4	4	6	8	8	10	10
15		2	2	4	4	6	6	8	10	10
15½		2	2	4	4	6	6	8	8	10
16		2	2	4	4	6	6	8	8	10
16½		2	2	4	4	6	6	8	8	10
17		2	2	4	4	6	6	8	8	10
17½			2	2	4	4	6	6	8	8
18			2	2	4	4	6	6	8	8

Arrow indicates measurement of finished size listed in chart. Yardage figures include ¼" seam allowances on patches.

Selvage

Selvage

Width of fabric

Yardage (44-inch fabric)

2¾	3	3¼	3½	3¾	4	4¼	4½	4¾	5
1792	1960	2128	2296	2464	2632	2772	2940	3108	3276
1008	1092	1197	1281	1386	1470	1554	1659	1743	1848
608	672	720	784	832	896	944	1008	1072	1120
448	490	532	574	616	658	686	728	770	812
324	360	384	420	444	480	504	540	564	600
240	260	280	300	330	350	370	390	410	440
189	207	225	243	261	279	297	315	333	351
152	168	176	192	208	224	232	248	264	280
119	133	140	154	168	175	189	196	210	224
112	119	133	140	154	161	168	182	189	203
84	96	102	108	120	126	138	144	150	162
78	90	96	102	108	120	126	132	138	150
60	70	75	80	85	90	95	105	110	115
60	65	70	75	80	85	90	95	100	110
44	48	52	56	60	64	68	72	76	80
40	44	48	52	56	60	64	68	72	76
40	44	48	48	52	56	60	64	68	72
36	40	44	48	52	56	56	60	64	68
36	40	40	44	48	52	56	60	60	64
24	27	30	33	36	36	39	42	45	48
24	27	27	30	33	36	39	39	42	45
24	24	27	30	33	33	36	39	39	42
21	24	27	27	30	33	33	36	39	42
21	24	24	27	30	30	33	36	36	39
21	21	24	27	27	30	33	33	36	39
18	21	24	24	27	30	30	33	33	36
12	14	14	16	18	18	20	20	22	24
12	14	14	16	16	18	18	20	22	22
12	12	14	14	16	18	18	20	20	22
12	12	14	14	16	16	18	18	20	22
10	12	12	14	16	16	18	18	20	20
10	12	12	14	14	16	16	18	18	20
10	12	12	14	14	16	16	18	18	20
10	10	12	12	14	14	16	16	18	18
10	10	12	12	14	14	16	16	18	18

Rectangles

Number of Rectangles
That Can Be Cut from Various Yardages

Finished Size (inches)	Yardage (44-inch fabric)									
	¼	½	¾	1	1¼	1½	1¾	2	2¼	2½
1 × 2	84	196	280	392	476	588	672	784	868	980
1 × 3	56	140	196	280	336	420	476	560	616	700
1½ × 3	42	105	147	210	252	315	357	420	462	525
1½ × 4½	21	63	105	147	168	210	252	294	315	357
1½ × 8	21	42	63	84	105	126	147	168	189	210
1½ × 9	16*	21	42	63	84	105	126	147	168	189
1½ × 10	16*	21	42	63	84	105	105	126	147	168
1½ × 12	12*	21	42	42	63	84	84	105	126	147
2 × 4	16	48	80	112	144	176	208	240	272	304
2 × 6	16	32	64	80	96	128	144	160	192	208
2 × 8	16	32	48	64	80	96	112	128	144	160
2 × 9	12*	16	32	48	64	80	96	112	128	144
2 × 10	12*	16	32	48	64	80	80	96	112	128
2 × 12	9*	16	32	32	48	64	64	80	96	112
2½ × 5	14	42	56	84	112	126	154	168	196	224
2½ × 7½	14	28	42	56	70	84	98	112	126	154
2½ × 8	14	28	42	56	70	84	98	112	126	140
2½ × 9	8*	14	28	42	56	70	84	98	112	126
2½ × 10	8*	14	28	42	56	70	70	84	98	112
2½ × 12	6*	14	28	28	42	56	56	70	84	98
3 × 6	12	24	48	60	72	96	108	120	144	156
3 × 8	12	24	36	48	60	72	84	96	108	120
3 × 9	8*	12	24	36	48	60	72	84	96	108
3 × 10	8*	12	24	36	48	60	60	72	84	96
3 × 12	6*	12	24	24	36	48	48	60	72	84

*In these cases you must turn the rectangle with its longest side parallel to the crosswise grain.

Arrow indicates measurement
of finished size listed in chart.
Yardage figures include ¼″
seam allowances on patches.

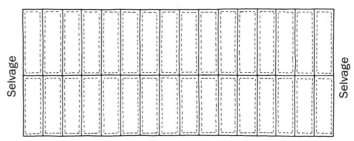

Selvage

Selvage

Width of fabric

Yardage (44-inch fabric)

2¾	3	3¼	3½	3¾	4	4¼	4½	4¾	5
1064	1176	1260	1372	1456	1568	1652	1764	1876	1960
756	840	896	980	1036	1120	1176	1260	1316	1400
567	630	672	735	777	840	882	945	987	1050
399	441	462	504	546	588	609	651	693	735
231	252	273	294	315	336	357	378	399	420
210	231	252	252	273	294	315	336	357	378
189	210	210	231	252	273	294	315	315	336
147	168	189	189	210	231	231	252	273	294
336	368	400	432	464	496	528	560	592	624
224	256	272	288	320	336	368	384	400	432
176	192	208	224	240	256	272	288	304	320
160	176	192	192	208	224	240	256	272	288
144	160	160	176	192	208	224	240	240	256
112	128	144	144	160	176	176	192	208	224
238	266	280	308	336	350	378	392	420	448
168	182	196	210	224	238	252	266	280	308
154	168	182	196	210	224	238	252	266	280
140	154	168	168	182	196	210	224	238	252
126	140	140	154	168	182	196	210	210	224
98	112	126	126	140	154	154	168	182	196
168	192	204	216	240	252	276	288	300	324
132	144	156	168	180	192	204	216	228	240
120	132	144	144	156	168	180	192	204	216
108	120	120	132	144	156	168	180	180	192
84	96	108	108	120	132	132	144	156	168

Isosceles Right Triangles

Number of Isosceles Right Triangles
That Can Be Cut from Various Yardages

Finished Size (inches)	Yardage (44-inch fabric)								
	¼	½	¾	1	1¼	1½	1¾	2	2¼
1	176	396	616	792	1012	1232	1408	1628	1848
1½	102	238	374	476	612	748	850	986	1122
2	84	168	252	336	420	504	588	672	756
2½	48	120	168	240	312	360	432	480	552
3	40	80	120	180	220	260	300	360	400
3½	36	72	108	144	180	216	252	288	324
4	16	48	80	112	144	160	192	224	256
4½	14	42	56	84	112	126	154	182	196
5	14	42	56	84	98	126	140	168	182
5½	12	24	48	60	72	96	108	132	144
6	12	24	36	60	72	84	96	120	132
6½	10	20	30	40	50	70	80	90	100
7	10	20	30	40	50	60	70	80	100
7½	10	20	30	40	50	60	70	80	90
8	0	8	16	24	32	40	48	56	64
8½	0	8	16	24	32	40	48	56	64
9	0	8	16	24	32	40	48	56	64
9½	0	8	16	24	32	40	40	48	56
10	0	6	12	18	24	24	30	36	42
10½	0	6	12	18	18	24	30	36	36
11	0	6	12	12	18	24	30	30	36
11½	0	6	12	12	18	24	24	30	36
12	0	6	12	12	18	24	24	30	36
12½	0	6	6	12	18	18	24	30	36
13	0	6	6	12	18	18	24	30	30
13½	0	4	4	8	12	12	16	16	20
14	0	4	4	8	8	12	16	16	20
14½	0	4	4	8	8	12	16	16	20
15	0	4	4	8	8	12	12	16	20
15½	0	4	4	8	8	12	12	16	16
16	0	4	4	8	8	12	12	16	16
16½	0	4	4	8	8	12	12	16	16
17	0	0	4	4	8	8	12	12	16
17½	0	0	4	4	8	8	12	12	16
18	0	0	4	4	8	8	12	12	16

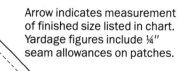

Arrow indicates measurement of finished size listed in chart. Yardage figures include ¼" seam allowances on patches.

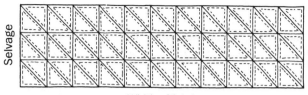

Selvage · Selvage · Width of fabric

Yardage (44-inch fabric)

2½	2¾	3	3¼	3½	3¾	4	4¼	4½	4¾	5
2068	2244	2464	2684	2860	3080	3300	3476	3696	3916	4136
1258	1360	1496	1632	1734	1870	2006	2142	2244	2380	2516
840	924	1008	1092	1176	1288	1372	1456	1540	1624	1708
624	672	744	792	864	936	984	1056	1128	1176	1248
440	500	540	580	620	680	720	760	800	860	900
360	396	432	468	504	540	576	612	648	684	720
288	304	336	368	400	432	448	480	512	544	576
224	252	266	294	308	336	364	378	406	434	448
210	224	252	266	294	308	336	350	378	392	420
156	180	192	204	228	240	264	276	288	312	324
144	168	180	192	204	228	240	252	276	288	300
110	130	140	150	160	170	190	200	210	220	230
110	120	130	140	150	160	170	190	200	210	220
100	110	120	130	140	150	160	170	180	200	210
72	80	88	96	104	112	120	128	136	144	152
72	80	88	96	104	112	120	120	128	136	144
64	72	80	88	96	104	112	120	128	128	136
64	72	80	88	88	96	104	112	120	128	136
48	48	54	60	66	72	72	78	84	90	96
42	48	54	60	60	66	72	78	78	84	90
42	48	48	54	60	66	66	72	78	84	84
42	42	48	54	54	60	66	72	72	78	84
36	42	48	48	54	60	60	66	72	78	78
36	42	42	48	54	54	60	66	66	72	78
36	36	42	48	48	54	60	60	66	72	72
24	24	28	28	32	36	36	40	44	44	48
20	24	28	28	32	32	36	40	40	44	44
20	24	24	28	32	32	36	36	40	40	44
20	24	24	28	28	32	32	36	40	40	44
20	20	24	28	28	32	32	36	36	40	40
20	20	24	24	28	28	32	32	36	36	40
20	20	24	24	28	28	32	32	36	36	40
16	20	20	24	24	28	28	32	32	36	36
16	20	20	24	24	28	28	32	32	36	36
16	20	20	24	24	28	28	28	32	32	36

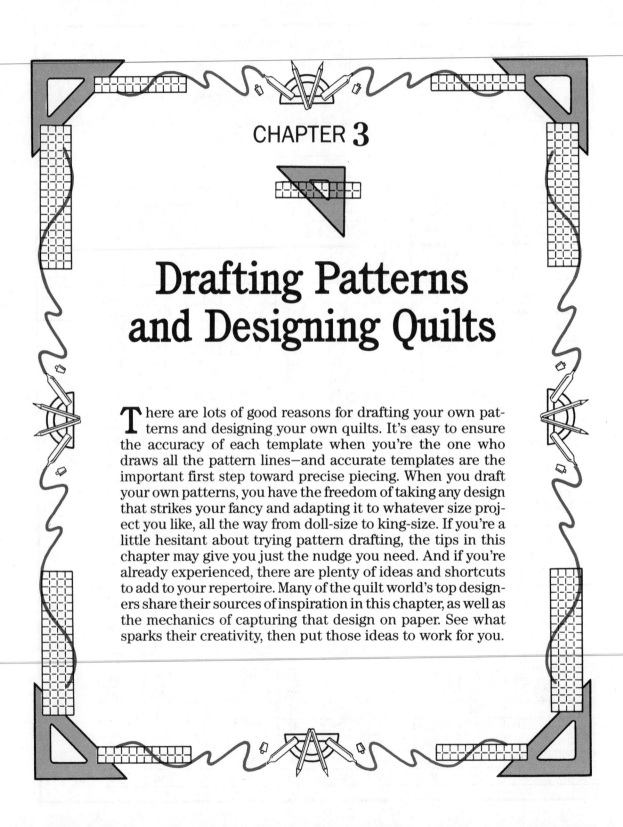

CHAPTER **3**

Drafting Patterns and Designing Quilts

There are lots of good reasons for drafting your own patterns and designing your own quilts. It's easy to ensure the accuracy of each template when you're the one who draws all the pattern lines—and accurate templates are the important first step toward precise piecing. When you draft your own patterns, you have the freedom of taking any design that strikes your fancy and adapting it to whatever size project you like, all the way from doll-size to king-size. If you're a little hesitant about trying pattern drafting, the tips in this chapter may give you just the nudge you need. And if you're already experienced, there are plenty of ideas and shortcuts to add to your repertoire. Many of the quilt world's top designers share their sources of inspiration in this chapter, as well as the mechanics of capturing that design on paper. See what sparks their creativity, then put those ideas to work for you.

Drafting Patterns

Patterns Based on Squares

❖ Oh, My Stars! ❖

Many beloved block patterns are based on the structure of an underlying grid of squares, including some stars. At first, it may not make much sense—how can a star be made up of squares? But once you learn how to look beyond the points and angles of the star shape and recognize that squares are the foundation, you'll be well on the way to drafting many star blocks that catch your fancy.

♦ Look at a star block and break it down into smaller divisions. To do this, count the number of *equal* sections across the top of whatever block you've chosen. The easiest underlying structures to recognize are the 4-patch and the 9-patch grids. If there are 2 equal sections, or a multiple of 2 equal sections, across the top, the block is a 4-patch, such as Evening Star. If there are 3, or a multiple of 3, equal sections, the design is a 9-patch, such as Variable Star.

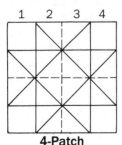

4-Patch
with 4 Equal Sections
Evening Star

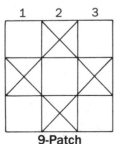

9-Patch
with 3 Equal Sections
Variable Star

♦ When you're ready to draft the actual block pattern, draw a square that equals the finished size of the block you want on a piece of graph paper. Next, draw in the equal divisions of the star as horizontal and vertical lines. With a straightedge, draw the lines on this grid to complete the shape of your star pattern. The diagrams below show examples of 4-patch and 9-patch grids and block designs.

4-Patch Grid

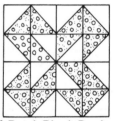

4-Patch Block Design

9-Patch Grid

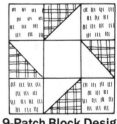

9-Patch Block Design

♦ Now you're ready to draft the individual pattern pieces you'll need to construct your star block. Draw them on another sheet of graph paper, remembering to add a ¼-inch seam allowance to each side of each pattern piece.

QNM Editors

❖ The LeMoyne Star ❖

This eight-pointed star is one of the most versatile designs in quiltmaking. Its grid has 3 divisions across the top, but the divisions are not equal. The grid is based on the measurement from the center of the square to one of its corners. To develop your own grid for one of these beauties, follow the guidelines below. From there, the possibilities are limitless for creating your own original star patterns.

Drafting an Eight-Pointed Star

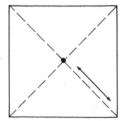

Step 1: *Draw a finished-size square on a piece of graph paper and mark lines dividing the square from corner to corner to find the center.*

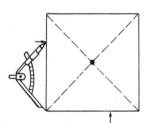

Step 2: *Place the compass point in the lower left corner of the square and adjust the compass until the pencil touches the exact center of the square. Use this measurement to mark the distance from the corner of the square to each of two sides.*

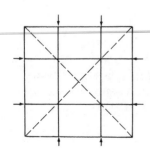

Step 3: *Repeat this process from the other three corners to mark the sides of the square. Then use the marks to draw lines from top to bottom and from side to side. This yields the basic grid for an eight-pointed star.*

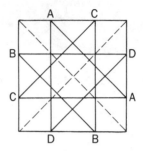

Step 4: *Use letters to connect the lines of the star, as follows: A to A, B to B, C to C, and D to D.*

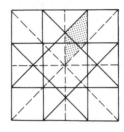

Step 5: *Draw light vertical and horizontal lines through the center of the square to divide it in half. Shade in the diamond shape this creates, and you have the most familiar eight-pointed star, the LeMoyne Star.*

Mary Klett Ryan

Patterns Based on Circles

❖ Circles in a Square ❖

Using a protractor can be a challenge to a beginning pattern drafter, but the mystery soon disappears as you learn how to use this tool to draft accurate patterns based on a circle. The traditional Grandmother's Fan block is actually based on one-quarter of a circle. With the aid of a compass in addition to a protractor, you can draft this kind of circular design in any size you like.

1. Draw the finished size of your block on a piece of paper and use a compass to draw a quarter circle that fills most of the square.

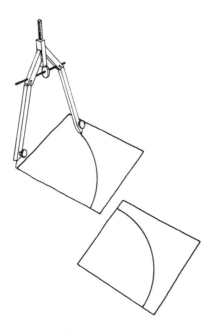

3. Mark a second quarter circle that is about one-fourth the width of the square. Use a ruler to connect the lower left corner of the square and the little section marks and then draw lines between the two quarter circles—and your Grandmother's Fan pattern will be complete. Whether your square is small or large makes no difference in the accuracy of your pattern, since a degree is a portion of a circle and never changes in size.

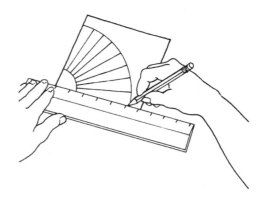

Rita Denenberg

2. Place the protractor on the block drawing, so that the 90 degree mark is on the left vertical line of the square and the ruler is on the horizontal line. Decide how many segments you want in the fan and divide that number into 90. For example, a fan with 9 sections would require 10 degrees in each section. Mark off the sections around the curved edge of the protractor.

❖ Protractors, ❖
Points, and Pentagons

A five-pointed star is really a series of points at 5 equal segments in a circle. It's easy to draft one, using just a pencil, paper, compass, and protractor.

1. Start by using a compass to draw a circle the size of the finished star and mark the center. To determine where to mark the points at 5 equal segments of the circle, divide 360 degrees

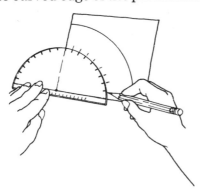

by 5 to discover that each segment will have 72 degrees. Place the point of your protractor on the center of your circle and mark a point at 72 degrees. Then rotate the protractor and mark off another 72 degrees.

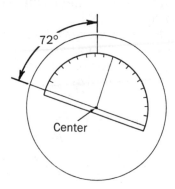

2. Continue until you've marked all 5 segments and then use a ruler to connect these marks with the circle's center. Then connect every other mark to complete your five-pointed star pattern.

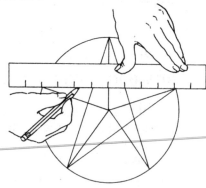

Rita Denenberg

❖ Star Light, Star Bright ❖

You can create an eight-, sixteen-, or twenty-four-pointed Mariner's Star pattern in any size you like without having the skills of a Nobel Prize–winning mathematician. You can also work with almost any other division, as well, though a multiple of four is especially suited to this technique. Here's how to draft a pattern for a basic four-pointed star.

Drafting a Basic Four-Pointed Star

Step 1: *Draw a circle the size of the finished star and mark the diameter across the middle. Place a protractor on the diameter and mark off 90 degrees, and continue until all 4 segments are marked.*

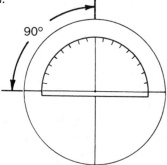

Step 2: *Draw a second circle inside the first one, to indicate the depth of the four star sections. Then use the protractor to mark points midway between the 90 degree marks, at 45 degrees. Now complete the lines of the star using the second circle and these 45 degree marks.*

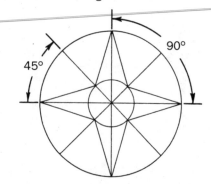

Step 3: *If you add a third circle between the first two, you can add four more star points.*

Step 4: *You can actually divide a circle into as many points as you like by using the protractor to mark equal divisions and by marking circles to indicate the depth of each star point. For example, a division of the 45 degree segments into halves of 22½ degrees will yield a sixteen-pointed star.*

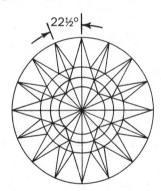

Rita Denenberg

Tools and Equipment for Drafting

❖ A Hole New Idea ❖

You can make a huge compass for drawing very large circles by drilling small holes along the entire length of a yardstick at 1-inch intervals. Put a pushpin or a tack in one of the holes to anchor the yardstick on a piece of paper or fabric. This point will become the center of the circle. Place your pencil in another hole to mark a circle with a radius of up to 36 inches.

QNM Editors

❖ Good Penmanship ❖

Sanford Sharpie marking pens are great to use for drafting patterns because they are opaque, show up easily, and will draw a very thin line.

Sue Rodgers

THE GREATNESS OF GRAPH PAPER

For pattern drafting, I like to use cross-section graph paper with 8 grids per inch. It's different from other graph papers because it has a heavier line at the 1-inch increments. The 8 grids per inch make it easier to draft patterns, especially for rotary cutting, which often deals with ⅛-inch measurements. You can purchase 17 × 22-inch cross-section graph paper at an art supply store, or contact Alvin & Co., Inc., at 1-800-444-2584 to find an Alvin Store in your area.

❖ Marsha McCloskey

The Process of Designing

❖ From Block to Top ❖

When you begin to draw on your own ideas for quilts, the possibilities are limitless. To do a design of your own for the first time, it's very helpful to start by making a graph paper "worksheet." Here are the supplies you need and some hints and helps to start you out on the designing road.

Supplies

♦ Accurate graph paper with either 4 or 8 squares to the inch
♦ Picture or drawing of a simple patchwork block
♦ Pencil and sharpener, or mechanical pencil
♦ Eraser
♦ Accurate ruler

How to Make a Graph Paper Worksheet

Step 1: *Using 1 square on the graph paper to represent 1 inch of the finished quilt, draw the block you've chosen.*

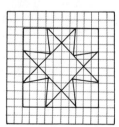

Step 2: *Make multiple photocopies of the block drawing and play with them to see how a design can develop.*

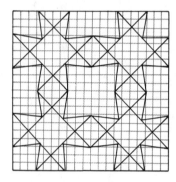

Step 3: *Experiment more with the design by adding another element, such as sashing between each block. Then add setting squares wherever two sashing strips meet.*

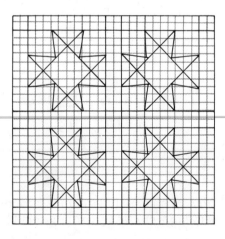

Step 4: *Add one or more borders of different widths. There are countless combinations and sizes that will yield new design possibilities.*

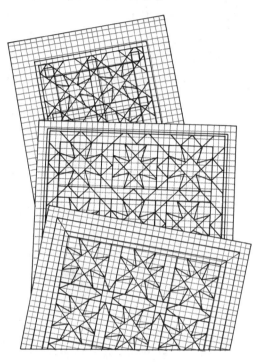

Step 5: *When you've decided on a design that pleases you, draw it on a large piece of graph paper, again maintaining the formula of 1 square of graph paper to 1 inch in the finished quilt. Write in the various measurements of blocks, sashing strips, and borders and check the finished size of the entire design.*

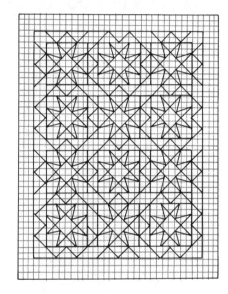

Using Your Worksheet

♦ Take your quilt drawing to a photocopy store and have several copies made of it. Color the entire drawing with colored pencils or felt-tip pens, or cover just enough to see the design begin to emerge. If you'd rather use fabrics than pencils or markers, cut up pieces of fabric and glue them in place on your worksheet.

♦ Let your worksheet be your guide to counting patches, figuring yardages, drafting templates, and assembling the quilt top. By counting the squares on the graph paper, you can determine the measurements of each piece in your quilt.

♦ When you draft your templates on graph paper, remember to add ¼-inch seam allowances to each piece. Now you're ready to start making your quilt!

QNM Editors

DO A SLEEP DOODLE

A lot of ideas come to me in the middle of the night, or toward early morning, so I always keep a large (8½ × 11-inch) pad of paper and a pencil by my bed. Whenever I wake up at night with an idea for a gorgeous quilt design, I sketch it out and write in big, bold letters. That makes it easy to read in the morning. It's helpful to use large sheets of paper, too, so you don't have to worry about making small or detailed drawings while you're sleepy.

❖ Debra Wagner

❖ Block It Out ❖

You can design very creative and original quilts by simply starting with traditional block patterns and introducing new shapes or elements from other blocks at the corners. Use the following variations as springboards for ideas to create your own unique quilts.

Creative Ideas for Block Designs

Turkey Track

In the classic Card Tricks pattern, adding traditional Turkey Track corners produces an entirely new block.

"Cone"

An Ohio Star has a totally different appearance when you add a "cone" at each corner to create a boldly dramatic block design.

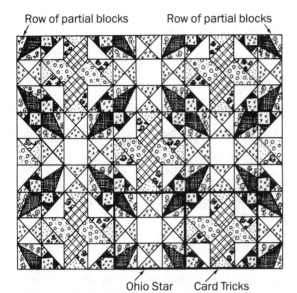

Row of partial blocks   Row of partial blocks

Ohio Star   Card Tricks

*When you've created two block designs that
please you, try experimenting with them to see
how they work together in the same quilt. Here, the
"cones" from the Ohio Star meet the Turkey Track
corners from the Card Tricks block to create a
design with an almost circular feeling. Adding a
row of partial blocks at each side of the quilt
completes the "circular" design.*

Stan Green

very lucky if 1 of them is something that
I'm happy with. I throw away the ones
that I don't like and keep the ones that I do
like in files in a drawer where I can go
through them some other time. Give yourself permission to do "play" drawings—just
have fun with them. And remember that
not every drawing you do has to be a
masterpiece. Think about what really
pleases you and makes you feel good.

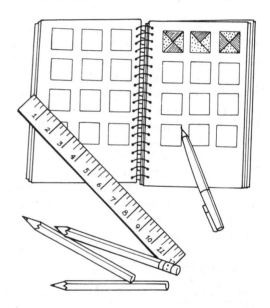

Caryl Bryer Fallert

❖ Sketches, ❖
Thumbnails, and Doodles

I like to sit and do small thumbnail
sketches. It's helpful to divide a piece of
paper into 2- or 3-inch squares and keep
the paper handy for doodling, especially
while you're watching television. I might
do 50 or 60 of these little sketches and feel

❖ Check Out the Stacks ❖

To get lots of inspiration for planning
a quilt design, go to your local library and
check out books that show collections of
antique quilts. Look through the pages
until you find three or four quilts you really

love. Photocopy the images and write out a list of the things you liked about each quilt. Keep your ideas filed together and pull them out whenever you begin to think about making a new quilt.

Debra Wagner

❖ Go Shopping for Designs ❖

Magazines and catalogs are a big source of inspiration for me. You never know what's going to strike you as having design potential. You can even come across great ideas when you're shopping. Illustrations on greeting cards, the colors and logo on a store's shopping bag, small gift items on display—all are fair game for creative inspiration. I'm always looking and thinking, "Is this something that could be incorporated into a design?" Sometimes another medium, such as wood crafts or painting, can influence you, too. I think it's important to keep your eyes open all the time, to take notes, and to collect your ideas and things you like in idea files.

Debbie Mumm

❖ Building Blocks ❖

I like to take an illustration of a single block from an anthology like Barbara Brackman's *An Encyclopedia of Pieced Quilt Patterns*. You can take a black-and-white drawing that excites you, draft it onto a piece of graph paper, and begin to create a quilt design with that as your starting point. I like Brackman's encyclopedia because it's full of hundreds of accurately documented, traditional blocks that

quilters are free to use and work with in any way they want.

Diana McClun

❖ One Picture Is ❖ Worth a Good Quilt Design

For great sources of design inspiration, try collecting greeting cards, magazines, and books on anything that appeals to you or excites you. I'm beginning to collect books on Chinese art and folk art, and I have a wonderful book about Chinese porcelain that shows hundreds of porcelain plates. It's an unending source of design ideas. Books can give you the kind of visual inspiration that will help you learn to create your own original images. You can find something you like in a book and take an individual element of some kind from it, such as a circle. If you change it, stretch it, enlarge it, or make it smaller, that will begin to make it your own unique design.

Sue Rodgers

❖ Quilts Are Natural Beauties ❖

If you'd like to start designing, why not begin by simply looking at the variety of colors and shapes in nature? Notice the rich earth tones in a range of mountains or the deep blue-greens in a lake. How would those colors look in a quilt? When you bring things that you see and like into your quilts, you're designing. Count the number of greens there actually are among the leaves of just one tree. What about adding a wide range of green shades to your next floral appliqué block? And you can even look further than nature's beauty. Are there design possibilities in the facade of a commercial building, a beautiful oak door, or an ornately trimmed window? Think about including some of those curved scrolls, flowers, or birds in a quilt. Have fun designing and creating your own unique legacy of beauty.

Jane Townswick

❖ Profile Your Style ❖

When you attend a quilt show, try writing down the things you *don't* like about certain quilts and taking photos of those you find *unappealing*, instead of just the quilts you find most attractive. Then you can take time later to analyze the things you didn't like, which will help define your personal style. For example, if you see an Irish Chain quilt, done in shades of yellow and brown, that you dislike, what are you really feeling? A negative reaction to the Irish Chain design? Or a dislike of the color combination of yellow and brown? When you can identify the elements you like most, as well as those you dislike, it will be easier to develop your own quilting style. And that will build your confidence in your own color, fabric, and design preferences.

Cyndi Hershey

❖ Save the Borders for Last ❖

I wait to plan the border until the main part of the quilt is done, because I think it's impossible to know what's going to look best until you have that part of the quilt completed. I have a design board on my wall where I can put up the interior part of the quilt and let my border design spring from that.

Jinny Beyer

❖ Three Sheets to the Wall ❖

To get a good sense of how your quilt design is coming together, you need a vertical surface where you can put up units and blocks to look at them. My large flannel design wall is actually a king-size flannel sheet. I just thumbtack it up at ceiling level, and that is where I do all my designing. If you have limited space, you can use a closet door or wrap flannel around a sturdy art canvas and prop the canvas against a couch or wall.

Sharyn Squier Craig

❖ Play with Paper Prints ❖

If you want to practice putting different fabric combinations together without having to actually cut up your fabrics, try making photocopies of your fabrics and cut up those instead. You can make several copies of each fabric, cut them into the shapes in the block, and try many different combinations in your block design before you commit to cutting your fabrics. In a black-and-white photocopy, you can evaluate the level of color contrast, without actually seeing the fabric colors, and you can compare the scales of prints and how they work together with plaids or solids.

Doreen Speckmann

❖ Be a Perfect Copycat ❖

When you want to have pattern pieces photocopied, it's a good idea to check that the copy machine to be used will actually reproduce at 100 percent. Always be sure to ask about this at commercial photocopy stores. Almost all major types of copy machines can be set to reproduce images at 100 percent, but if you don't ask, they have to build in an error factor by law. If that happens, any of your designs or templates will be reproduced at approximately 98.8 percent. That's very close to 100 percent, but for pattern pieces, it is not acceptable. Being off by even that little bit can cause distortion in the patterns. This distortion usually shows up in one direction.

Sharyn Squier Craig

Quick and Creative Designs

❖ Quick Crib Cuddlers ❖

You can make a baby quilt in the twinkling of an eye by appliquéing a simple design from a child's coloring book to a large piece of prequilted fabric. Bind the edges in a fabric that matches the appliqué patches, and you'll have a super-fast gift for a little one.

QNM Editors

❖ Isn't That ❖
Uncle John's Jacket?

Recycle, recycle, recycle! Old suits, coats, and blankets, especially wool ones, can be transformed into warm and durable tied quilts for camping, football games, and other outdoor activities.

QNM Editors

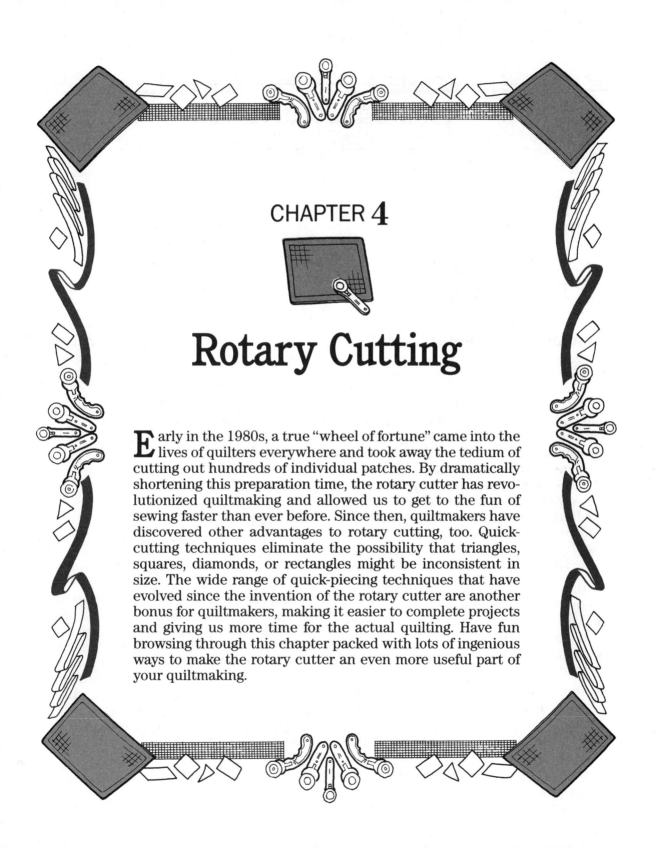

CHAPTER 4

Rotary Cutting

E arly in the 1980s, a true "wheel of fortune" came into the lives of quilters everywhere and took away the tedium of cutting out hundreds of individual patches. By dramatically shortening this preparation time, the rotary cutter has revolutionized quiltmaking and allowed us to get to the fun of sewing faster than ever before. Since then, quiltmakers have discovered other advantages to rotary cutting, too. Quick-cutting techniques eliminate the possibility that triangles, squares, diamonds, or rectangles might be inconsistent in size. The wide range of quick-piecing techniques that have evolved since the invention of the rotary cutter are another bonus for quiltmakers, making it easier to complete projects and giving us more time for the actual quilting. Have fun browsing through this chapter packed with lots of ingenious ways to make the rotary cutter an even more useful part of your quiltmaking.

Tools and Equipment

Maintaining and Using a Rotary Cutter

❖ Anatomy of a Rotary Cutter ❖

A rotary cutter deserves the same kind of attention you lavish on your sewing machine; it, too, needs to be cleaned and oiled. Taking apart and reassembling your rotary cutter for the first time may be reminiscent of the first time you threaded your machine—you may be slightly confused about what goes where. To help you get to know your rotary cutter better, here's a crash course on cutter anatomy, along with some hints on getting all the pieces back together in the right order. Cutters have the same basic parts, including the following:

♦ Handle (the colored part that you grip as you move the cutter)

♦ Blade (the sharp edge that cuts through layers of fabric)

♦ Washer, screw, and nut (the parts that hold the cutter together)

♦ Tension disk (not all cutters have one; in those that do, it can be used to adjust the tension)

♦ Shield (the part that goes between the blade and the handle; keeps the sharp blade covered when not in use)

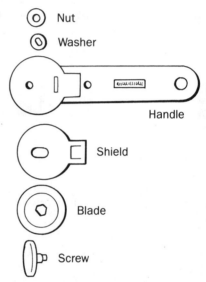

Rotary Cutter Anatomy

Save yourself a lot of headaches by paying close attention to how the various pieces come apart. Lay them out in a line, in order as they come off the cutter. A good rule of thumb is to always work so that the cutter handle faces right side up (the blade side, or side on which the manufacturer's name appears). Then, after you've cleaned and oiled the cutter, it's simply a matter of putting the pieces back together in order.

QNM Editors

❖ Oil Be Seeing You ❖

All new rotary cutters are slightly oiled when you buy them, and that little bit of lubrication keeps the blade operating cleanly and smoothly. To keep your rotary cutter in top working order, it's a good idea to take it apart periodically to clean and oil it, to prevent rusting and allow the blade to work smoothly.

1. First, clean out all lint from behind the blade. It's difficult to use a rotary cutter if you're fighting lint buildup as the blade moves across the fabric.
2. Put just one tiny drop of sewing machine oil on the plastic surface that sits next to the blade.
3. Reassemble the cutter, keeping in mind that the nut should be loose enough to allow the blade to rotate very freely. If cleaning and oiling do not make a significant improvement in the way your rotary cutter works, it's time for a new blade.

Sharyn Squier Craig

❖ Get the Nick in Time ❖

To get good results in rotary cutting, it's crucial that you keep your cutting blade sharp and in good condition. Replace a blade immediately if it begins to develop burrs or nicks (you'll know the blade is nicked when it doesn't cut cleanly and you have to go back and recut portions of the strip). It should become an automatic reflex to close the blade guard on your cutter each and every time you lay it down, even if only for a moment. This guards against nicking the blade—and also keeps *you* safe and in one piece.

Diana McClun

❖ A Cut Above ❖

When you begin making the first cutting stroke with your rotary cutter, position it so that it's in front of the fabric fold rather than right on top of it. And *always* be sure to cut *away* from your body, because a pushing motion is stronger than a pulling motion. Hold the cutter at approximately a 45 degree angle, which is a natural angle for the human arm to extend from the body. If you hold your cutter too straight or at too low an angle, it isn't comfortable to cut. When you start to cut, make your cutting motion across the fabric a clean one, rather than use short, choppy strokes.

Sharyn Squier Craig

❖ Reinventing the Wheel ❖

The new rotary cutter from Fiskars is great for people who are feeling the fatigue of being at the cutting table too long. This cutter has a handle that is specially designed to be very easy to hold. To use it, you don't need to tip your wrist as high as you do with other cutters, and you can hold your elbow and wrist parallel to the table. You don't need to apply as much pressure to the blade as you cut through your fabric, either, so it creates less fatigue in your hand. With a little practice, this cutter will be very comfortable to use, and you will be able to enjoy cutting for a much longer period of time with less stress in your arms and wrists.

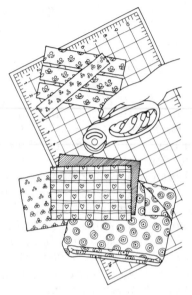

Eleanor Burns

❖ Fast Aid for First Cutters ❖

When I teach a class or workshop in which people will be learning rotary-cutting techniques, I like to take some first aid supplies with me. Whenever a rotary cutter is involved, there is always a chance that someone might be cut by a blade, so I like to keep sterile gauze pads right in the classroom. That way, if a student nicks or grazes a finger, I can reach for the gauze to help stop bleeding and minimize any discomfort as quickly as possible. Even if you're not a teacher, it could be helpful to tuck some of these pads into your quilting tote when you go to a workshop or guild meeting.

Diana McClun

Working with Fabrics

❖ A Grain of Truth ❖

To straighten and true up the angle of the cross-grain edge of your fabric before you start cutting strips, try using this two-ruler method. Simply place the rulers so that one falls just over the cross-grain edge of the fabric and the other lies right next to the first. One line on each ruler should be lined up with the fold of the fabric. Move the ruler that lies completely on the fabric out of the way, and the other ruler will be in the correct position to cut the edge of the fabric so that it is straight and perpendicular to the folded edge. If you are right-handed, straighten the left edge of the fabric, and if you're left-handed, the right edge.

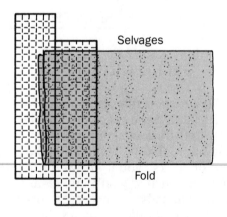

Selvages

Fold

QNM Editors

❖ Straight Cuts ❖ for a Head Start

I like to make sure one edge on each piece of fabric is straightened for rotary cutting before I store it. If I want to cut bias strips, I'll be able to work from the other end of the fabric. I like knowing that whenever I pick up a piece of fabric from my shelf, there will always be one straight edge ready to go and one edge I can use for bias cuts. That saves me a lot of preparation time.

Nancy J. Martin

❖ Soothe the Selvage Beast ❖

Folding your fabric correctly is one of the most important things you can do to avoid cutting strips with "the bends." To prepare your fabric, fold it so that the selvages are together. Then pick the fabric up with the selvages in both hands and slide the selvages from side to side until the fold of the fabric is flat. Lay the fabric back down on your work surface and fold the fabric in half again, bringing the fold to the selvage edges so that they line up. Now you have one edge that is all folds and the other one that is a fold and two selvage edges. Those must all be lined up and lying flat before you begin to cut your strips.

Sharyn Squier Craig

❖ A Pressing Situation ❖

I like to press a piece of fabric with the selvage edges together and then fold it over lengthwise again. Having a double fold in the fabric means that you can use shorter strokes with the rotary cutter each time you make a cut. And if you press each piece of fabric this way before you store it, it will always be ready for rotary cutting whenever you need it.

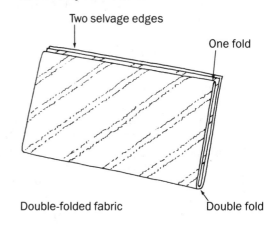

Two selvage edges

One fold

Double-folded fabric

Double fold

Nancy J. Martin

❖ A Real Time Shaver ❖

When you're cutting multiple pieces for many blocks, you can shorten your cutting time if you keep your fabric strips folded double. First, determine the total number of pieces you'll need, based on how many pieces are in the block and how many blocks you plan to make. Then leave the fabric strip folded double, so you are working with approximately 10 inches of fabric when you cut out the pieces. Most patchwork blocks have pieces that occur in multiples of two or four, and if your fabric strip is folded to cut through four layers at once, you can save quite a lot of time by cutting around a template a fewer number of times. If you cut four triangles from a strip when you actually need only two for your block, I think you are still several minutes ahead. You may end up with a couple of extra triangles, but you'll save time by not unfolding the fabric strip to cut just the two pieces you need.

Sharyn Squier Craig

❖ Short Strips ❖

I've devised a method of my own for rotary cutting fabric, which I call "short strips." Start by layering four or five pieces of fabric, each 18 inches long by the width of the fabric, and align the selvages. Use a rotary cutter and ruler to trim off the selvage edges, and then cut strips of whatever width you need.

There are a number of advantages to working with short strips. Cutting strips parallel to the selvage edge of the fabric allows you to take advantage of the more stable lengthwise grain of the fabric for your patches. Prints often align better with lengthwise grain, so you'll ensure the best possible appearance for each patch. Plus, with this cutting technique you can create a beautiful scrap look by using small pieces of many different fabrics to cut your short strips.

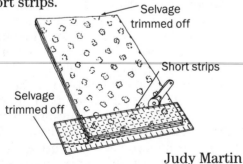

Selvage trimmed off

Short strips

Selvage trimmed off

Judy Martin

❖ Go Figure! ❖

Here's an easy method for figuring yardages based on rotary-cutting methods:

1. Check your quilt directions to find the total number you will need of each pattern piece.

2. On a piece of paper, draw a rectangle to represent the width and length of one fabric strip, and calculate the number of pattern pieces you can cut from that strip. Make the width of the fabric strip in your sketch the same as the width of the desired pattern piece. In the example shown, 3½-inch squares are needed, so the rectangle measures 3½ inches × 44 inches. Divide the length of the strip by the length of the pattern piece to get the number of pieces per strip. The example shows you can get twelve 3½-inch squares from a 44-inch strip.

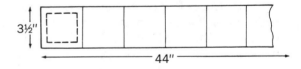

44" ÷ 3½" = 12 squares

3. Divide the number of shapes you can get from one strip into the total number of pieces in the quilt to determine the number of strips you will need to cut for that particular pattern piece.

4. Multiply the width of the strip by the total number of strips needed, to figure out how much of that fabric to buy. Be sure to calculate the yardage for all pattern pieces and to combine yardage amounts when more than one

pattern piece will be cut from the same fabric.

5. Divide the total amount of fabric (in inches) by 36 to calculate the actual number of yards you'll need. It's always a good idea to give yourself the security of a little extra fabric to use as a "fudge factor," in case you make a mistake in cutting.

Helen Whitson Rose

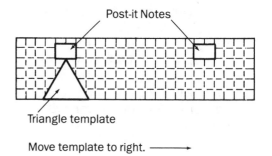

Post-it Notes

Triangle template

Move template to right. ———→

Doreen Speckmann

Using Rulers and Mats

❖ A Noteworthy Idea ❖

When you're making a project that contains isosceles triangles (triangles with two equal sides), you can quickly and easily cut these shapes using your rotary cutter and ruler. The basic technique is to line up a template of the triangle you want to cut on your rotary ruler; this marks the exact width of the strip you need to cut, which will be cut again into the individual triangles.

I place my triangle template on top of my ruler, about an inch in from the left end, so that the ruler base and the triangle base are even. Then I put a little Post-it Note on the ruler at the very tip of the triangle, slide the template along the ruler to the right, and place another Post-it Note at the other end of the ruler, approximately an inch from this end. This method marks the exact width of the strip you need to cut for your triangles, which is helpful if the height of the triangle does not fall neatly on a ruler line.

❖ You Have to ❖ Draw the Line Somewhere

If you need to cut fabric into strips with measurements that don't fit neatly onto the lines of your ruler, you can use a fine-line permanent marker to add lines to the ruler.

Marsha McCloskey

❖ Got That on Tape? ❖

Even if the measurement line you need for cutting strips is actually on your rotary-cutting ruler, it can be helpful to place a piece of masking tape on the underside of the ruler at whichever line you're using. The edge of the masking tape becomes an instant visual guide that keeps you from having to look at all the other lines on the ruler each time you move it across the fabric.

QNM Editors

❖ Going over the Top ❖

Position your rotary ruler on the fabric so that the end closer to you extends beyond the fold of the fabric. That way, when you begin cutting, you'll avoid nicking the corner of your ruler with your blade.

QNM Editors

❖ Let Your ❖ Fingers Do the Walking

It's a good idea to cut your fabric strips by using one continuous motion, never lifting the cutter from the fabric. It's helpful to move your noncutting hand along the surface of the ruler when you cut, with a "walking" motion to hold the ruler securely in place on the fabric.

QNM Editors

❖ Put On the Brakes ❖

If you position your hand on top of your rotary-cutting ruler so that your ring finger and thumb are just next to the outside edges, and your index and middle fingers remain on top of the ruler, you can "park" the ruler, so it won't slide out of control on slippery fabric surfaces.

QNM Editors

❖ A Tale of True Grit ❖

Try gluing pieces of fine-grit, self-adhesive sandpaper to the backs of all your rulers to help avoid slippage. You can buy this kind of sandpaper at any hardware store.

QNM Editors

❖ Recommended ❖ by Skateboarders

You can use the grid tape that skateboarders put on their skateboards to help stop rotary-cutting rulers from sliding on fabric when you cut strips. This is a clear tape, so it allows you to see through a ruler to align it with the edge of the fabric.

QNM Editors

❖ Does It Need Realignment? ❖

One thing I've done to improve my accuracy with the rotary cutter is to be careful when aligning a line on my ruler with the edge of my fabric. If you simply bring whichever ruler line you want to use to the very edge of the fabric, you actually undercut your fabric strip by the width of that line. The actual measurement of a ruler line goes to the outside of the line. It will help your cutting accuracy to take that little bit into account. I like to leave just a tiny "hair" of fabric sticking outside the ruler line I'm using. That way, I know I'll get the full width.

Lynn Lewis Young

❖ Grids with Gusto ❖

I like to use a cutting mat that has a network of grids on it, because I like working with the horizontal and vertical lines. For example, to prepare a piece of fabric for rotary cutting, and to straighten the cross-grain edge, I start by positioning the fold of the fabric on one of the horizontal lines on the grids. Then it's easy to place a ruler over the cross-grain edge of the fabric and line up one of the lines on the ruler with the fabric fold on the cutting mat.

Sharyn Squier Craig

❖ Duct Tape to the Rescue ❖

If you're cutting particularly long pieces of fabric, longer than the size of your cutting mat, consider borrowing a mat from a friend and taping it onto yours. Lay both mats face down and slide the edges so they abut; join them together with a strip of duct tape.

QNM Editors

❖ Keep Out of the Sun! ❖

Don't learn the hard way that rotary mats don't like the sun or extreme heat. Anytime you leave a mat in a warm or sunny place and the mat is not perfectly flat, it may warp or buckle. If you're on your way to a guild meeting or workshop and you stash your mat in the trunk of your car, don't leave it there for long. If you store your mat leaning against a wall in your sewing room and the room gets hot during the summer, try to find a place where you can rest it flat while not in use.

QNM Editors

❖ On Behalf of Lefties ❖

When you're left-handed, you quickly learn that the world is set up for right-handers. This holds true for directions for rotary cutting, as well. On behalf of the left-handed minority, here are a few tips that can help when you're working with a rotary cutter:

◆ Make your first cut to even the end of the fabric with the length of folded fabric extending to your right. Subsequent cuts, when you're slicing your strips, will need to be made with the length of fabric turned around so it's on your left.

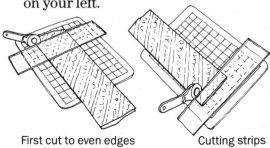

First cut to even edges   Cutting strips

◆ If you're ambidextrous, you can have the best of both worlds and never have to rotate the fabric between the first even-it-up cut and the following cuts. Make the first cut as described above, with the cutter in your left hand. Then, instead of turning the fabric around, switch the cutter to your right hand to cut the strips. Practice on some scrap fabric to see how comfortable this is for you.

◆ If you're working on a group quilt or cutting in the company of a right-handed quilter, take advantage of your southpaw orientation. Lay the fabric on the cutting mat with the length extending to the right. You make the first cut to even the edges, then turn the ruler and cutter over to the rightie, who will finish slicing the strips. Both of these cuts can be done without having to rotate the fabric in between.

Mary Green and Suzanne Nelson

Techniques for Rotary Cutting and Quick Piecing

Squares and Triangles

❖ The Bias Square ❖

This quick and accurate technique for cutting half-square triangles is featured in the book *Rotary Riot—40 Fast and Fabulous Quilts*, by Judy Hopkins and Nancy J. Martin. It yields squares cut from two fabrics with the straight of grain along the outside edges.

This method consists of sewing together two bias strips, pressing the strips open, and cutting squares from the strips. The advantage of this technique is that you do the pressing before you cut the squares, so there's less chance of distortion.

1. Cut a square or a rectangle from each of two fabrics. An 18-inch square or an 18 × 44-inch rectangle will work well.

2. Determine the *finished* size of the square you want to cut, and cut the fabrics into bias strips that are ¾ inch wider. For example, to end up with a 3-inch finished square, cut the bias strips 3¾ inches wide.

3. Sew four strips of fabric together with ¼-inch seams, alternating the fabrics.

Press the seam allowances to one side, pressing toward the darker fabrics.

4. The ruler for cutting the bias squares should be an acrylic square with a 45 degree diagonal line marked on it, such as the Bias Square. Begin at the lower end of the stitched strips and align the 45 degree line on the ruler with the first seam line on the fabric strips. Extend the ruler over two strips, so that you can cut a segment *larger* than the *cut* size of your square. For example, if you want a 3-inch finished square, place the bottom edge of the ruler at approximately the 3¾-inch line on the ruler. Cut the first two sides of the square.

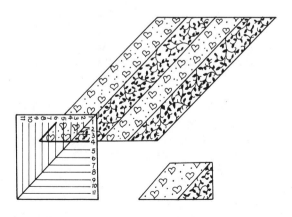

5. Move the ruler to the right and cut a second segment in the same way, and then a third. From four fabric strips, you can cut three squares across each row.

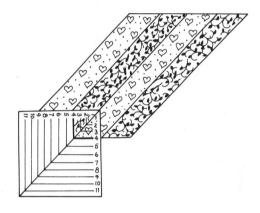

6. Moving upward, continue cutting out as many rows of squares as you can. Be sure to save the leftover edges of fabric. They're great for cutting single triangles.

7. Turn each segment and place the cut edges on the correct ruler markings for the *cut* size of the square. Cut the remaining two sides of each square.

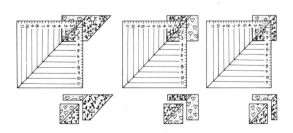

8. You can use this same cutting method for making scrap quilts. Just cut a variety of fabrics into bias strips, stitch them into bands, and cut out bias squares in the same manner.

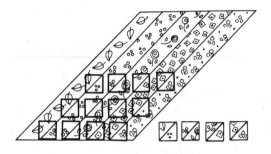

Nancy J. Martin

❖ **Quarter-Square Triangles** ❖

A close relative of the half-square triangle, the quarter-square triangle is used in many block patterns and can be time-consuming to construct, not to mention vexing, as you try to get all the seams and pieces to align. Borrowing the same basic technique described in "The Bias Square" on page 68, quarter-square triangles become a snap using a rotary cutter and the technique that follows.

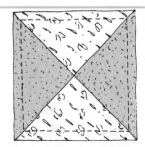

1. Determine the *finished* size of the quarter-square triangle unit you want. Add 1⅛ inches to that measurement and cut four bias strips that wide. For example, if you want to have 3-inch finished quarter-square triangle units, cut the bias strips 4⅛ inches wide. Sew the strips together with ¼-inch seams and press the seam allowances toward alternating strips.

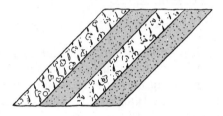

2. Use the Bias Square to cut two-color square units that are ⅞ inch larger than the finished size you're working toward. Then cut those units in half diagonally into quarter-square triangles.

Finished size + ⅞"

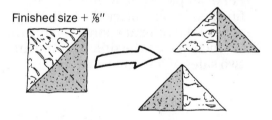

3. Sew the resulting triangles together into the finished-size quarter-square triangle unit.

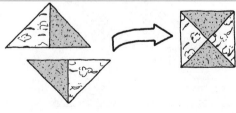

Nancy J. Martin

IT'S AS E-Z AS 1-2-3!

I like the Easy Angle tool for rotary cutting half-square triangles. Let's say you're making a block that has 2-inch finished squares in it, as well as some 2-inch finished half-square triangles. You can use a 2½-inch strip of fabric to cut out the squares, and with the Easy Angle tool, you can cut your triangles out of that same 2½-inch strip. With other rotary rulers, you'd need to cut strips of a different width to accommodate the points of the half-square triangles. Being able to cut all your squares and triangles from the same strip size simplifies things. I also like the fact that the tool takes off that little bit of "extra" fabric at the point of a triangle. Measurements are printed on the front and the back, so you can use either side. You can buy this tool in quilt shops, or contact EZ International, 95 Mayhill Street, Saddle Brook, NJ 07662, for a source.

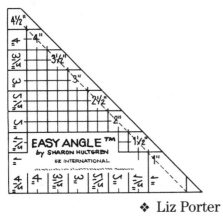

❖ Liz Porter

❖ Double-Sewn Bias Strips ❖

This method of cutting half-square triangles involves sewing two bias strips together and cutting stitched triangles from those strips. The advantage to this method is that you can use small amounts of fabric, which can be very helpful when making a scrap quilt.

Cutting Half-Square Triangles from Double-Sewn Strips

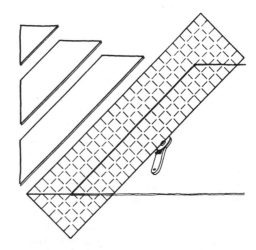

Step 1: *Layer two contrasting fabrics right sides together. Align the 45 degree line on your ruler with the bottom edge of the fabric and cut bias strips, using the required width indicated on the chart on page 72. If you're working with scraps, be sure to cut on the bias grain.*

Step 2: *Place two fabric strips of the same length right sides together. Stitch a ¼-inch seam along both long edges, using thread that contrasts with the lighter fabric so you can see the seam easily.*

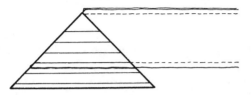

Step 3: *Using a triangle template such as the Quilter's Rule Mini-Triangle (or you can make your own, as explained in "Make Your Own Triangle Template!" on page 74), find the line that shows the finished size of the square you want. Position that line exactly on top of one seam, just at the end of the bias strip. The tip of the template will fall on or just past the stitching line on the other side of the strip.*

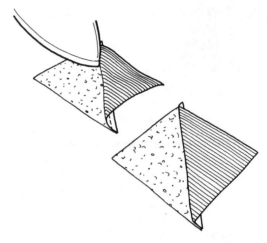

Step 6: *Press the square unit open, making sure that the seam allowance goes toward the darker of the two fabrics.*

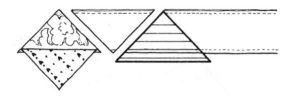

Step 4: *With a rotary cutter, cut across the strip on both sides of the triangle template. Then turn the template around to cut another triangle. Each time you cut a triangle, the line that shows the finished size of your square on the triangle template must match the stitching line on the bias strip. This may mean you'll have to cut both sides of each new triangle.*

Width of Bias Strips	Finished Square
1½"	1"
2"	1½"
2¼"	2"
2¾"	2½"
3"	3"
3¼"	3½"
3¾"	4"
4"	4½"
4½"	5"
4¾"	5½"
5¼"	6"

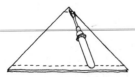

Step 5: *If you find that one or more stitches remain from the seam on the other side of your bias strip, you can remove the threads with a single pull from a seam ripper.*

Judy Duerstock

GIVE YOUR BLOCKS A MAKEOVER

Rotary cutting and strip piecing can contribute creative new elements to your block designs. The trick is looking at standard blocks and figuring out where you can add the visual excitement of strip piecing.

You can instantly change the look of any patch in any block by making it from a strip-pieced band of fabric instead of from a single fabric. To get your creative juices working, here are some ways to add strip piecing to a portion of a patchwork block. Once you start thinking along these lines, you're bound to come up with more ideas of your own.

Frame the center. *Strip-pieced patches at the outer edges of a block, such as in this Nine-Patch Star, can make a very effective frame around the center portion of the block.*

Change the focus. *If a block contains several elements of nearly equal design importance, strip piecing can bring your eye to one particular element by emphasizing it, as in this Aunt Sukey's Patch block.*

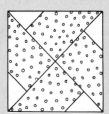 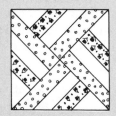

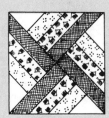

Add movement to the block. *This Pinwheel block seems to spin in joyful abandon simply by the addition of pieced strips to the larger patches. And by varying the color contrast from light to dark, you can create a feeling of even more motion.*

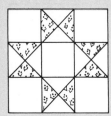 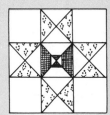

Fill an "empty" spot. *Sometimes a block that has a large center square can look a bit barren. You can liven it up with interesting strip-pieced triangles, as in this Variable Star block.*

❖ QNM Editors

❖ Make Your ❖
Own Triangle Template!

Here's a way to make your own tool for cutting half-square triangles, to be used with the double-sewn bias strip technique described in "Double-Sewn Bias Strips" on page 71.

1. Purchase a clear acrylic or plexiglass 45/90 degree triangle at an art supply store.

2. On a piece of paper taped to your work surface, draw a right triangle that is the size of the purchased triangle. On this drawing, use a ruler to mark the lines for various finished square sizes. Laying an 18-inch rotary ruler over the triangle, mark ½-inch increments.

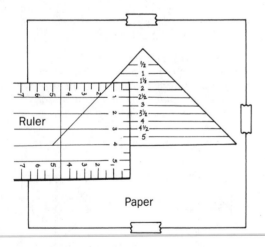

3. Place your purchased triangle over the drawn triangle, matching short

edges, and use a utility knife to carefully etch the lines.

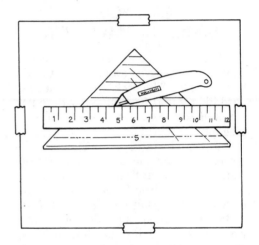

4. Turn your triangle over and place a narrow strip of masking tape labeled with the finished square sizes perpendicular to your etched lines.

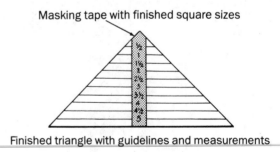

Masking tape with finished square sizes

Finished triangle with guidelines and measurements

Judy Duerstock

❖ Shortcuts for Cutting ❖ Triangles from Squares

Shortcuts can come in handy when you need to cut a number of setting triangles and corner triangles for a quilt top. Rather than cutting them all out individually, start by cutting strips of fabric. Then cut the strips into squares and cut the squares diagonally in half or quarters. Each of the diagrams below tells you how much to add to the finished size of your piece to arrive at the correct strip width to cut.

Rotary Shortcuts for Triangles

Short side + ⅞"

To cut half-square triangles, measure the finished size of the short side of the triangle and add ⅞ inch to this number. Cut a strip of fabric this width and cut a square from the fabric strip. Then cut the square in half diagonally to create half-square triangles.

Longest side + 1¼"

To create quarter-square triangles from a square, first measure the finished size of the longest side of the triangle. To that measurement, add 1¼ inches and cut a fabric strip that wide. Cut a square from that strip and cut the square in half diagonally both ways.

QNM Editors

Using Templates for Rotary Cutting

❖ Con"template" This Idea ❖

It's a good idea to make a set of master templates in sizes and shapes that you use frequently. I find that certain sizes of squares and triangles are found in many different quilt blocks, which means it usually isn't necessary to draft a whole new set of templates each time you design a new block.

Sharyn Squier Craig

❖ Template Sandwiches ❖

I like to show people how to make template "sandwiches" that they can use with a rotary cutter and ruler. You can start by drafting your pattern piece—a square, triangle, or rectangle—on a piece of graph paper, including the seam allowances. Run a fairly thick line of glue stick all around the outside edges of your graph paper template, without leaving any little "clumps" of glue. (I like the Dennison brand glue stick because it doesn't get hard or dry out easily. Rubber cement works well, too, but it does give off fumes. If you use it, it's a good idea to keep the room well ventilated.)

Then place a piece of heavyweight, see-through template plastic (nongridded) on your graph paper pattern. Turn this glued unit over and run a line of glue stick around the back side of the graph paper template. Place a piece of heavyweight, fine-grit, see-through sandpaper on top of the graph paper, rough side out. This will create a durable 3-layer template sandwich.

Let the layers dry completely, which can take several hours. To cut out the template accurately, cut right down the middle of the cutting line. This kind of template sandwich is sturdy and durable enough to use with a rotary cutter.

Sharyn Squier Craig

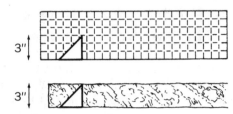

Sharyn Squier Craig

❖ Getting the Proper Fit ❖

I cut my fabric strips to fit my templates exactly. The easiest way to do this is to take a template and lay it on your ruler and measure its width. The width of the template then becomes the width of the strips you cut. If you are cutting rectangles, it won't matter which measurement you use for placing the pieces on the fabric strip. If you're cutting triangles, however, you'll need to decide which side of the triangle will go on the straight grain, in order to measure for the correct strip width. If you're working with half-square triangles, in most cases the straight grain goes on the two short sides. Then the strip should be cut as wide as the measurement of the short side. If you're working with quarter-square triangles, or if you want the straight grain of your half-square triangles along the long edge, then you should position the triangle on the ruler so that you measure the *height* of it, rather than the sides.

❖ Let Your Fingers ❖ Do the Checking

If you want to check for accuracy when you're cutting around templates on fabric strips, use your fingers to feel the edges of the template and the fabric strip. That way, each time you cut, you'll know that your template fits the fabric strip exactly. If you've cut your strip incorrectly and it's somewhat skimpy or a bit too large, that fact will show up immediately, *before* you have cut out dozens of pieces incorrectly. It's a good checks-and-balances system for accurate cutting.

Sharyn Squier Craig

❖ This End Up! ❖

It's possible to use rotary methods for cutting directional pieces that face the same way, such as the parallelogram-shaped roof used for many Schoolhouse blocks. Just start with a strip of fabric that is a little bit wider than it needs to be to accommodate the template, and cut rectangles from this strip that are a tiny bit larger than the template, as well. (Add this little extra space around the edges to give you some leeway when you stack up the fabrics and find that their edges don't exactly match. The extra room allows you to position the template so that it can be cut from all the layers.) Separate the rectangles and stack them so that each layer of fabric is right side up. Then when you cut around the template, each parallelogram will be cut directionally to match all the others.

Sharyn Squier Craig

Some Quick-Piecing Shortcuts

❖ Know When to Strip ❖

The rotary cutter makes cutting strips a cinch. Learn to look at a quilt block to analyze whether all or part of it might lend itself to strip piecing (where strips of fabric are cut, sewn together to create strip sets, and then cut apart into units that are assembled into a block). Using strips wherever you can will streamline construction of the block. The diagrams below provide examples of blocks containing units that are perfect for strip piecing.

Analyzing Blocks for Strip Piecing

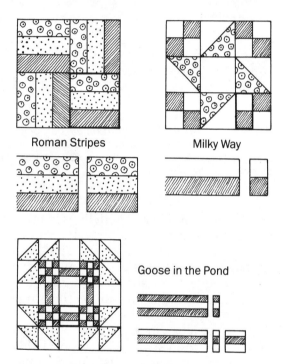

Roman Stripes

Milky Way

Goose in the Pond

If part of a block is made up of 4-patch or 9-patch units or just plain strips, you can strip piece those and rotary cut the segments needed for the block. The parts of the block that aren't suitable for strip piecing can be completed with traditional cutting and piecing methods. The dark lines in the diagrams show the units in the blocks that translate readily into strip piecing.

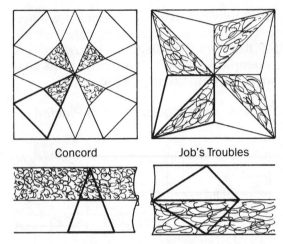

Concord   Job's Troubles

Blocks with set-in patches often contain portions that can be strip pieced. The dark lines in the diagrams isolate the parts of the blocks that are suitable for strip piecing.

Keep the following guidelines in mind as you determine whether you can use strip piecing for a quilt block. First, and perhaps most obvious, patches must have straight edges to be strip pieced. Also, the same fabrics must appear in the same sequence in several blocks. If you plan to make every block in your quilt from different fabrics, then strip piecing is probably not the best method to use. You can use strip piecing to make scrap quilts, however, simply by cutting shorter strips from a greater number of fabrics and arranging the pieced segments so that they're scattered randomly throughout the quilt.

QNM Editors

❖ Change Directions ❖ to Stay Straight

When I'm sewing several long strips together for a project, I like to alternate the sewing direction with each strip. I find that helps avoid the "warping" that can occur when you're working with long strips.

Debbie Mumm

❖ Rack 'Em Up! ❖

With two small children and two feisty cats in the house, it didn't take me long to discover that I needed to find a way to keep my sets of rotary-cut strips organized and out of the way until I got the chance to sit down at the machine and do some strip piecing. A simple wooden drying rack was the perfect answer. I bought an inexpensive one, and I drape my sets of strips (grouped according to fabric and length) over the wooden dowels. The best part is that I can set the whole thing in the closet, out of the way of fingers and paws, until the next time I'm ready to sew.

Suzanne Nelson

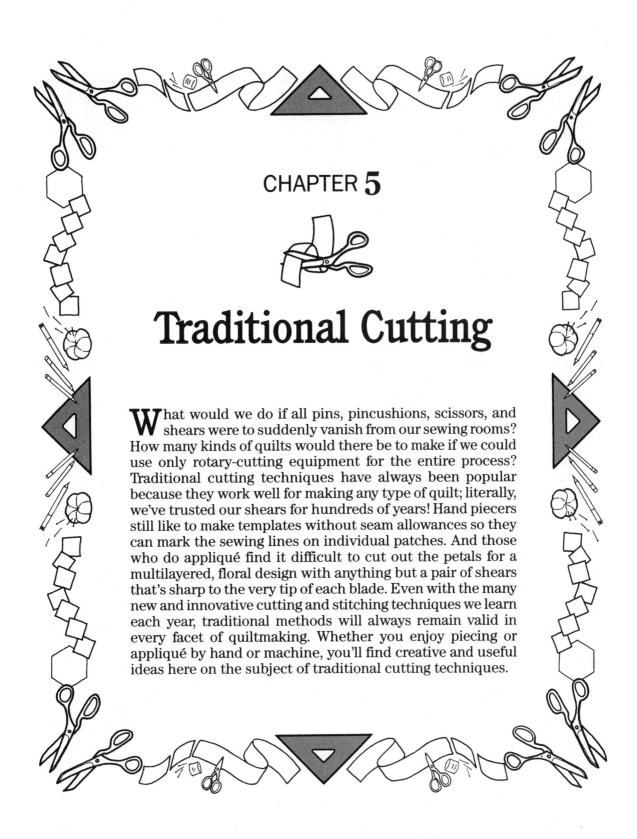

CHAPTER 5

Traditional Cutting

What would we do if all pins, pincushions, scissors, and shears were to suddenly vanish from our sewing rooms? How many kinds of quilts would there be to make if we could use only rotary-cutting equipment for the entire process? Traditional cutting techniques have always been popular because they work well for making any type of quilt; literally, we've trusted our shears for hundreds of years! Hand piecers still like to make templates without seam allowances so they can mark the sewing lines on individual patches. And those who do appliqué find it difficult to cut out the petals for a multilayered, floral design with anything but a pair of shears that's sharp to the very tip of each blade. Even with the many new and innovative cutting and stitching techniques we learn each year, traditional methods will always remain valid in every facet of quiltmaking. Whether you enjoy piecing or appliqué by hand or machine, you'll find creative and useful ideas here on the subject of traditional cutting techniques.

Making Templates

The Importance of Grain

❖ Straight Talk ❖

The way you arrange templates on fabric has a great deal to do with how straight your quilt blocks will be when you're finished sewing. It's hard to overstate the importance of cutting accurately on the straight grain. The term "length of grain" refers to threads that run parallel to the selvage edges of a piece of fabric, and the term "cross grain" refers to the fibers that run at a 90 degree angle to the lengthwise threads. Both are straight grains of the fabric. "Bias" is the fabric grain that lies at a 45 degree angle to the selvages. It's best to have length of grain or cross grain along the outside edges of a block whenever possible. Here are some guidelines to consider for cutting pattern pieces that are straight and true:

♦ Study the block you want to make and determine which edges of the patches fall on the outside edges of your block.

♦ Place your templates on the fabrics so that these edges lie along either the cross- or lengthwise grain of the fabric.

♦ Place as many straight edges of your templates as you can along a straight grain. (Note the placement of Triangle A in the diagram on the right, for example.)

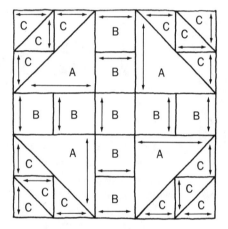

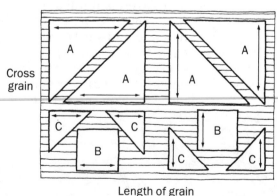

Length of grain

Outside edges on straight of grain

80

♦ Wherever possible, avoid having to sew two bias edges together. The inherent stretchiness of bias makes it difficult to keep the pieces true to shape.

QNM Editors

❖ TLC for Bias Edges ❖

Bias has a great deal of stretch, which makes it wonderful for sewing around curves, but at the edges of a quilt block, it can cause distortions. It's possible to work with bias edges, however, when the design of your fabric is a more important consideration than the placement of templates on the grain line. Just remember to handle bias edges very gently as you stitch, to avoid pulling them out of shape, and press these seams very carefully when you're finished sewing.

QNM Editors

❖ Stable Stay Stitches ❖

If the grain lines on the outer edges of a block are not straight, you can machine stitch them outside the seam line to increase stability.

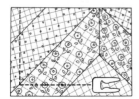

QNM Editors

Terrific Template Tips

❖ Precision Pattern Pieces ❖

I feel strongly about drawing the exact finished-size pattern pieces first and adding seam allowances all the way around to make accurate templates. For more complicated blocks, it's a good idea to draw the finished block in its entirety, as well. Then you can cut the whole pattern apart, glue the individual pieces of the block onto template plastic, and add ¼-inch seam allowances.

Doreen Speckmann

❖ Hand-Piecing ❖ Templates for Machine Piecers

I have found that even when I'm machine piecing, I sometimes like to use finished-size templates and mark around them on the wrong sides of the fabrics, as if I were cutting out patches for hand piecing. That gives me a visible sewing line and lets me pin-match each seam as I sew.

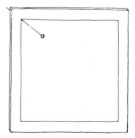

Marianne Fons

❖ One Patch at a Time ❖

I like to use templates to cut my pieces one at a time for a scrap quilt, rather than cutting strips of fabric. I like to make each block a pleasing and balanced unit in itself. By cutting all the patches for a block individually, I can think of a scrap quilt first in terms of smaller units, before putting it together as a whole quilt. I lay out the patches on a Pellon fleece or cotton flannel surface to view the block as an individual unit. By viewing the entire block before I stitch it together, I can make sure that the darks and lights are balanced within it.

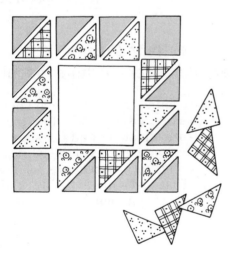

Jeana Kimball

❖ Get a Grip ❖ with Rubber Cement

All my templates have rubber cement on the back, to stop them from slipping on the fabric. Just coat the entire back surface of each template you make and let the glue dry. The rubbery coating will make the template stay firmly in place on the fabric while you mark or cut around it. It won't discolor or harm the fabric in any way, and you can peel it off and put a new coating on your template whenever you like. But don't put rubber cement on the back of a ruler, because it can take off the ink.

John Flynn

❖ Using X-Ray-ted Film ❖

If you have access to hospital X-ray film, it makes great template material. When I work with curved shapes, I find it useful to draw those shapes on graph paper and trace them onto X-ray film. The advantage is that it is an easy weight to cut accurately. Some other types of plastics are a bit too thick for that.

Marsha McCloskey

❖ Precise, ❖ Pressable Freezer Paper

If you're going to make only one block from a given pattern, or if you're working a complicated pattern that has set-in pieces, try using freezer paper templates. Freezer paper is easy to draw on and cut, and you can press it on the wrong side of your fabric, so you'll know exactly where the seam lines in your block are.

1. Draw the block full-size on a piece of freezer paper and label each piece.

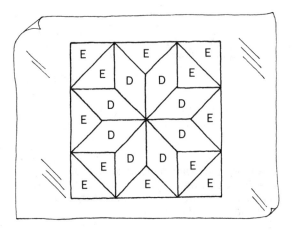

2. Cut your paper pattern apart and press the pieces onto the *wrong* sides of your fabrics. Be sure to leave at least ½ inch between adjacent pattern pieces.

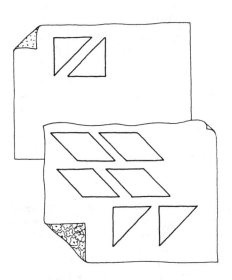

3. Add the seam allowances to each piece with a pencil or marker and cut the pieces out by hand. (Or you can use a rotary ruler to add the ¼-inch seam allowances as you cut with a rotary cutter.)

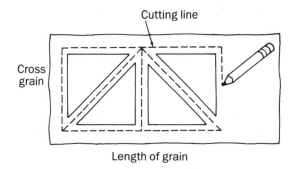

4. When you sew the block together, leave the freezer paper on the fabric and use the edges of the paper to guide your seam lines. Your corners will meet perfectly, and the freezer paper stabilizes the bias edges of your fabric, so the pieces won't stretch as you sew them together.

Liz Porter

❖ Merry Olde English Piecing ❖

More quilters should give the gentle art of English paper piecing a try. Although it takes time, it almost guarantees a perfect fit for the pieces in your quilt. This method is most often used for piecing Grandmother's Flower Garden quilts, but you can sew other shapes, such as diamonds, triangles, trapezoids, and parallelograms, together this way, too.

The Step-by-Step for English Paper Piecing

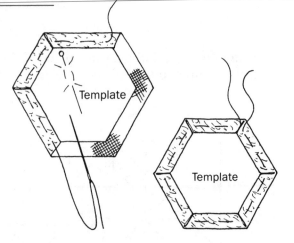

Step 3: *Center a paper template on the wrong side of a fabric patch and fold the seam allowances over it snugly. Baste the seam allowances in place with a neutral thread. It isn't necessary to begin and end the basting with a knot.*

Step 1: *Make a paper template that is exactly the size of your finished piece. Heavy writing paper, greeting cards, or index cards—or as tradition suggests, old love letters—will work well. You can also purchase precut paper templates in many standard sizes.*

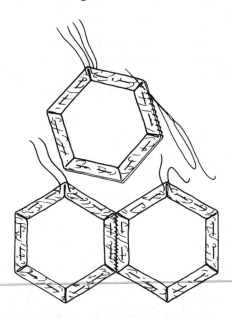

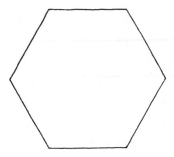

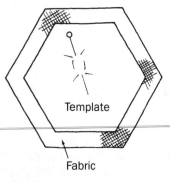

Template

Fabric

Step 2: *Cut fabric patches that are at least ¼ inch larger than the paper template on all sides. These seam allowances need not be exact, because the template will control the finished size of the patch.*

Step 4: *After you've basted several pieces, place two patches right sides together and overcast the edges, catching just two or three threads from each patch at a time. To finish this seam, run the thread through to the back side and cut it. Then you can open up the pieces and finger press them.*

plates. The innovative and creative part lies in how you piece fabric strips onto the paper templates and how you piece those parts together with the non-string-pieced fabric parts of your design. You can make any size quilt you like with string-piecing techniques, from a small wall quilt to a very large design. For my quilt "Corona II: The Solar Eclipse," I taped big sheets of paper together, so that the whole piece of paper was 76 inches × 94 inches, which was exactly the size of the finished quilt. Here are some guidelines and ideas to consider when you incorporate string piecing into one of your quilts.

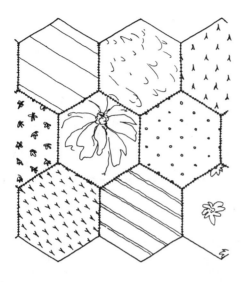

Step 5: *Position the next patches so they match precisely and sew them in the same manner. Each seam should be sewn along the straight edge; do not try to sew around corners, or the pieces will not lie flat. After you've finished piecing, remove the basting stitches and the paper templates and press your work.*

QNM Editors

The Step-by-Step for String Piecing

Step 1: *Start by drawing a full-size picture, including the borders, so that everything is lined up exactly the way you want it in your finished design.*

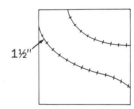

1½"

Step 2: *On curved lines in your design, mark little orientation lines at 1½- to 2-inch intervals along the curves. These will help you later, when you join the string-pieced portion to the adjacent fabric sections. Since these lines need to be visible on the back of the template, place carbon paper face up under the template as you draw the lines.*

❖ Stringing Things Out ❖

What really revolutionized my ability to make the quilts I wanted to make was discovering string piecing, which is sewing strips of fabric, or scraps, onto a paper base. You can string piece almost anything you can draw on paper, and you can incorporate any number of prints and color gradations into your quilt.

Basically, string piecing is just like cutting with traditional, old-fashioned tem-

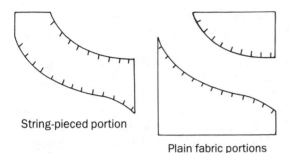

String-pieced portion

Plain fabric portions

Step 3: *Decide which part of your design you want to be string pieced, and cut that shape from your paper drawing. It will become the paper template base to which you string piece your strips of fabric. The other two paper shapes that are left over will be used as templates for the plain fabric portions of your design.*

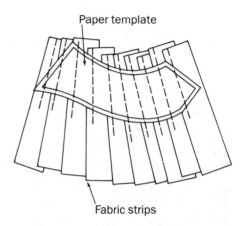

Paper template

Fabric strips

Step 5: *When you've finished sewing strips to your paper template, flip the template over to the back and draw around the edges of the template to create the seam lines, and trim ¼ inch outside these lines.*

Putting the Pieces Back Together

Sew your string-pieced portions to the other fabric parts of your design. To get these pieces to fit smoothly, line them up so that the orientation marks match on adjacent templates. (Remove the paper before you stitch the seams. The paper should come out very easily because it's been perforated by your stitching.) On any curved seam, you'll have to clip the seam allowance so that it will stretch to fit the outside curve of the seam on the adjacent piece. This means you'll have to clip almost to the seam line, ideally within a couple of threads. And on a seam that has a really tight curve, it's a good idea to hand baste the pieces together. For a seam with a gentle curve, just pin the first two orientation marks together and sew to the second pin. Then move the pins to the next two orientation marks, and continue pinning as you sew. When all the pieces are

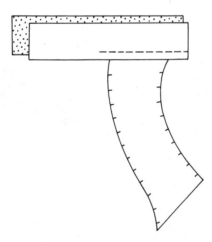

Step 4: *To begin the string piecing, lay a strip of fabric right side up on your paper template. Then place another fabric strip on top of that one, right sides together. Sew these two strips together with a ¼-inch seam allowance. Then open the fabrics and press from the top. Continue sewing and pressing in this manner until your paper template is covered with fabric. The fabric must extend ¼ inch beyond the paper on all sides.*

sewn together, the result will be exactly the size of your paper drawing.

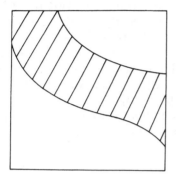

Caryl Bryer Fallert

Marking Methods

❖ That's a Good Point ❖

It helps to use a very sharp pencil for marking around templates. I like the #4 Karisma Aqua-rel pencil from Berol, rather than a harder or softer lead pencil, because it's water soluble. Another marking tool I like a lot is the Sanford Sharpie permanent marker with the ultrafine point. I use it only for marking cutting lines on fabric, however, so those lines do get cut off as I cut my pieces out. I wouldn't recommend it for marking seam lines.

Doreen Speckmann

❖ Chalking It ❖
Up to Experience

I like using the triangular tailor's chalk by Clover for marking around templates.

There is very little "drag" on the fabric with this type of marker, and you can sharpen the edges by moving them back and forth against a flat surface.

Jinny Beyer

GOING 'ROUND THE BEND

If you're designing or drafting quilts or blocks with curved lines, a quilter's memory curve can be helpful. Quilt shops usually have this kind of flexicurve tool, but if you need a long one, an art supply store or a drafting supply store is a good source for flexicurves that are longer than 12 to 18 inches.

❖ Caryl Bryer Fallert

❖ Punch a Hole in It! ❖

I *include* seam allowances when I make templates for hand piecing. I like to cut more than two layers of fabric at a time, which greatly reduces the preparation time. If you use traditional templates for hand piecing, which have no seam allowances included, it takes so long to line up and pin the pieces that you spend twice as much time sewing. Because I don't use marked seam lines, I can just line up the raw edges of two patches and start sewing.

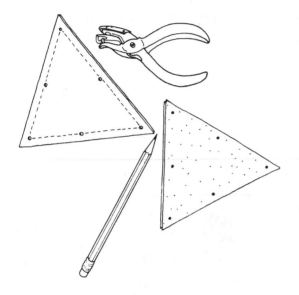

If you need help in "eyeballing" a ¼-inch seam allowance, I recommend using a ⅛-inch hole punch to put little holes in certain places on the template seam lines, such as at the points where corner seams meet and at the midpoints on the seam lines. That way, when you line up two pieces together to sew, you can put your template on top of one piece, use a pencil to mark a dot through the holes, and sew from one dot to the next.

Jinny Beyer

Cutting Techniques

❖ "Scrap Iron" Takes ❖ On a New Meaning

I sort my scraps according to size and then stack them on the ironing board in layers of equal or similar sizes. Then I press them together, which makes it easier to cut patches from all of the layers of fabric at once. I do that with all of my quilt fabrics, too, not just scraps. For instance, when I make a Kaleidoscope quilt, I start by cutting 5-inch strips and then place them in pairs, right sides together, before pressing. When I cut out the triangles, they're bonded like glue, right sides together and ready for sewing.

Eleanor Burns

❖ Borders First ❖

I think a good general cutting rule of thumb is to cut border pieces before you cut the other pieces. I think it's nice to have a full length of fabric for seamless borders. Although I know some people prefer crosswise strips, I usually cut my long borders on the length of grain for strength and stability. Cutting borders first also helps avoid having to go out and buy more fabric later.

Marianne Fons

❖ Spritz, Steam, ❖ Stretch, and Sew!

I cut my borders along the lengthwise grain whenever I can. If I *have* to cut them on the crosswise grain, however, I like to spray them with water and press them after they've been cut. And I like to stretch them as I press, because the crosswise grain of fabric has more give. And that stretching will happen by itself if you don't do that step before you sew the borders on your quilt.

Nancy J. Martin

❖ Hold an ❖ Audition on Your Block

It's always good to cut enough pieces for one block and make a sample before you plunge ahead and cut pieces for the whole quilt. This gives you a chance to make sure that the block is correct, that you like the way the block looks, and that you're going to have enough fabric. Making a sample block will reveal any problems immediately, such as a template that is incorrect.

Marianne Fons

❖ Making a Matched Set ❖

Getting pieces to match accurately and easily comes from good cutting. If you cut something right, it's going to align and it's going to match. When pieces are not cut right, that's usually when you have to try to "fudge" to get them together. Taking care right from the very start, from your very first cut, will make your piecing so much easier.

Nancy J. Martin

BOOKS ON TAPE FOR BETTER QUILTS!

I cut pieces for many of my quilts using templates and scissors. While I'm spending the time marking and cutting, it's wonderful to listen to books on tape. My library carries approximately 800 to 900 unabridged books on tape, and I like everything from *Clan of the Cave Bear* to Dick Francis mysteries to works by Tony Hillerman and Isaac Asimov. I find that listening to books while I'm working frees my creativity. While my left brain is listening to the book, my right brain seems to be a little freer to try things that I otherwise might not have done.

❖ Doreen Speckmann

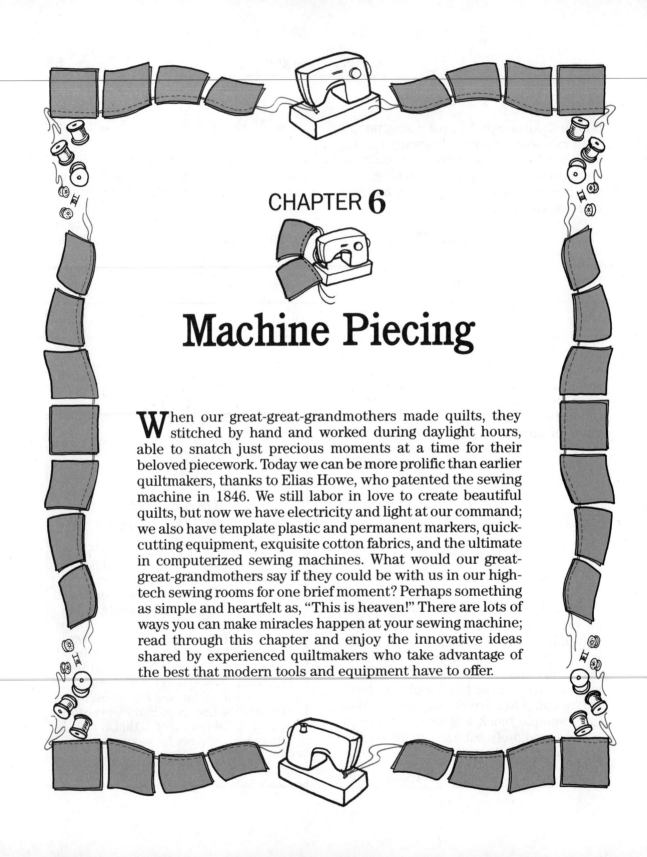

CHAPTER 6

Machine Piecing

When our great-great-grandmothers made quilts, they stitched by hand and worked during daylight hours, able to snatch just precious moments at a time for their beloved piecework. Today we can be more prolific than earlier quiltmakers, thanks to Elias Howe, who patented the sewing machine in 1846. We still labor in love to create beautiful quilts, but now we have electricity and light at our command; we also have template plastic and permanent markers, quick-cutting equipment, exquisite cotton fabrics, and the ultimate in computerized sewing machines. What would our great-great-grandmothers say if they could be with us in our high-tech sewing rooms for one brief moment? Perhaps something as simple and heartfelt as, "This is heaven!" There are lots of ways you can make miracles happen at your sewing machine; read through this chapter and enjoy the innovative ideas shared by experienced quiltmakers who take advantage of the best that modern tools and equipment have to offer.

Mastering Machine Patchwork

Handy Hints on Cutting and Piecing

❖ Cutting Corners ❖

Precise cutting is an important key to producing accurate machine patchwork. When you are piecing triangles and squares together, however, even perfect cutting is not always enough to ensure success. You also need to know how to align pieces correctly so they'll fit together perfectly. Follow this sequence of diagrams and captions to learn how to get the best fit from your patchwork pieces.

Tips to Ensure the Perfect Fit

If you're not careful, mismatching a triangle to a square can result in a block that looks something like this.

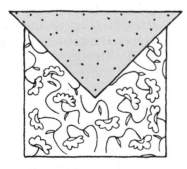

When triangle points extend far past the edges of a square, it's difficult to know exactly where to position them.

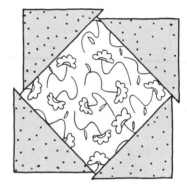

Machine piecers can solve this problem by aligning templates so that the marked seam allowances meet precisely where they should at each corner, and then cutting off the corners of the triangle template to fit the edges of the square template.

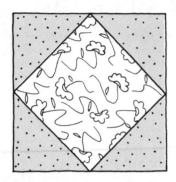

Using this kind of trimmed template means that your patches will fit together with precision, even in the trickiest of situations, producing a block like this one, with triangles meeting exactly where they should around the square.

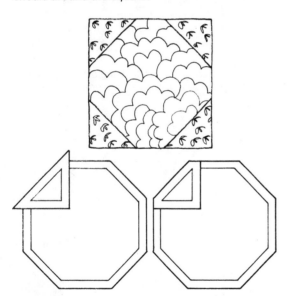

You can use this template-trimming technique whenever you're working with a patch that has angles that are more acute than 90 degrees. Just place the template you wish to trim over the template you want to match it to, and trim the corners to fit. On this Snowball block, you would trim the triangle points to match the octagon. The octagon needs no trimming since it has no sharp points.

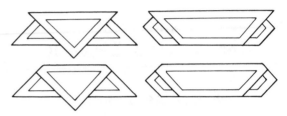

In this King's X block, two of the three templates could use a trim. Position the triangle over the neighboring trapezoid and trim the triangle to fit. Then place the trapezoid over the center lozenge shape and trim the trapezoid to fit. The center lozenge needs no trimming.

QNM Editors

❖ How Wide ❖
Are Your Stitches?

When you mark a line for a ¼-inch seam allowance on your sewing machine, be sure to include the actual width of your stitching line. If your seam allowance does not include the width of your stitches, you'll be altering the size of the finished work at every seam you sew. For example, if there are five seams across a block, you can sometimes remove as much as $5/32$ inch in one block. If you multiply this distance by the number of blocks in a large project, you may substantially change the dimensions in your quilt.

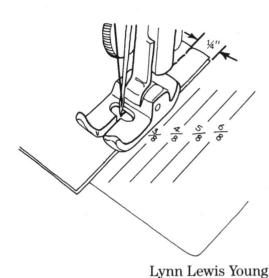

Lynn Lewis Young

SEWING WITH SUPER SPOOLS

Don't overlook sewing machine dealerships as sources for thread. Dealers often stock brands that your local fabric stores do not carry. For machine piecing, I like Star Mercerized thread, which is a 50-weight 100 percent cotton fiber. It's available in 65 different colors, and each spool gives you 1,200 yards of thread. You can also get neutral shades (black, white, natural, and navy) in 6,000-yard spools. If this thread isn't available where you live, contact Wheeler's Sewing Machine Company, 218 S. Grand Avenue, Santa Ana, CA 92701; (714) 547-0743.

❖ Doreen Speckmann

❖ Consider Going Gray! ❖

I like to use a medium gray 100 percent cotton thread for all my machine patchwork, even for working with black fabric. It blends with almost every color tone and print imaginable, and using such a neutral shade takes away the need to buy many different colors of thread. It also means you can save some time by not having to thread your machine as often.

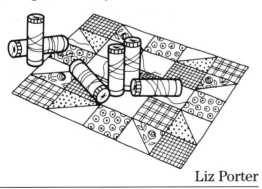

Liz Porter

❖ A Snip Here, a Clip There ❖

It's a good idea to trim all threads when you're piecing by machine. If you can train yourself from the beginning to clip each thread as it comes out of the machine, you won't have little snippets of thread showing behind light-colored patches in your finished quilt.

Marsha McCloskey

❖ A Great Thread Catcher ❖

A 3- or 4-inch piece of masking tape makes a great catchall for threads and bits of scrap fabric. Just make a loop of tape with the sticky side of the tape facing outward and stick it wherever you like, to catch snippets of thread, scraps, and even stray pins or needles. When you're finished working for the day, just toss the tape away.

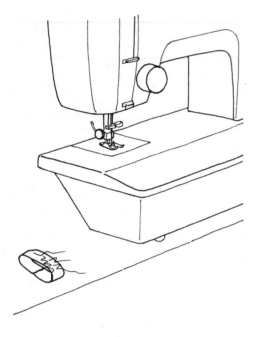

QNM Editors

❖ Halt the ❖
Spread of Bias Edges

If you use freezer paper templates that are the finished size of your pieces, try leaving the freezer paper in place while you machine sew the patches together. It will stabilize any bias edges and keep them from stretching out of shape as you stitch,

and you can remove the paper easily after you've sewn the seams.

Liz Porter

Chain and Unit Piecing

❖ Scraps Make ❖
Great Thread Savers

When I'm chain piecing many patches together, I use what I call a "thread saver" at the beginning and end of my piecing sequence. This is a scrap of fabric that I use to start sewing on, so that there are no "tails" of thread to clip later. I start by sewing across the fabric scrap and then place the first patch I want to sew next to the edge of it, so there is no space between the scrap and my next patch. When I've finished the entire chain-piecing sequence, I place another scrap of fabric next to the edge of my last patch, so that the end of my seam will be on the scrap. That way I can begin my next seam on that same scrap of fabric. It's amazing how much time and thread you can save with this method of beginning and ending a seam line.

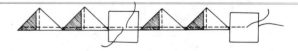

Nancy J. Martin

❖ Chain of Command ❖

You can make chain piecing go faster by arranging your patches next to your machine so they're in position to be easily aligned, with a minimum of wasted motion. Place one stack of patches right side down at the left of your machine, where you can pick them up with your left hand. Put another stack of patches at the right of your sewing machine needle, making sure that these patches are facing right side up. That way, when you pick one patch from each stack, they'll line up easily and quickly. After you've finished sewing and pressing all the seams, you can carry this process further by stacking your completed units next to the machine in the same manner, in position to be picked up and aligned with the following patches in your sewing sequence.

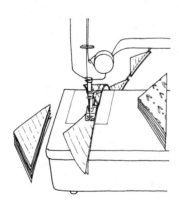

Judy Martin

❖ Make a Practice Block ❖

I like to machine piece blocks in units, so that each unit is completed before I go on to the next. Then I assemble the various units into the completed block. To help me determine which sewing methods I like best, I often make a practice block. I construct the block in more than one way and decide which one I prefer. This process is very instructive; it tells me how flat my work will lie when I'm finished and helps me decide which direction the seams should face. My goal is always to find the most efficient way to sew the pieces together to get the most accurate results.

Diana McClun

❖ Multiple Stacks ❖

When I make several blocks from the same pattern, I like to use an assembly line approach to piecing. I start by laying out all the patches for one block right side up, positioned as they will appear in the block. Then I match the patches for the rest of the blocks I want to make to those, placing them on top of the first patches, still right side up. I usually set up about six to eight blocks at a time; that way, I can piece individual units for each block and then assemble those units into completed blocks.

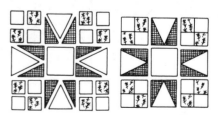

Liz Porter

Setting In Seams

❖ Seeing Things ❖ from a New Angle

The best incentive to learn how to set in patches at an angle is that it brings all patterns easily within your grasp. Sewing angled patches together is not difficult if you give careful thought to the piecing process and use precise ¼-inch seams. The first step in learning to set in pieces at an angle is to analyze a quilt block and see if there are any patches in it that cannot be sewn with straight seams. Once you've determined that, you can then look for the piecing sequence that will allow you to work with the gentlest angles. Take some time to analyze a few quilt blocks, using the examples that follow.

Analyzing Angles

This Eight-Pointed Star block has outer triangles and squares that will need to be set in because the diamond-shaped pieces beneath them are angled.

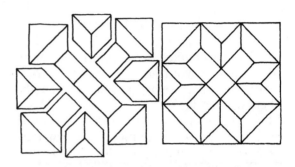

In this Star and Cross block, the small 3-patch units at each side of the block will need to be set in at an angle to the corner units, before the corner portions of the block are joined to the center unit, which also will require setting in.

Option 1   Option 2

Option 3

Here are three piecing options for this Album Flower block, all of which feature patches set in at an angle. If your goal is to find the sequence that gives you the gentlest angles, you'll see that Option 3 is the best choice for assembling the block.

QNM Editors

❖ No-Fail Angles ❖

Once you've analyzed a block pattern and determined that you'll need to set in the patches, here are the simple steps to create perfect angles.

The Step-by-Step for Setting In

Step 1: *Mark the seam lines precisely on each patch and begin your first sewing line at the corner where the piece will be set in. Start exactly ¼ inch from the edge of the patch. Sew forward a few stitches, backstitch, and then continue sewing to the opposite end of this seam line, backstitching and stopping exactly at the corner point (¼ inch from the edge of the patch).*

Stitch direction

Stitch direction

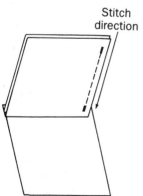

Step 2: *Open these pattern pieces and place the pattern piece to be set in right sides together with one of the first two pieces. Begin sewing this seam by backstitching ¼ inch from the edge of the piece and then sew to the exact point where the first seam ended, backstitching again.*

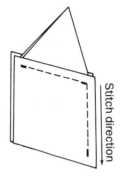

Step 3: *Rotate the pattern pieces to sew the third and last seam. Keeping the seam allowances free, sew from the point where the last seam began to ¼ inch from the edge of the piece.*

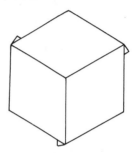

Step 4: *Open up the three patches and press the seams to one side, so they lie flat.*

QNM Editors

❖ Blazing Stars ❖

When you piece together rows of diamond-shaped patches for a Blazing Star quilt, the key to piecing accuracy lies in the preparation of your templates. Here are some helpful hints for making templates and piecing stars that lie smooth and flat, without bulges or puckers.

The Step-by-Step for Piecing Diamonds

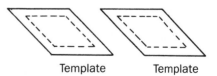

Template   Template

Step 1: *Draft or trace your pattern on heavy tracing paper and add ¼-inch seam allowances. Make a second template exactly like the first one.*

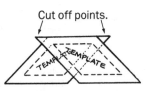

Cut off points.

Step 2: *Lay one template over the other, matching seam lines. Then trim the points of each template to fit the other.*

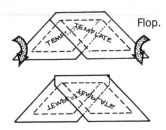

Flop.

Step 3: *Rotate each template in the direction of the arrow, so that the edges that were on top before are now on the diagonal.*

Step 4: *Trim both templates to fit each other.*

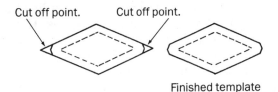

Cut off point.   Cut off point.

Finished template

Step 5: *Lay one diamond on top of the other, as shown, and trim the pointed ends to fit each other. This method creates two identical templates, one to use and another to keep as a spare.*

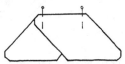

Step 6: *When you sew the first two diamonds, pin the patches right sides together, and the ends will match perfectly. Repeat this pinning and matching for the rest of the diamonds in your star.*

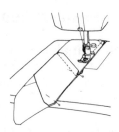

Step 7: *When you join rows of diamonds, carefully match the points where seams will intersect. The seam allowances of the top row of diamonds should lie toward the presser foot; those on the underside should lie away from it. Pinning at each intersection will hold each patch in position. It's a good idea to press the rows of diamonds as you complete each seam, taking care not to stretch them out of shape.*

Judy Martin

❖ Eight-Pointed Stars ❖

If your diamond-shaped templates have trimmed points (as in the "Blazing Stars" tip above) and you sew with accurate ¼-inch seam allowances, you can machine piece an eight-pointed star with a center seam that lies as flat as if you had sewn it by hand. Here's a handy piecing sequence to keep in mind for your next star project:

1. Pin two diamond-shaped patches together and stitch them with a ¼-inch seam allowance. At one point, which will later become the center of your eight-pointed star, the seam should extend all the way to the edge. At the other end of this seam, the sewing line must begin ¼ inch in from the edge. This will allow you to set in the corner square later. Press this seam to one side.

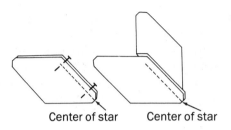

Center of star   Center of star

2. Sew the remaining pairs of diamonds together in the same manner and press each seam lightly, making sure that all of the seams lie in the same direction.

3. Sew together two pairs of diamonds to make half of the eight-pointed star. Begin and end this seam ¼ inch in from the edges of these patches.

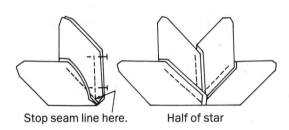

Stop seam line here.   Half of star

4. Press this seam to one side, keeping all seam allowances lying in the same direction, as before. Repeat this step to make the other half of your eight-pointed star.

5. To sew the center seam that completes the eight-pointed star, pin the two half stars right sides together. Rather than sew from one side of the star across to the other side, sew from one outside edge toward the center, stopping exactly at the point where all of the eight seams meet. Finger press the seam allowances out of the way. Sew the remaining seam, from the opposite side to the star center, ending exactly at the center point. By leaving all of your seam allowances free, you will be able to press this final seam in your star by fanning out all of the seam allowances in the same direction.

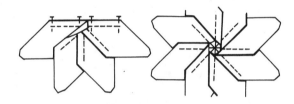

QNM Editors

❖ Mariner's Compass ❖

In machine piecing circular designs, you really can't take any liberties in the width of your seam allowances. If a Mariner's Compass pattern is drafted to have ¼-inch seam allowances and you do not sew exactly ¼-inch seams, you'll be removing a certain number of degrees from your finished work and you'll have a "mountain" rather than a block that lies flat. The stitch length you set on your machine can sometimes distort your ¼-inch seam allowances, while hand-pieced seams, which do not have as much thread in them, distort less, are easier to press, and tend to lie flatter. To reduce the "thickness" of machine seams, you can increase your stitch length. Another thing to remember is that when you draft a pattern using templates, what you're actually drawing is the outside of each shape. It's best to sew exactly on stitching lines rather than inside or outside; if you sew inside these lines, your finished work will be distorted.

Judy Mathieson

❖ Piecing That's ❖ a Notch Above

Curved seams, such as in the Clamshell pattern, pose some logistical problems for quiltmakers. You need to join the pieces so they are properly aligned with a smooth curve. Here are three hints that can help you handle those curves:

♦ To align curved seams, it's helpful to have notch marks in the seam allowances of both the concave and convex templates. These notches need to be cut or marked at a depth of only ⅛ inch.

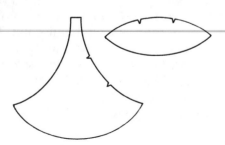

♦ On a concave patch, you can use embroidery scissors to make the ⅛-inch clips into the seam allowance, and then make tiny ⅟₁₆-inch clips between notches to score the seam allowance and make it easier to manipulate during the piecing process.

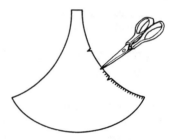

♦ When you piece a curved seam, sew slowly, removing pins as you come to them, and lightly press the seam allowances toward the convex curve.

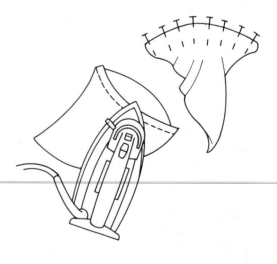

QNM Editors

Pressing Essentials

❖ Press Down, Iron Across ❖

Pressing is an important step in making each portion of your quilt, from sewing a single block to assembling the entire top. There really is a difference between pressing and ironing, and the technique you use can affect the appearance of your finished work. In machine-pieced blocks, seam allowances are most often pressed to one side, usually toward the darker of two fabrics. To press this kind of seam, it's best to lift your iron and press it down on each area, without sliding your iron across the fabric. This will prevent the seams from becoming distorted. After you've finished pressing all of the seams in a block, you can then turn the block right side up and iron it, by moving your iron across the fabric in the direction of the fabric grain.

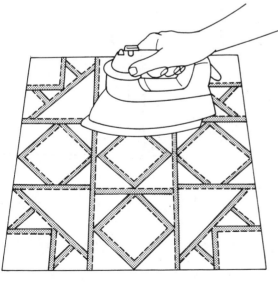

QNM Editors

❖ Deciding Which ❖ Direction to Take

When you're pressing seams, it's a good idea to think about which direction you want the seams to face when the quilt is finished. It's easier to put a quilt together when the seams of neighboring units are lying in opposite directions. Look at your quilt blocks and your setting and analyze how your quilt will go together. If possible, press the seams of neighboring blocks and/or sashing strips so that they will face in opposite directions when you assemble the quilt top. This may sometimes mean that you'll be pressing a seam toward the lighter of two fabrics rather than the darker to avoid having the bulk of several seams coming together under one dark patch. One helpful idea for when your patches are very small is to press those seams open and flat rather than toward one side. It can create too much bulk if more than one seam allowance lies under a 1-inch finished square.

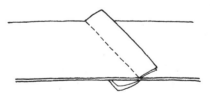

Nancy J. Martin

❖ Seat Your Seams ❖

When you're piecing strips of fabric together by machine, try this pressing technique to make sure the seams will lie flat and your strips will be straight. Lay two fabric strips on your ironing board with the seam lying away from you and the darker fabric on top. Press this seam while it's closed; this will "seat" the stitches into the fabric, preventing distortions. Then open up the fabric strips and begin pressing this seam by placing your iron on the lighter fabric, which is closest to you, and moving the iron over the seam line, pressing it carefully along the entire length of the fabric strips. This will make the seam lie toward the darker fabric. This two-step pressing ensures that your strips will be straight, without ridges, pleats, ripples, or puckers. You can use this technique for pressing any number of strips; just remember to press each seam before adding your next strip of fabric.

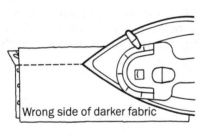

Wrong side of darker fabric

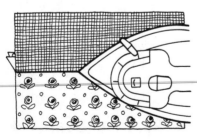

Sharyn Squier Craig

❖ Water Works ❖

Whenever four or more seams come together at one point, I like to press the seams open. Here's a trick I learned from tailoring that makes this process easier. Dip one finger into a bowl of water and apply just a bit of extra moisture right in the area where multiple seam allowances come together and fan out. The few drops of water help to "compress" the seams and make them lie flatter when you press them. If you press your iron down very firmly and hold it a moment at the juncture of the seams, that will help flatten the seams out nicely, too. This method works well for designs like Kaleidoscope, Pinwheel, and LeMoyne Star, where many seams come together at one point.

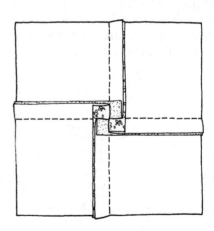

Diana McClun

❖ A Steamy Story ❖

I prefer not to use any steam when I press, because it can stretch and distort fabric. If you need to steam a portion of your quilt, however, it's a good idea to leave the piece on your ironing board for a moment and let it dry completely before picking it up. Then it will be blocked and won't stretch out of shape.

Lynn Lewis Young

❖ Portable Pressing ❖

An ironing table right beside your sewing machine makes it easy to press immediately after stitching a seam. I've discovered a simple and inexpensive way to make a lightweight and portable pressing table. Visit your local quilt shop and ask for an empty bolt board. Pad the bolt board with a piece of Pellon fleece, cotton batting, or an old cotton mattress pad, and then wrap muslin or another cotton

fabric around the padding and tape or staple it in place. A padded bolt board makes a very sturdy and portable ironing surface that will last for years.

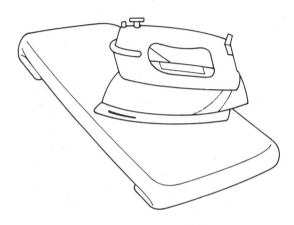

Sharyn Squier Craig

Making the Best of Your Piecing Time

❖ Easy Does It! ❖

If you have only a little time in your day to devote to machine piecing, you can make the most of those precious minutes by always keeping something cut out and next to your machine. As long as you have something prepared and ready to sew at a moment's notice, you'll be able to turn even a couple of minutes into productive time. And you can make the most of your cutting time, too, by dividing it into small, workable units. Set yourself a goal of cutting just the number of pieces you can sew in one day. You'll probably find that you're able to accomplish a great deal in very short segments of time.

Nancy J. Martin

MIDNIGHT MASTERPIECES

The muse of creativity can speak at any hour of day or night, but my own inspiration often comes when I least expect it—usually on a Saturday night at 10:00 P.M.! When that happens, I'm grateful to have a good stock of ready-to-use fabrics close at hand so I can go directly to my machine and start piecing.

Since you never know when the urge to piece a new quilt will strike, it's best to be prepared. You can learn to give yourself permission to purchase fabrics for your collection on a regular basis, without feeling any guilt. And while you're shopping, remember that the fabrics you see in a shop today will probably not be there next year, or possibly even next month. Remember—if you see it and you like it and there's a place in your collection for it, it's a good idea to buy it! Someday a clock may strike midnight, and you'll find yourself loaded with inspiration—and the resources—to sit right down at your sewing machine and make a masterpiece.

❖ Marsha McCloskey

hands and wrists. When you have a couple of hours set aside to sew, try to vary the kinds of sewing tasks you do within that time. Stand and cut pieces at your cutting table and then sit down at your machine for a while and do some piecing. It's best to avoid repetitious motions, because that's the kind of thing that can aggravate problems in your hands and wrists.

Nancy J. Martin

❖ Stretch and Sew ❖

If you feel tension in your shoulders from leaning over your work for too long, stop sewing and do some stretching exercises, like moving your shoulders in a circular motion. And when your arms and hands are tired, take a break and hold them out and shake them vigorously to release stress and tension. You'll be able to sew longer and more comfortably if you take periodic stretch breaks.

Mary Mashuta

❖ Vary Your Motions ❖

If you have trouble with tendinitis or carpal tunnel syndrome, it's very helpful to vary the motions you make with your

❖ Cushion Your Contours ❖

It's easy to become tired from sitting at your sewing machine for a long time. Try to listen to what your body is telling you, so you can figure out what you're doing that makes you feel tired and achy and remedy the problem. For instance, if your back hurts from leaning over your work for too long, try using a contour pillow to cushion and support your back while you sew.

Mary Mashuta

❖ At Arm's Glance ❖

When you reach "that certain age" when your arms aren't long enough any more for you to read a newspaper or magazine easily, you may find that reading glasses are in order. And there can be a difference in the amount of magnification you need for machine sewing than you need for reading a book or magazine. To find out if this is the case for you, sit at your sewing machine and piece something while you're wearing your glasses, and see whether you feel the need for more correction to work comfortably. If you think different lenses would help for working at the sewing machine, ask your doctor about getting two pairs of glasses—one for "reading distance" and a second pair for "sewing distance."

Marsha McCloskey

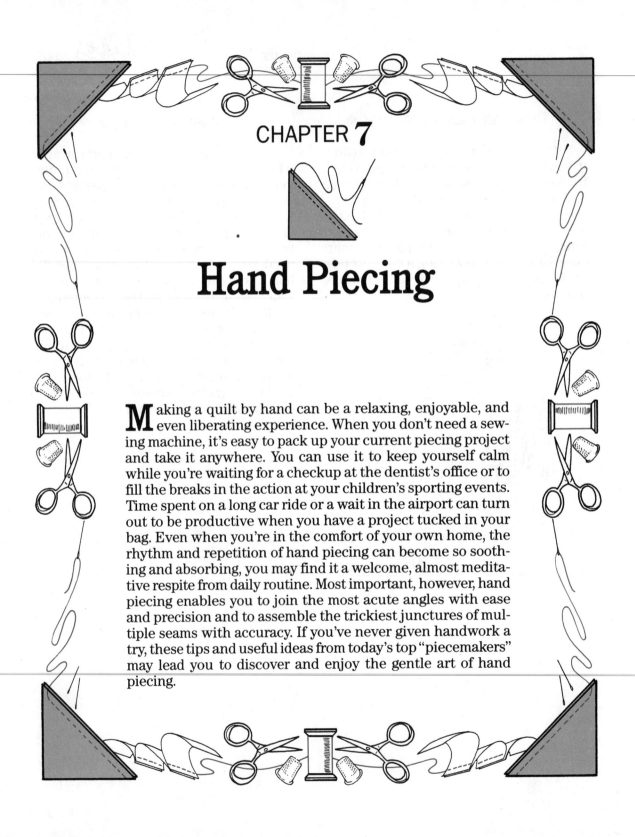

CHAPTER **7**

Hand Piecing

Making a quilt by hand can be a relaxing, enjoyable, and even liberating experience. When you don't need a sewing machine, it's easy to pack up your current piecing project and take it anywhere. You can use it to keep yourself calm while you're waiting for a checkup at the dentist's office or to fill the breaks in the action at your children's sporting events. Time spent on a long car ride or a wait in the airport can turn out to be productive when you have a project tucked in your bag. Even when you're in the comfort of your own home, the rhythm and repetition of hand piecing can become so soothing and absorbing, you may find it a welcome, almost meditative respite from daily routine. Most important, however, hand piecing enables you to join the most acute angles with ease and precision and to assemble the trickiest junctures of multiple seams with accuracy. If you've never given handwork a try, these tips and useful ideas from today's top "piecemakers" may lead you to discover and enjoy the gentle art of hand piecing.

Mastering Hand Patchwork

Marking Basics

❖ A Corner on Accuracy ❖

Templates made for hand piecing do not include the seam allowances. This enables you to draw around a template, marking the finished seam lines of each patch on your fabric. To mark the exact corner points of each seam line, try using a mechanical pencil, which maintains its line width with no variations as you mark. You can also increase your marking precision by placing your pencil at the exact corner point on a template and marking from that point along each side of the template.

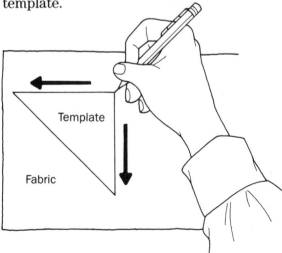

Cindy Zlotnik Oravecz

❖ Upright Is Best ❖

When you mark seam lines on fabric for hand piecing, it's a good idea to keep your pencil perpendicular to the marking surface while you mark. Holding it at an angle can move the seam line out of position, which means that your finished work will be inaccurate.

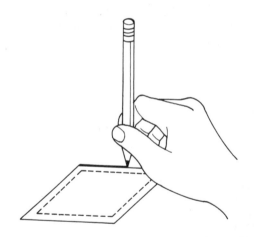

Cindy Zlotnik Oravecz

Hand-Piecing Pointers

❖ Perfect Piecing 101 ❖

There are no tricky techniques to master to be able to hand piece seams together beautifully. To piece by hand, all you need to be able to do is sew exactly on marked seam lines. Here's a rundown of the basics, from the supplies you need to the step-by-step of piecing.

Supplies

Obviously, you don't need a big-ticket item like a sewing machine when you're stitching seams by hand. Hand piecers' needs are more modest (and more portable!). Here's a list of the basic supplies you need to get started:

♦ Patches with seam lines marked on the wrong side of the fabric

♦ Good-quality sewing thread

♦ Fine needles, such as sharps or betweens

♦ Fine, sharp pins, such as silk pins

♦ Small pair of scissors

♦ Thimble

The Step-by-Step for Hand Piecing

Step 1: *Place two patches right sides together and put a pin through the corner point, making sure that the pin enters the same point on the seam line of the underlying patch.*

Step 2: *Place a pin at the other end of the seam line, and also place one at the midpoint if the seam line is longer than 2 inches.*

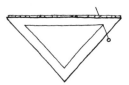

Step 3: *Thread a needle with a 20- or 24-inch strand of thread that matches the darker of the fabrics in your patches. At the beginning of the marked seam line, make a single stitch, pulling the thread through and leaving a tail approximately 1 inch long.*

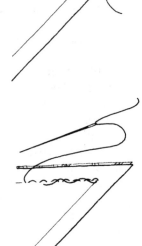

Step 4: *Bring the needle to the front again and make a backstitch at the beginning of the seam line. Then begin to make a series of running stitches, securing the tail of thread by stitching over it.*

Step 5: *Continue sewing to the end of the seam line using approximately 8 to 10 running stitches per inch.*

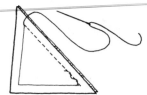

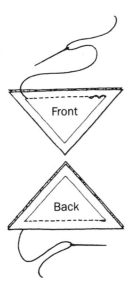

Step 6: *The most important thing you can do to ensure accuracy in hand piecing is to turn your work over often, so that you can see both the front and back of your work as you sew. This will help make sure that your stitches lie exactly on the marked seam lines.*

Step 7: *When you reach the end of a seam line, make two backstitches, pulling the needle through the final loop to secure the thread. Clip the thread, leaving a tail that is less than ¼ inch long.*

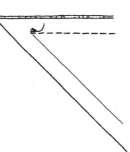

Step 8: *It's a good idea to finger press each seam as you sew. To finger press, lay the seam allowance toward the darker fabric and use your thumb to crease the seam line, holding your index and middle fingers underneath the patches. Then turn your patches over and crease the seam line gently from the right side.*

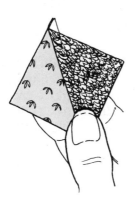

QNM Editors

❖ Piecing Units by Hand ❖

When you sew units of two or more patches together by hand, you can match the seams and leave the seam allowances free so you can determine which way to press them later.

1. Sew up to the point of a seam allowance and make a backstitch, anchoring the patches together at that point. Slide your needle through the intersection of the seams.

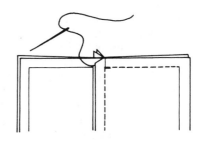

2. Make a backstitch on the other side of the seam allowance. Continue stitching to the end of this seam. You can now go back and press the seam in any direction you desire.

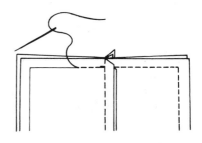

QNM Editors

A THREAD OF DISTINCTION

My favorite brand of thread for hand piecing is Conso, which is usually sold for working with drapery fabrics. I like it because it's stronger than standard sewing thread, yet it isn't as coarse as quilting thread. There are 1,200 yards of thread on a tube, and this brand is available in a wide variety of colors. I don't like to change threads constantly when I sew; I prefer to work on soft, muted colors and use only two or three different colors of thread in any quilt. I use this brand of thread for quilting, too, particularly if I can't find the thread color I want in a regular quilting thread. If you can't find this thread where you live, you can write to Jinny Beyer Studio, P.O. Box 488, Great Falls, VA 22066; (703) 759-0250.

❖ Jinny Beyer

the right side of the fabric, it's easy to align the seams and check for correct fabric placement as you stitch.

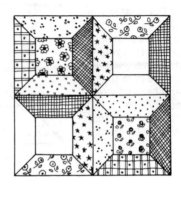

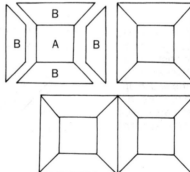

Spools pattern with acute angles

❖ "Appli-piece" ❖ a Perfect Seam

When you want to tackle an advanced design with patches set in at acute angles (like the Spools block used in this example), the technique of "appli-piecing" may be just what you need to help create perfect points and corners. This method of piecing consists of sewing one patch to another with a blind stitch. Because you work from

1. Mark seam lines on the right side of each patch with markings that you can remove easily. Extend the seam lines to the edges of each patch. The seam lines will cross at each corner point.

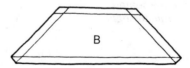

2. Fold under one seam allowance of the patch you want to appli-piece to another patch. Baste this seam allowance in place so that the marked seam line is just barely turned under.

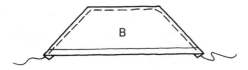

3. Place the basted edge of this patch over the marked seam line on the adjoining patch, matching the corner points. Pin the basted patch in place. With thread that matches the top patch, sew the top patch to the underlying patch with a blind stitch.

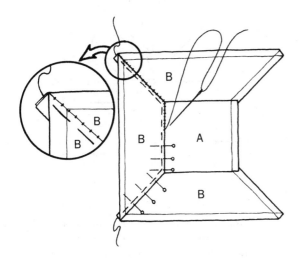

QNM Editors

❖ Lump-Free Center Seams ❖

The true test of a perfectly pieced LeMoyne Star block is a center point that lies flat with no telltale lumps. Hand piecing is a nearly "goof-proof" way to stitch a stunning star.

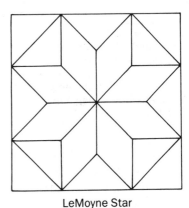

LeMoyne Star

The Step-by-Step for a LeMoyne Star

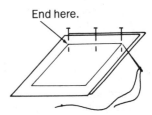

End here.

Step 1: *Place two diamonds right sides together and pin the end points of the seam line together to align them. Place a pin at the midpoint on the seam line, as well. Sew this seam from end point to end point with small running stitches, backstitching at the beginning and end of the seam line.*

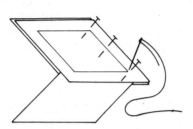

Step 2: *Open up the first two diamond patches and pin a third diamond over the second one, right sides together. Insert your needle into the same spot where the first seam line began. Join this seam with small stitches, beginning and ending with a backstitch.*

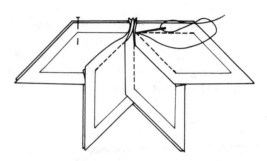

Step 4: *Place the two halves of the star together and pin the beginning point of this seam line, the exact center point, and the end point. Stitch this seam, beginning and ending with backstitches, as before. When you reach the center juncture of the seams, lift the seam allowances so your stitches will go through the exact center point of each diamond. When you open up the star, you'll be able to fan out all seam allowances freely in the same direction. This method eliminates a lot of bulk and allows all seams to lie flat.*

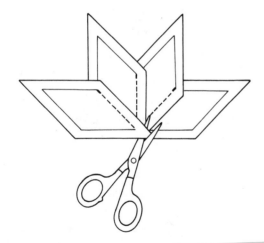

Step 3: *As you add each diamond, finger press the seam to one side, keeping all seam allowances lying in the same direction. When you have pieced together four diamonds, lay them aside and piece the other half of the star in the same manner. Clip off the points of each seam to reduce bulk.*

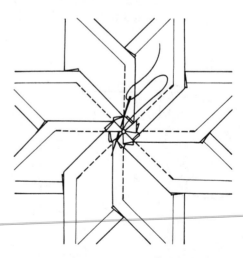

Step 5: *If you take tiny stitches around the "pinwheel" of seams, just catching the seam allowance of each patch, you can pull the thread gently to close a tiny gap in the center of your star.*

QNM Editors

Helpful Hints on Piecing and Pressing

❖ Step Up Your ❖ Stitching Speed

You can sew a hand-pieced seam more quickly if you hold your needle in one hand and move the fabric back and forth, so that you're putting the fabric onto the needle rather than inserting the needle into and out of the fabric. You can take approximately an inch of fabric onto the length of a needle.

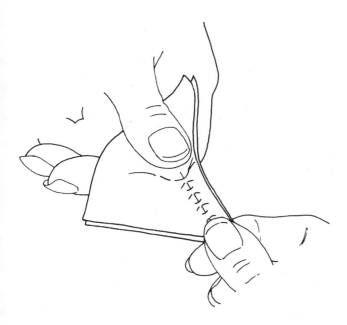

QNM Editors

❖ Backstitching at a Slant ❖

When you backstitch at the beginning and the end of a hand-pieced seam, you can give the seam more strength by slanting your backstitches so they fall into the seam allowance rather than lie on top of one another. You can still press these seams in any direction you like, and seams will lie more smoothly because there will be fewer threads coming together to create bulk at the juncture between two seams.

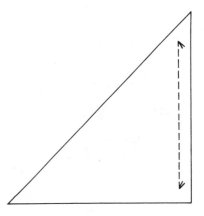

Mimi Dietrich

❖ That's Sew Straight ❖

When you're hand piecing a seam, the thread should control the fabric so that it lies in a relaxed position, without any tiny pleats or puckers. To achieve smooth seams, make sure that your needle consistently pierces the exact drawn line, not points above or below it. And don't tug one piece of fabric to fit another piece; correct any errors in templates before you sew the patches of your quilt together. If stitches in your seam lines are as straight as an arrow, your finished quilt will be precise and true, too.

QNM Editors

FOUND MOMENTS

I always keep something that is ready to be worked on close at hand so I can make use of "found" moments—such as when I'm sitting in the waiting room of a doctor's office, carpooling with friends, or just talking on the telephone. Whether you quilt at a floor frame during a phone conversation or piece something by hand while you wait out a traffic jam, it's amazing how much you can do in small time segments. Here's how to make the most of your own extra moments for quiltmaking: Gather the supplies you'll need for piecing one block—fabrics, threads, needles, scissors, and thimbles—and put them into a plastic bag. Keep them ready to go at a moment's notice, and you'll be surprised at how creatively you can use your time.

❖ Jinny Beyer

❖ Oh, What a Tangled Web ❖

When you thread your needle for hand piecing, it's a good idea to knot the end of the thread that you cut, or the end closest to the spool. That will keep your thread from tangling and twisting as much while you sew each seam.

QNM Editors

❖ Eye Can See That Now ❖

Put something white, like a sheet of paper or a piece of fabric, behind your needle when you thread it, and you'll find that it's easier to aim your thread accurately toward the eye of the needle.

QNM Editors

❖ Leather Fingers ❖

When you're pressing hand-pieced seams directionally, try wearing a leather thimble on the index finger of your left hand. The leather will protect your finger while you work with the placement of seam allowances and keep you from being burned by steam from the iron.

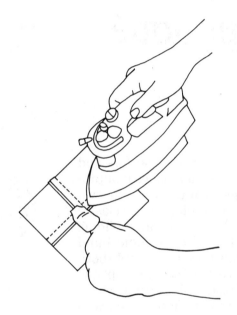

QNM Editors

❖ Keep Your Work in Sight ❖

I find that the biggest problem in getting something finished often comes from putting projects away and out of sight. If you keep your current piecing project where it's highly visible in your home, you'll be more likely to pick it up and start stitching whenever you have a spare moment or two.

Jinny Beyer

❖ Take It from the Top ❖

I like to wait to do any pressing until my entire block is finished. Then I place the block on a fluffy towel that has been folded over to create a lot of depth, and I press the block from the top, which makes the seams lie very smooth and flat.

Jinny Beyer

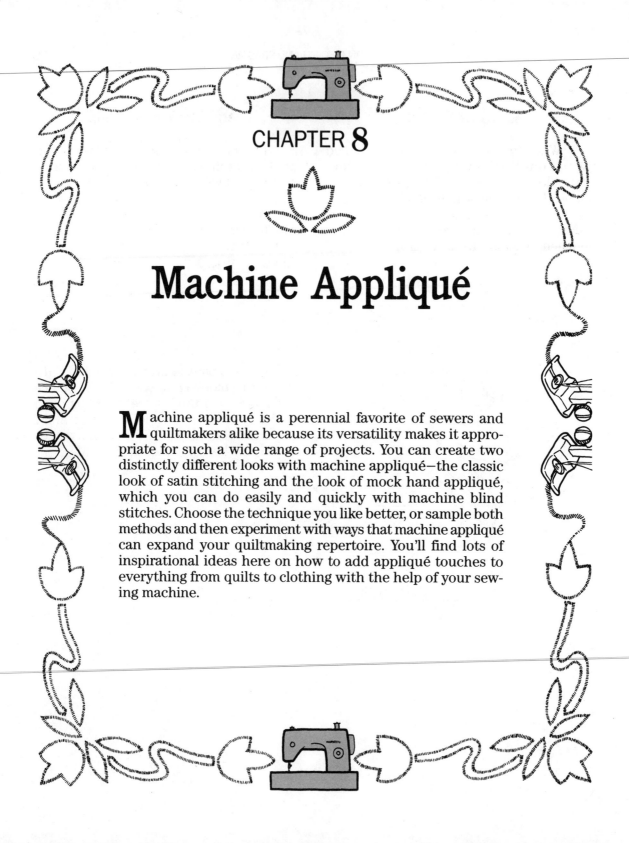

CHAPTER **8**

Machine Appliqué

Machine appliqué is a perennial favorite of sewers and quiltmakers alike because its versatility makes it appropriate for such a wide range of projects. You can create two distinctly different looks with machine appliqué—the classic look of satin stitching and the look of mock hand appliqué, which you can do easily and quickly with machine blind stitches. Choose the technique you like better, or sample both methods and then experiment with ways that machine appliqué can expand your quiltmaking repertoire. You'll find lots of inspirational ideas here on how to add appliqué touches to everything from quilts to clothing with the help of your sewing machine.

Mastering Machine Appliqué

Satin Stitch Techniques

❖ Learning the Basics ❖

If your sewing machine can do a zig-zag stitch, you're well on your way to satin stitching decorative and durable quilts, clothing, and home-decorating projects quickly and easily. Here are the supplies you need and the step-by-step for creating masterful machine appliqué.

Supplies

♦ Background fabric
♦ Finished-size appliqué shapes with no seam allowances added
♦ Good-quality cotton or poly-cotton thread to match your patches
♦ Fine machine-embroidery-weight cotton thread for the bobbin
♦ Fusible interfacing to stabilize appliqué shapes (optional)
♦ Fabric glue stick or spray adhesive (optional)

The Step-by-Step for Satin Stitching

It's a good idea to practice stitching until you establish a good tension for the top thread on your machine. Here's how to go about creating a smooth line of satin stitching using a close zigzag stitch:

1. Keep in mind that the fabrics you choose will determine how wide your stitches should be. Finer fabrics will lie more smoothly and look better with a narrower line of stitches, while medium-weight cottons can support wider stitches. For your first venture into machine appliqué, work with medium-weight cotton fabrics. If you are using fusible interfacing, press it to the wrong sides of your fabrics before cutting out the appliqué shapes.

2. Loosen the top tension on your machine a bit. That way, your stitches will interlock on the underside of your work, with no bobbin thread visible on the right side of your fabric.

3. Use glue stick, spray adhesive, or hand basting to position your finished-size patches on the background fabric. Leaving approximately 3 inches of thread free at the beginning, sew a line of zigzag stitches that are approximately ⅛ inch wide just over the edges of each patch.

4. When you reach a corner, lower your needle into the background fabric, lift the presser foot, and turn the fabric so you can stitch in the next direction. Lower the presser foot and continue stitching.

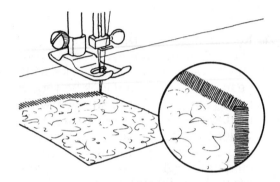

5. To end a line of satin stitches, leave another 3-inch tail of thread free, pull it to the back of your work, and tie a knot. Use a needle to weave these threads into the back of your line of stitches for an inch or two and then clip off the excess thread. Do the same with the tail of thread at the beginning of your line of stitches.

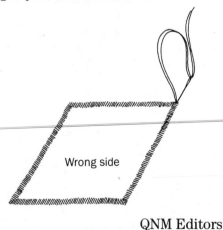

Wrong side

QNM Editors

❖ On a Sliding Scale ❖

One of the most helpful sewing machine features to have for machine appliqué is a variable zigzag stitch, because it allows you to select a stitch width that pleases you. Look for a machine with a control knob that allows you to choose from a sliding scale of stitch widths and lengths, rather than one with only a few preset widths and lengths.

Debra Wagner

❖ Channeling Your Stitches ❖

If your sewing machine has a zigzag presser foot that has a channel or slot on the underside of the foot, try using it for satin stitching. The channel allows a ridge of stitches to feed smoothly through the foot. If you use a regular presser foot to do satin stitching, the zigzag stitches can build up into a ridge that won't slide as easily through the foot. If you don't have a special appliqué foot for your machine, you can improve your satin stitching by using a buttonhole foot.

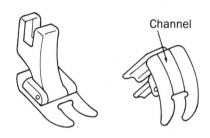

Channel

Liz Porter

❖ Wound Up Tight ❖

When you do machine appliqué, it's a good idea to use very fine cotton thread in the bobbin and to tighten the tension on the bobbin thread so that the thread has a heavy "drag" on it. Otherwise, little white "bubbles" of thread will come up through your fabric as you sew. Check your sewing machine manual to see how you can adjust the bobbin tension. On my Bernina, there is a small hole in the finger of the bobbin case that I can put the thread through to increase the tension. If your machine uses a bobbin case, it can be helpful to buy an extra one, on which you adjust and tighten the tension exclusively for machine appliqué. If you dab on a dot of colored fingernail polish, it will be easy to tell this bobbin case apart from the one you use for your other sewing.

Harriet Hargrave

❖ Stop and Pivot ❖

When you machine appliqué around the small curves of a flower, the background fabric can become distorted and stretched out of shape. Instead of trying to "push" the background fabric to make your stitches go around a curved shape, it's best to stop at the peak of a curve and lower your needle, raise the presser foot, and pivot the fabric slightly. That way, you can change the angle of your stitches and continue stitching around the curve without distorting the background fabric.

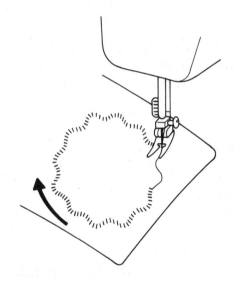

Harriet Hargrave

❖ A Short Fuse ❖

To place patches in position for appliquéing them on a background, I sometimes turn under the edges of the patch, as for hand appliqué, and then anchor the patch lightly with a bit of fusible thread. You can zigzag over the edges of a patch with fusible thread in your bobbin and regular cotton thread on top. Then lightly press to hold the patch in place. This anchors it so you can use regular cotton thread to stitch over the edges with satin stitching or a decorative stitch.

Lynn Lewis Young

❖ A Wonder-Underful Thought ❖

A line of satin stitching that is too heavy can sometimes detract from the appearance of the appliqué. I prefer the look of a looser satin stitch, one that resembles a featherstitch. You can lighten the stitching and still keep the appliqué in place by first fusing the appliqué shape to the background using a fusible material such as Wonder-Under. Because the appliqué has already been adhered to the background, you won't need as much satin stitching around the edges and you can go for the lighter look.

Lynn Lewis Young

❖ Look beneath the Surface ❖

Stabilizing sweatshirt fabric from the underside makes it quicker and easier to machine appliqué shapes on the right side of the fabric. I like to cut a piece of freezer paper larger than the design area I want to appliqué. I iron the shiny side of the paper onto the wrong side of the sweatshirt. This layer of paper keeps the knitted fabric in

place while I satin stitch the patches, and it tears away almost effortlessly when the stitching is completed.

Liz Porter

❖ "Papered-Over" Appliqué ❖

For my quilt "Life in the Margins #2: After Autumn," I used a machine appliqué technique. Using some equilateral diamond patches left over from a series of quilts I had made in peaches, turquoises, and mauves, I pieced the background for this quilt in a variation of the Baby Blocks pattern. Then I did a drawing of an abstract, free-form design on paper and pinned a piece of black fabric over my pieced background. I pinned the paper over the black fabric and used a darning foot to stitch through the paper drawing with very small stitches. Then I pulled the paper off and cut one section of the design at a time from the black fabric, very close to my stitching lines. Finally, I satin stitched over the edges to create the finished design.

Caryl Bryer Fallert

Mock Hand Appliqué

❖ Blind Stitch Basics ❖

Invisible machine appliqué can look very much like its twin sister, hand appliqué. Invisible appliqué with the machine is simple and easy to learn, though quite different in nature from the appliqué you do by hand. Here's a rundown of the supplies you need and the techniques for creating beautiful mock hand appliqué with machine blind stitches.

Supplies

♦ Lightweight fusible interfacing to stabilize appliqué shapes
♦ Clear nylon thread for the top
♦ Fine embroidery-weight cotton thread for the bobbin
♦ Template plastic
♦ Freezer paper
♦ Fabric glue stick or spray adhesive

The Step-by-Step for Invisible Stitches

See pg 146

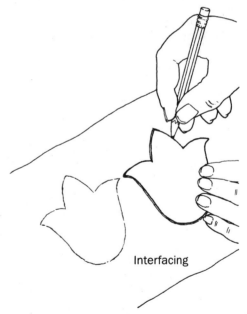

Step 1: *From freezer paper, cut a finished-size template for each patch you wish to appliqué.*

Step 2: *For each shape you're working with, cut a plastic template that has ¼-inch seam allowances added to it. You will use these plastic templates to trace the shapes for the patches you need. (Don't trace or cut anything yet.)*

Interfacing

Step 3: *Press lightweight fusible interfacing to the wrong side of each of your fabrics. Use the plastic templates to mark each patch on the interfacing, and cut out each patch.*

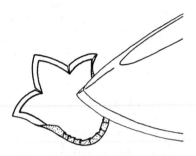

Step 4: *Place a freezer paper template, shiny side up, on the wrong side of one of your patches. Carefully press the seam allowances over the edges of the freezer paper to hold them in place. Remove the freezer paper when you have pressed the patch, being careful not to distort the shape of the patch.*

Step 6: *Replace your regular presser foot with an open-toed appliqué foot and set your machine to do a blind hem stitch with 20 stitches per inch. With clear nylon thread on the top and fine embroidery-weight cotton thread in the bobbin, sew around the folded edges of each patch. The straight stitches should fall in the background, with the "jump" stitches catching the fold of the patch at ¼-inch intervals. This method of invisible machine appliqué can be very hard to distinguish from hand appliqué.*

QNM Editors

Step 5: *Use glue stick or a bit of spray adhesive to position each patch on the background fabric.*

YOU DESERVE THE VERY BEST!

It's important to use the very best in supplies to get the best results in machine appliqué. For mock hand appliqué, I recommend using Sew Art International nylon .004 thread on top and 60-weight, 2-ply, extrafine machine embroidery thread by Mettler in the bobbin. If you can't find these threads in a shop where you live, you can contact Harriet's Treadle Arts, 6390 W. 44th Avenue, Wheat Ridge, CO 80033; fax (303) 424-1290.

❖ Harriet Hargrave

❖ Adjustable Stitch Width ❖

One of the most common mistakes people make in doing mock hand appliqué is using a stitch that is too long and wide. It's best to set your stitches only about 3 threads wide, with a maximum length of ⅛ inch. This means that on many sewing machines with preset stitch widths and lengths, the controls should be set at "1 and 1", or 1 width and 1 length.

Harriet Hargrave

❖ The Eye of the Needle ❖

For doing fine blindstitching on the sewing machine, it's best to use fine thread and a small needle, such as a size 60, so that you're piercing very small holes in your fabric as you stitch. A sewing machine needle for blind stitch appliqué needs only to be large enough to carry the thread you're using.

Harriet Hargrave

❖ Curved ❖ Piecing with Appliqué

You can "piece" beautifully curved seams with mock hand appliqué. For example, to assemble a Drunkard's Path block, just make a template for the curved portion of the block from freezer paper, turn under the fabric along the curve, and use a blind stitch to piece the curve onto a square of fabric. Mock hand appliqué enables you to piece other curved patterns, like Clamshell, easily, and you can miter corner seams easily with this method, too.

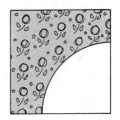

Blindstitch curved edge.

Curved edge folded under

Use mock hand appliqué on curved seams.

Harriet Hargrave

GRACEFUL EMBELLISHMENTS

I think the new "hand-look" stitches on many sewing machines are really versatile. Many of today's machines have the capability to make stitches that really look like such old-fashioned favorites as the buttonhole stitch, cross-stitch, and faggoting stitch. Why not go creative and try incorporating some of these and other decorative machine stitches into your next machine appliqué quilt? Check out the stitch options your machine offers and be on the lookout for creative new ways to embellish some of the patches in your quilt. Use sparkling metallics or brilliant variegated threads to satin stitch around your patches, or try machine embroidery threads to simulate the look of hand embroidery found in a traditional crazy quilt. Your imagination is the only limit in creating beautiful embellishments for your quilts.

❖ Debra Wagner

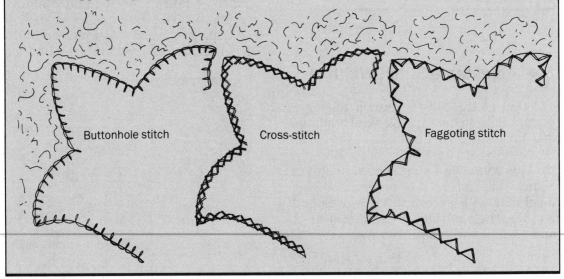

Buttonhole stitch   Cross-stitch   Faggoting stitch

❖ The Many Faces of Appliqué ❖

I like to use iron-on interfacing for doing a kind of faced machine appliqué. I place the interfacing right sides together with my fabric and trace the appliqué shapes on the wrong side of the interfacing. Then I cut the shapes from these two layers. I stitch all the way around the turning lines of each patch, clip the interfacing, and turn the patch right side out. The fusible side of the interfacing is now at the back of the patch, so you can press the patch in place easily on the background. This method takes away the need for pinning or turning under seam allowances. Now you're ready to machine appliqué the patch, using your favorite stitch.

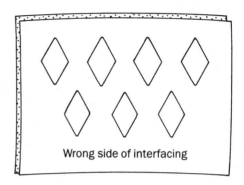

Wrong side of interfacing

Eleanor Burns

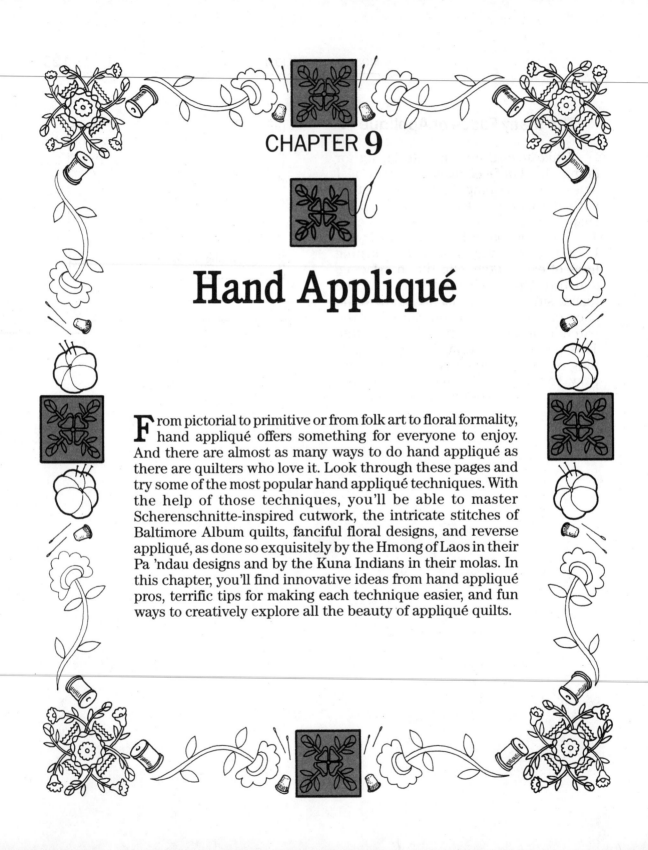

CHAPTER 9

Hand Appliqué

From pictorial to primitive or from folk art to floral formality, hand appliqué offers something for everyone to enjoy. And there are almost as many ways to do hand appliqué as there are quilters who love it. Look through these pages and try some of the most popular hand appliqué techniques. With the help of those techniques, you'll be able to master Scherenschnitte-inspired cutwork, the intricate stitches of Baltimore Album quilts, fanciful floral designs, and reverse appliqué, as done so exquisitely by the Hmong of Laos in their Pa 'ndau designs and by the Kuna Indians in their molas. In this chapter, you'll find innovative ideas from hand appliqué pros, terrific tips for making each technique easier, and fun ways to creatively explore all the beauty of appliqué quilts.

Mastering Hand Appliqué

Stitching Essentials

❖ Get Ready, Get Set, Stitch! ❖

The word *appliqué* means literally "to apply." In hand appliqué, it means to apply one layer of fabric to another with hand-stitches. There are many different ways to do hand appliqué, and often, the design you choose will tell you which method will work best. To learn the basics, start with shapes that have gentle, rounded curves, which are easier to stitch than deep indentations and inner points. To get you started, here is a listing of the general supplies you'll need, along with the four-step basics of the blind stitch. Read the remainder of the tips in this section for pointers on some of the most popular hand appliqué techniques. Try them all and see which ones you like best.

General Appliqué Supplies

For any method of hand appliqué, you will need several of the following supplies:

- ◆ Background fabric
- ◆ Patches with marked turning lines
- ◆ Cotton sewing thread to match the fabrics in your appliqué patches
- ◆ Template plastic
- ◆ Freezer paper

- ◆ Fine, long hand-sewing needles
- ◆ Fine straight pins
- ◆ Scissors for cutting fabric
- ◆ Scissors for cutting paper
- ◆ Small embroidery scissors for clipping seam allowances and threads
- ◆ Fabric glue stick
- ◆ Permanent fabric marker
- ◆ Removable fabric marker

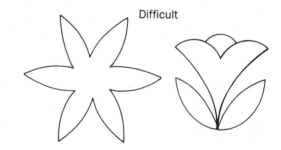
Difficult

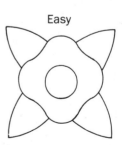
Easy

Start with gently curved shapes.

127

The Step-by-Step for the Blind Stitch

One of the most basic and popular appliqué stitches is the blind stitch. You can use this stitch with success for any of the methods described in "Stitching Essentials."

Step 1: *Knot your thread and bring the needle up through the folded edge of a patch, so that the knot is concealed inside the fold. Begin stitching by inserting your needle into the background fabric, just under the fold of your appliqué patch, right next to the point where the needle comes out of the patch. Bring the needle up through the background fabric and catch the very edge of the fold, approximately ⅛ inch away.*

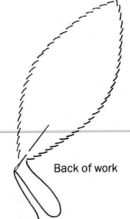

Step 2: *Continue stitching in this way around the entire patch. To end your stitching line, bring the needle to the wrong side of the background fabric and take one small stitch just inside the stitching line. Do not pull the thread all the way through; leave a loop on the surface of the fabric.*

Back of work

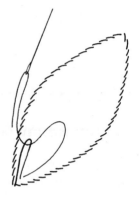

Step 3: *Run your thread through this loop and then tighten it into a knot on the surface of your fabric.*

Step 4: *Insert your needle into the background fabric, run the thread between the background and the appliqué patch, and cut the thread even with the surface of the fabric to hide it.*

QNM Editors

❖ Basted Appliqué ❖

This traditional appliqué technique takes a bit more preparation time than some of the other methods, but it offers the security of working with perfectly shaped patches.

The Step-by-Step for Basted Appliqué

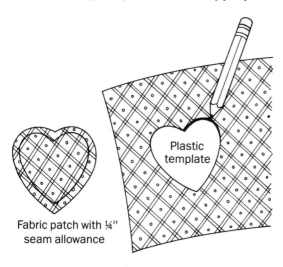

Fabric patch with ¼"
seam allowance

Plastic
template

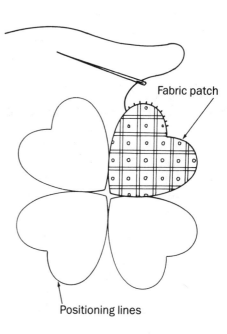

Step 3: *When you've clipped the seam allowances, turn them under and baste them in place with thread.*

Step 1: *Trace finished-size appliqué shapes onto template plastic and cut them out. Draw around each template on the right side of your fabric and cut out each patch with approximately ¼-inch seam allowances outside the drawn lines.*

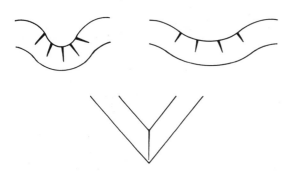

Fabric patch

Positioning lines

Step 2: *Clip into the seam allowances of inner curves and inner points to make them easier to turn under. The deeper the curve or sharper the point, the deeper your clip should be.*

Step 4: *Mark the lines of your design on your background fabric and pin each basted appliqué patch in position. Sew each patch in place with a blind stitch along the folded edges.*

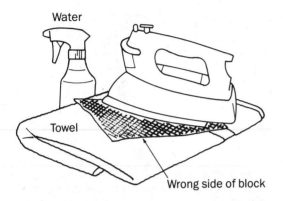

Water

Towel

Wrong side of block

Step 5: *After you've stitched the entire design, place your work face down on a folded towel, spray it lightly with water, and press.*

QNM Editors

❖ Needle-Turn Appliqué ❖

One of the oldest of all appliqué techniques, needle turning needs relatively little preparation time before you begin to sew. If you find it easy to manipulate a seam allowance with your needle, this may become one of your favorite methods of stitching.

1. Make a finished-size plastic template for each different shape in your design. Trace your templates onto the right sides of your fabrics and cut the patches out with either ³⁄₁₆- or ¼-inch seam allowances outside the turning lines, whichever you prefer.

2. Mark the lines of the design on the background fabric and pin your patches in place, matching the turning lines of

each patch to the lines on the background square.

Patch with seam allowance for turning

Design outline

Background fabric

3. With the point of your needle, turn under about ¼ to ½ inch along the fold of your appliqué patch at a time and hold it in place with your thumb while you stitch it.

4. When you're finished stitching, spray your work lightly with water and press it face down on a towel.

QNM Editors

❖ **Freezer Paper Appliqué** ❖

You may find freezer paper so wonderful for appliqué that you'll wonder what you ever did without it. You can use it to make sure that all of the hearts in a quilt are shaped identically, to stabilize specialty fabrics like silk or lamé and make them easier to work with, or to cut out symmetrical designs for Hawaiian appliqué. Here's how to use it for making wonderful templates:

1. Trace your finished-size patches onto the matte "paper" side of a piece of freezer paper and cut out a finished-size template for each piece in your design. If there are ten diamond shapes in your quilt, make ten diamond templates from freezer paper.

2. Press the shiny side of each freezer paper template onto the wrong side of your fabric and cut out each patch with ¼-inch seam allowances outside the freezer paper.

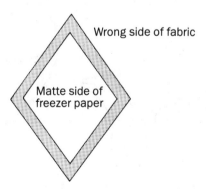

Wrong side of fabric

Matte side of freezer paper

3. Put a line of glue stick around the edges of each freezer paper template and use your iron to press the seam allowances over the edges. (An alternate way to accomplish the same thing would be to pin the freezer paper onto your fabric patch with the shiny side up. That way, the seam allowances stick to the freezer paper when you press them over the edges.)

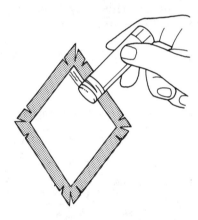

4. Mark the lines of your design on the background fabric and pin your patches in place, matching the folded edges of your patches to the lines. Stitch each patch in place with a blind stitch. From the backside, clip away the background fabric behind the patch and carefully remove the freezer paper. Spray your finished work lightly with water and press it face down on a towel.

QNM Editors

❖ Reverse Appliqué ❖

This method consists of turning under the edges of the top layer of fabric to reveal a layer of fabric beneath. Since the fabric of the design shape lies *below* the background fabric rather than on top of it, you can create an illusion of depth with this technique. It works very well for small shapes, too, so if you like the look of layered appliqué, this may become one of your favorite techniques.

The Step-by-Step for Reverse Appliqué

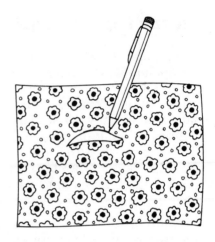

Step 2: *Make a finished-size plastic template for each shape you've chosen. Then position the templates on your background fabric and trace around them lightly with a marker that can be removed easily. Mechanical pencils (using hard lead) make very fine lines, and silver artist's pencils make very light markings, both of which are simple to remove. Be cautious about using a water-soluble marker of any kind unless you've tested it on your own fabric for removability.*

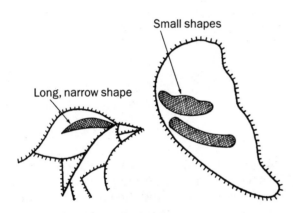

Small shapes

Long, narrow shape

Step 1: *Analyze a design and decide which shapes might be easier to stitch by reverse appliqué and also which ones would be enhanced by a layered look. Long, narrow shapes and very small pieces are often good candidates for reverse appliqué.*

Step 3: *Make a clip into the background fabric in the middle of your traced shape and cut away the excess fabric in the center if there is any, leaving approximately 3/16-inch seam allowances inside your drawn lines. With small, sharp scissors, clip into the seam allowances of inner curves and points.*

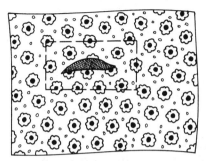

Light upper layer of fabric

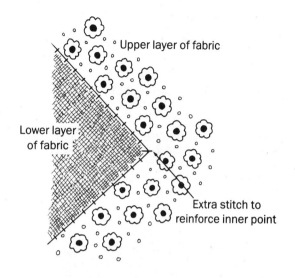

Upper layer of fabric

Lower layer of fabric

Extra stitch to reinforce inner point

Step 4: *Cut a piece of fabric that is at least 1 inch larger on all sides than your finished-size template. This is the fabric that will show through the background and appear as your appliqué shape when you're finished. Baste the background fabric over this fabric.*

Step 6: *At inner points where there is no seam allowance to turn under, make an extra stitch, catching a couple of threads of the background fabric to reinforce the point.*

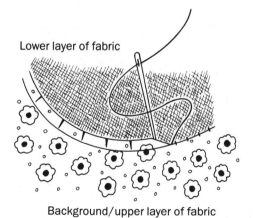

Lower layer of fabric

Background/upper layer of fabric

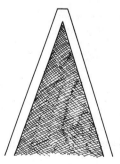

Step 5: *Use the point of your needle to turn under the seam allowances, and blindstitch them in place.*

Step 7: *At outer points, trim away excess fabric at the tip, leaving approximately a ⅛-inch seam allowance to turn under.*

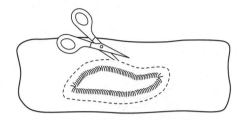

Step 8: *When you're finished stitching, turn your work over and trim the lower layer of fabric to approximately ¼ inch of your stitching line.*

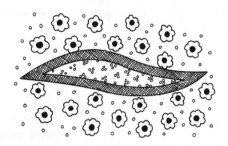

Step 9: *You can create another layer of reverse appliqué beneath your first appliqué patch by tracing a finished shape onto the right side of the patch and following the same process with a third layer of fabric underneath it.*

Step 10: *When your reverse appliqué is finished, spray it lightly with water and press it face down on a towel.*

QNM Editors

❖ Hawaiian Appliqué ❖

Doing Hawaiian-style appliqué is a lot like cutting out paper "snowflakes." This whole-cloth appliqué technique involves folding fabric and cutting out a design that is then appliquéd to a background fabric. You can also draw a design on fabric and use the cut-as-you-go method to apply it to your background. Either way, Hawaiian appliqué gives you a chance to enjoy the fun of stitching symmetrical, single-fabric designs. Follow these steps to try Hawaiian appliqué on a small scale before working with very large pieces of fabric:

1. Cut a piece of freezer paper large enough for your finished design. Fold the paper into quarters and open it up again. On the matte "paper" side, trace one-fourth of the design in one of the quadrants. Fold the freezer paper back up and cut out your symmetrical snowflake design.

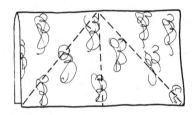

2. Open up your design and press it onto the right side of your fabric. Draw around the edges of the freezer paper to mark the turning lines and cut out your fabric snowflake with ¼-inch seam allowances outside the drawn lines. Remove the freezer paper.

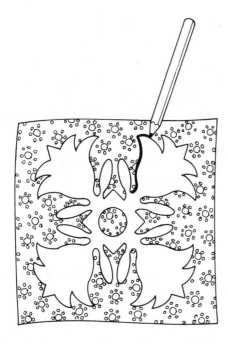

3. Center your cut appliqué fabric on your background fabric and pin or baste it in place. Turn under the seam allowances with your needle and blindstitch them.

4. Spray your finished work lightly with water and press it face down on a towel.

Marjorie Kerr and the QNM Editors

Special Techniques

❖ Template Appliqué ❖

Template appliqué is an appealing technique for anyone who wants to cut down on time spent in preliminary ironing, basting, and pinning. Another great benefit is that it's easy to create consistently shaped patches with this method.

The Step-by-Step for Template Appliqué

Plastic templates

Step 1: *Make a plastic template for each shape in your design. As for any appliqué method, the easier the curves and the gentler the angles in a shape, the easier it will be to stitch.*

Wrong side up

Wrong side of fabric

Step 2: *Cover the entire surface of the right side of a template lightly with glue stick and then position it on the wrong side of your fabric.*

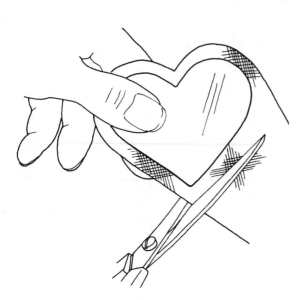

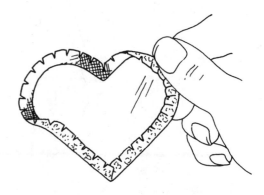

Step 3: *Cut out the fabric patch with ¼-inch seam allowances outside the edges of the template.*

Step 5: *Fold the seam allowances over the template, checking the fabric in your patch to make sure that it is smooth and free of wrinkles.*

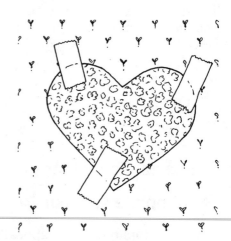

Step 4: *Make ⅛-inch clips into the seam allowances, spacing them about ¼ inch apart. Do not clip outer points or straight edges. Put a line of glue stick on the seam allowances and the outer edges of the template.*

Step 6: *With the template still inside it, position your prepared patch on the right side of the background fabric with several short pieces of masking tape.*

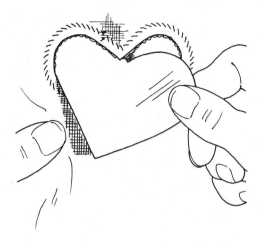

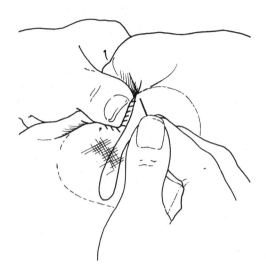

Step 7: *Unlike for traditional appliqué methods, you will do all of your stitching on the wrong side of the background fabric, letting the edges of the template guide your stitches. Using thread to match the background fabric, make your first stitch about ⅛ inch in from the edge of the template, directing the point of your needle toward the outer edge of the template. Let your needle touch the surface of the template until it reaches the edge, so you're assured of catching the seam allowance of the appliqué patch on the right side.*

Step 8: *Make all stitches in the same way, spacing them at approximately ⅛-inch intervals on straight edges or gentle curves and placing them closer together on deeper inner curves or sharp outer points.*

Step 9: *When you're finished stitching, remove the template by cutting the background fabric ¼ inch inside your stitching line and pulling it out gently.*

Step 10: *Spray your finished work with water and press it face down on a towel.*

Rob Benker-Ritchie
and Janice G. Cooke

❖ Running Stitch Appliqué ❖

I like to work most of my floral designs with a method I call needle-turn appliqué with a visible running stitch. It gives a "ripple" effect to the contours of each shape, which is attractive when accented by quilting stitches. And it's fast and easy to do; the secret lies in turning under enough seam allowance to prevent raveling, but not so much that you change the contour of the shape. You also need to make your running stitches very close to the edge of the fold, without going over it. After a few practice pieces, you'll see how easy it is to do beautiful running stitch appliqué.

1. Make a plastic template for each shape, *including* a ⅛-inch seam allowance on all sides. Trace the templates on the right sides of your fabrics and cut out the patches.

2. Pin your patches on the background fabric. To start stitching a patch, turn under a small portion of the seam allowance and hold it in place with your thumb. Sew on the side of the patch that is farther away from you; bring your needle up through the background fabric and the turned seam allowance, surfacing about ⅛ inch from the starting point. Make small running stitches along the folded edge of the patch, turning under the seam allowance just a short distance at a time.

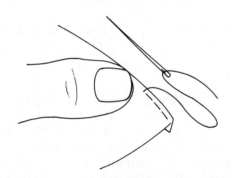

3. To sew an outer point, sew right up to the place where your finished point will be, approximately ⅛ inch in from the unturned seam allowance, and stop.

4. Use the point of your needle to turn under a short distance along the next side of the patch, and do a few whip-stitches directly through the point. To do this, insert your needle through the background fabric just off the point and bring it back up through all layers of the patch. Make another whipstitch in the same place.

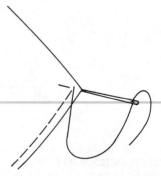

5. The third time, insert the needle into the background fabric and bring it up along the next side of the patch; then continue the line of running stitches along that side.

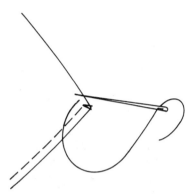

6. To make your last stitch, bring the needle to the back underneath the appliqué patch and secure your thread with a few knots on the back, running your needle through a loop before knotting it.

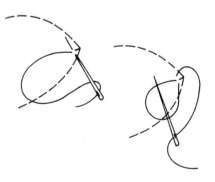

7. About ½ inch away, secure the tail of your thread with a few more knots and cut off the rest of the thread. Be sure to run your thread underneath the appliqué shape, so that none of it will show through the background fabric.

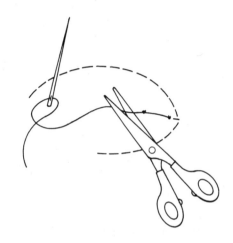

Jeanne Benson

❖ Twisted Fabric Appliqué ❖

When you want to make appliquéd petals, leaves, or ribbons that appear to be folded or overlapped, twisted fabric appliqué is the perfect answer. Normally, you would have to stitch very long, narrow outer points to achieve this appearance, but here's a way to create the same look without having to struggle with those sharp angles:

1. Cut a finished-size pattern for each shape that you wish to appear folded or overlapped. In this example, you would cut a plastic template for each side of the tulip.

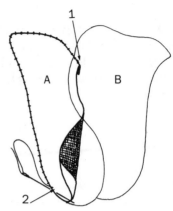

Stitch outer edges of A in place first.

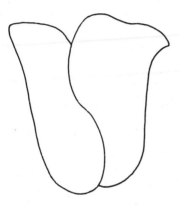

2. Choose two contrasting fabrics and draw around each template on the right side of one of the fabrics. Cut out each patch with ³⁄₁₆-inch seam allowances outside the drawn lines.

3. Mark the finished lines of the tulip on the background fabric. Begin appliquéing patch A at point 1, leaving the edge that will be overlapped by patch B unstitched. Continue your line of stitching to point 2, which is ³⁄₄ inch from where patch B will meet patch A.

4. Turn your work upside down and fold back as much as you can of patch A, holding it in place with your needle. Thread another needle with thread to match patch B and start stitching at point 3. Continue sewing to point 4, which is ³⁄₄ inch from where patch B will meet patch A. Note that you've now stitched the outer edges of both patches and that the inner edges are still open, ready to be overlapped.

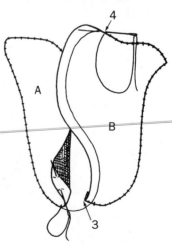

Stitch outer edges of B.

5. Turn your work to the upright position again and find the midpoint of each of the unstitched inner seam allowances. Make clips in those areas for a distance of approximately ¼ inch. Each clip should be about ¹⁄₁₆ inch apart from the next and reach about ⅞ of the way into the seam allowance. Fold under both clipped areas of the seam allowances and crease them with your thumbnail. The ¼-inch areas on each piece should be butted smoothly against one another. Return to point 4 at the top of patch B and continue stitching until you reach the middle of the clipped area at point 5. Then bring your thread to the back of your work, knot it, and cut it.

twisted in the center, appearing to overlap smoothly.

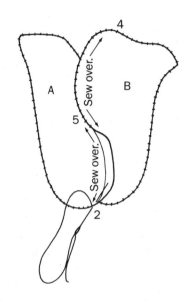

Nancy Pearson

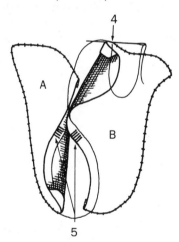

6. Starting at point 2, stitch the remaining portion of patch A, continuing until you meet your previous stitches in the middle of the clipped area at point 5. Bring your thread to the back of your work, knot it, and cut it. The two petals of your tulip are now

Using Fabrics Effectively

❖ A "Scrap-liqué" Collection ❖

Starting a scrap collection is one of the best things you can do to have a good stock of fabric for appliqué projects. If you haven't started to collect bits and pieces of fabric yet, find a box or a container and begin to put all of your scraps into it, even those so small that you might normally throw them away. This kind of fabric collection is great for all of those little shapes that go into an appliqué project.

Debbie Mumm

SUBTLE SURPRISES

I like to study old quilts and analyze the elements that give them charm and individuality. One interesting thing in many antique appliqué quilts is that not every block is identical. I think there often is more "energy" in a quilt if every shape in every block is *not* exactly the same. You can create this same kind of feeling in your own quilts. Think about putting in a few unexpected variations in your blocks or making some shapes slightly different from others. If each block is slightly different, it can make your quilt all the more interesting to look at. Little "surprises" are sometimes the very things that give old—and new—quilts their feeling of uniqueness.

❖ Gwen Marston

❖ A Print of Many Colors ❖

For a good starting point in selecting fabrics for an appliqué project with many small pieces, start by finding one multicolored print you really like. Then choose your other fabrics to go with that print. It can give you a feeling of security to know that because these colors look great together in one multicolored print, they'll work together well for your project, too.

Debbie Mumm

❖ Through a Print Window ❖

To find the perfect portion of your fabric for an appliqué patch, I recommend using a "print window," which is a template with the finished shape of the patch cut out of it. This allows you to see exactly how the finished patch will appear in any given fabric, which is especially helpful with directional prints.

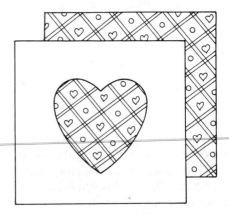

Elly Sienkiewicz

General Hints and Helpful Pointers

❖ Stop Short of Your Thumb ❖

When you're appliquéing curves by needle turning the seam allowances, it's helpful to fold under, crease, and stitch only a little bit of the seam at a time. Hold your thumb at the point where the folded part of the seam ends, and when you stitch, stop just short of that point. This will help you to avoid pleats or puckers. Then you can fold under the next part of your appliqué patch and continue stitching a smooth curve.

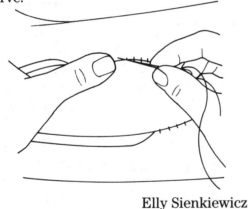

Elly Sienkiewicz

❖ Stick Those Inner Points ❖

When you appliqué an inner point and you want to control the threads that sometimes appear when you clip the seam allowance, you can run the point of your needle across a glue stick and then sweep the threads under easily. The glue holds all "fuzzies" in place and controls them while you appliqué a perfect inner point.

Mimi Dietrich

❖ Subtle Skyscapes ❖

You can sometimes add richness and depth to an appliqué design by piecing the background, or part of the background. For instance, rather than put a single piece of fabric as a sky in the background, think about how you could piece that same background, using simple traditional blocks and fabrics in soft shades of similar color value. The effect of a pieced sky can be very subtle; from a distance you might not see the piecing, but as you approach the quilt, you become aware of the pieced blocks in the background.

Mary Mashuta

❖ Use a Paper Oval ❖

It's easy to appliqué patches onto a *very* large piece of background fabric. Just cut a 3×5-inch oval out of heavyweight paper, like a manila folder. Position your appliqué patches precisely where you want them on your background fabric and then place the paper oval underneath your exact stitching area. That way, you can place your hand around the edge of the paper oval while you work and your needle will come into contact only with the paper oval as you stitch through the background fabric. Your thread will catch only the part of the background fabric that it should, and you won't have to wrap your hand around the outer edge of a large piece of background fabric all the way into your stitching area in order to appliqué. This will enable you to do precision appliqué on any size piece of fabric—even one that's a mile square!

Anne Oliver

❖ A Large Pepperoni ❖ to Go; Hold the Pizza!

If you're making an appliqué quilt and you need a place to store your blocks where they can lie flat, visit your neighborhood pizza parlor and ask for a clean pizza box! These handy boxes make great temporary storage for quilt blocks. Many restaurants have them in several sizes and are happy to give them away or let you buy them for a small charge. If you want to be creative, you can glue colorful wrapping paper to the box top or cover it with fabric.

Mimi Dietrich

❖ "Black-liqué" Magic ❖

You can sidestep the need to mark appliqué placement lines on dark fabrics by using very lightweight fusible interfacing. Just place a piece of interfacing over your appliqué design and trace the finished lines of your design onto it with a permanent fabric marker. Then cut out each shape on your drawn lines and press the shapes in position on your background fabric. Make templates for each of your appliqué shapes and cut them out, as you would for any method of appliqué. When you stitch each patch onto your background, the fused interfacing shapes provide exact stitching lines. And when your appliqué is finished, the lightness of the interfacing keeps your light appliqué colors light. The interfacing also acts as a stabilizer for the patches, enhancing each shape with a tiny bit of added loft.

June Culvey

❖ Appliqué Straight Up! ❖

When I do hand appliqué, I like to sit on the edge of a straight-backed chair, which brings my arms to a higher level as I work and helps me to keep my back straight while I stitch, avoiding the backaches that can come from bending over for a long time. I also try to sit by a window whenever possible, because my stitches are always smaller and more even when I work in natural lighting.

Kathy Berschneider

❖ Pillow Your Stitches ❖

To see better while you appliqué, and to make the stitching more relaxing, try using a pillow in your lap to raise your work. The pillow serves as a great "pin-cushion," and it keeps your work flat, which makes it easy to clip into inner curves and points accurately, without accidentally snipping the background fabric. The stitching process itself is more enjoyable, because your shoulders are free of the stress that can come from bending over your work for a long time. And instead of turning the appliqué block as you stitch, you turn the pillow. I've found that a 14- to 16-inch pillow works best.

Margaret Lydic Balitas

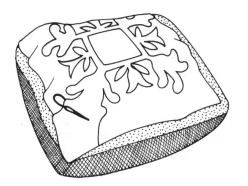

Equipment and Tools

On Pins and Needles

❖ Short Pins, No Tangles ❖

Try using small ¾-inch sequin pins to hold appliqué patches in place on the background square. Your thread won't tangle around these short pins as easily while you stitch. Another thing you can do to prevent thread from tangling while you sew is to put pins in from the wrong side of the background square when you pin your patches in place.

Mimi Dietrich

❖ Undercover Work ❖

If you have several patches pinned on a background square while you appliqué, it's easy to get your thread tangled and caught on pins and patches. It can be really helpful to cover the top of your work with another piece of fabric, so that the patches are not exposed. Just use a piece of muslin about the same size as your background fabric and cover the top of your square with it, pinning it in place, so that you expose only the part you want to work on, and you'll be able to stitch easily and have fewer thread "snarls."

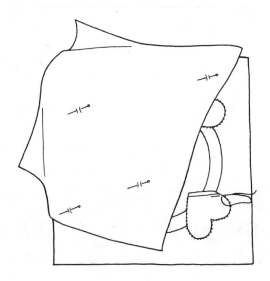

Carol Doak

❖ Thin Is In! ❖

To do very small stitches, use very thin needles. I like the Piecemakers brand of needles, especially their size 12 hand appliqué needles, size 12 sharps, and size 10 milliners needles. Thin needles glide smoothly through the edge of a fold, pick-

ing up only one or two threads at a time. If you can't find Piecemakers needles where you live, you can contact Piecemakers Country Store, 1720 Adams Avenue, Costa Mesa, CA 92626; (714) 641-3112.

Mimi Dietrich

❖ A Needle in a Straw Stack? ❖

I like straw needles for appliqué because they are very long, which can give you more leverage in turning under a seam allowance. They are also very thin needles, which helps in appliqué because they don't leave big holes in the fabric. And straw needles are the same width along the entire shank from the eye to the point, which makes them glide through fabric smoothly and easily. If you have a hard time locating straw needles, you can contact Foxglove Cottage, P.O. Box 18294, Salt Lake City, UT 84118.

Jeana Kimball

❖ Recommended ❖ by Embroiderers

For basting appliqué patches in place or for demonstrating something in a workshop, I like to use size 8 embroidery needles made by Piecemakers. The eye of this needle is quite large and easy to thread, which is especially helpful for teachers who need to stand in front of a group of people. (See "Thin Is In" above for a source listing.)

Mimi Dietrich

❖ Needle Your Thread ❖

I recommend "needling the thread," rather than threading the needle. Usually you hold the needle in your left hand (assuming you're right-handed), the thread in your right, and you try to aim the thread at the needle's eye. If this doesn't work well for you, try switching hands. Put the thread in your left hand, holding it between your thumb and your first finger so that only about ¼ inch is sticking up between your fingers. That makes it fairly stable. Holding the needle in your right hand, put the eye of the needle over the thread. If you're left-handed, you would do just the opposite, starting with the thread in your right hand.

Jeana Kimball

❖ Turn It Around ❖

One side of a needle has a larger opening than the other side. If you're having trouble threading a needle, turn the needle around and try inserting your thread from the other side.

Jeana Kimball

Thoughts on Thread

❖ Tuck in Your Tails ❖

When you begin to appliqué, you can hide the knot in your thread by sliding your needle inside the seam allowance.

The knot will stay inside your appliqué, which keeps the back of your work smooth and neat. To end a thread, make a knot on the wrong side of the background fabric and run the thread between the appliqué patch and the background fabric for about ½ inch to completely hide the tail of the thread. This will prevent threads from showing through the background fabric when your quilt is finished.

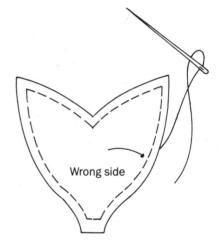

Wrong side

Mimi Dietrich

❖ Embroidery ❖
Floss to the Rescue

If you can't find the right thread color to match the fabric in an appliqué patch, try using a single strand of embroidery floss. Floss is a bit heavier than regular cotton sewing thread, but the range of colors makes it possible to find shades that aren't available in other threads.

Carol Doak

❖ A Darker Shade of Pale ❖

When you have trouble finding a thread to match the fabric in your appliqué patch, you can go a shade darker and have good results. A darker shade tends to blend in a bit lighter after it has been stitched. If you absolutely cannot find anything that comes close to the color you need, choose a neutral gray or tan thread, which will blend quite well with many colors, especially in a multicolored fabric.

Mimi Dietrich

❖ Invisible ❖ Thread, Hidden Stitches

I sometimes like to use clear nylon thread for appliqué, because it works well for dimensional appliqué with red ribbon or fabrics that change colors often. You can press it, too, if you use a press cloth and your iron is not on an extremely hot setting like "cotton" or "linen." It can be a bit wiry, so it's a good idea to use a firm knot at the beginning of a thread and a French knot at the end.

Elly Sienkiewicz

❖ Nothing Glides Like Silk ❖

If your quilt shop carries Tire brand silk thread, you're in for an appliqué treat! It's a truly wonderful Japanese thread that's available in a wide range of beautiful colors, and it glides through fabric so easily that stitching is almost effortless. The cost is higher than for many other threads, but the delight you'll feel in appliquéing with it will probably make it worth every penny to you. If you want to investigate the wonders of silk thread and you can't find the Tire brand in your area, ask your local quilt shop to contact Quilter's Resource, Inc., P.O. Box 148850, Chicago, IL 60614; (312) 278-5695 or 1-800-676-6543.

Jane Townswick

Freezer Paper and Other Fusibles

❖ A Freezer Paper Bias ❖

Here's a quick and easy way to cut bias stems that uses freezer paper and an iron instead of a rotary cutter and mat (this is a great trick to remember if you're taking an appliqué class and don't have your rotary-cutting equipment with you). Draw lines ½ inch apart, or whatever stem width you need, on freezer paper with a ruler and cut the strips apart with scissors. Press the strips on the bias grain of your fabric (leaving space for seam allowances), draw around the edges of the freezer paper strips, and use scissors to cut out perfect bias stems with ³⁄₁₆- or ¼-inch seam allowances outside the drawn lines.

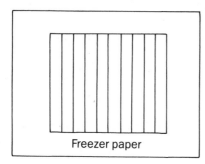

Freezer paper

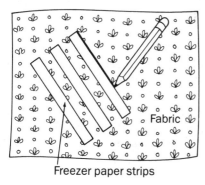

Fabric

Freezer paper strips

Mimi Dietrich

❖ Stabilizing ❖
Specialty Fabrics

You can appliqué fabrics like silk and lamé more easily by stabilizing these fabrics with fusible interfacing or freezer paper. If you choose fusible interfacing, press the side with "beads" onto the wrong sides of your fabrics before you cut out your appliqué shapes. If you use freezer paper, cut a finished-size freezer paper template for each of your shapes, using the shiny side of the freezer paper as the right side of your shape. Then press the freezer paper templates to the wrong sides of your fabrics and cut out each patch, adding ¼-inch seam allowances beyond the freezer paper. Turn the seam allowances over the edges of the paper, using glue stick to hold them in place, and press the patches. Pin your patches on the background and blindstitch them in place. Then cut a slit in the background fabric behind each patch and remove the freezer paper.

QNM Editors

❖ Two-Sided Sticky ❖

When you use freezer paper to make templates for appliqué, spray the matte "paper" side with Spray Mount brand adhesive (made by 3M) to create a template that's sticky on both sides. First, draw your templates on the freezer paper and then spray on the adhesive and cut them out. Press the paper side of each template to the wrong side of your fabric and cut out the patch, leaving ¼-inch seam allowances. Iron the seam allowances over the shiny side of the freezer paper to hold them in place. When you remove the freezer paper, the sticky residue will stay on the freezer paper, without penetrating the fabric.

Sue Rodgers

APPLIQUÉ MAGNETISM

Magnetic photo albums are a great source of template material for hand appliqué. They're inexpensive, too, and easy to find in any discount store. Look for an album that has cardboardlike pages with clear plastic sheets over them for keeping photos in place. To make appliqué templates, peel off one clear plastic sheet and place it over a pattern you want to appliqué. Trace your patches onto the plastic sheet and place the sheet back over the magnetic cardboard page. Smooth the pages together and cut your patches out through both the plastic and the cardboard. Discard the plastic when you're finished. These templates will be slightly sticky on both sides, which means they'll be easy to position securely on your fabric while you cut out your patches with seam allowances, and it will be easy to press the seam allowances over the edges of the templates because your fabric will stick to the other side, too. And the best part is that you can pull out the template after pressing each shape and use it again and again.

❖ Carol Doak

❖ Call On the Butcher ❖

If you're having difficulty finding plastic-coated freezer paper at your grocery store, investigate butcher shops, restaurant supply stores, and janitorial supply stores.

Sue Rodgers

❖ Office Dot Magic ❖

Self-stick office dots are wonderful for making perfect circle shapes for appliquéd grapes or berries. You can press seam allowances over the edges, and the seams will stick in place easily. Just place the sticky side of the office dot on the wrong side of your fabric and cut out your grape or berry with a ³⁄₁₆-inch seam allowance. Next, turn the dot over so that the sticky side is face up. Then use small scissors or a seam ripper to press the seam allowance to the sticky side of the dot, to "hem" the fabric circle over the office dot template. It will give you a perfectly rounded edge to appliqué, and the dots are easy to remove when you're finished stitching.

Elly Sienkiewicz

❖ Stick-to-Your-Ribs Appliqué ❖

Wash-away basting tape is wonderful for positioning the pieces of a woven basket in place for a Baltimore appliqué block.

When you've made the bias bars (bias strips folded in half and stitched together with the seam pressed to the back), or "ribs," for your basket, place a piece of double-stick wash-away basting tape on the back of each one and peel off the protective layer of paper. Then you can position the vertical ribs of your basket and the tape will hold them in place on your background fabric. It's also helpful to put a pin at the top and bottom of each vertical rib. Put the tape on your horizontal pieces, too, and weave them through the vertical ribs, pressing the pieces in place gently as you work. You can find wash-away basting tape in ⅛- and ¼-inch widths at your local quilt shop.

Elly Sienkiewicz

Marking Tools

❖ "X" Marks the Spot! ❖

When you're working with layered appliqué shapes, it can be helpful to mark your templates with an "X" on an edge that won't need to be stitched because the fabric of another patch will overlap it. The "X" on your template can help you remember to mark the correct edge on your appliqué patch, so you can stitch your patches in place without having to stop each time and decide which edges will be overlapped.

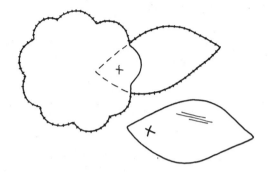

Carol Doak

❖ Super Stenciling ❖

Quilt stencils often make great appliqué patterns. For example, if you find a stencil for a quilted border that has a pretty flower and leaf, you can use the stencil to make appliqué templates of those shapes. You can also use the stencil to position and mark the shapes onto a background square, just as you'd use a stencil to center and mark the quilting design on the border of a quilt.

Carol Doak

❖ Mark Lightly ❖

When you prepare a background square for appliqué, it's a good idea to use as few markings as possible, or mark *inside* the lines of your pattern, so that none of the markings will show when your block is finished.

Elly Sienkiewicz

❖ Pigma Perfection ❖

For marking the turning lines on appliqué patches, I like the Pigma permanent marker. It's great to work with because it doesn't "drag" on the fabric as you mark, it doesn't bleed, and it doesn't wash out. The fine, thin line the pen makes doesn't show at all, because the markings lie in the seam allowances after you've stitched the patch in place. And you can see the marks on most medium and dark fabrics, even printed deep reds and purples—on almost anything except black. On pale fabrics, I'd recommend the brown Pigma marker, but for other fabrics, the black one is wonderful.

Susan McKelvey

❖ Only You Know Best! ❖

Many of my students want to know what kind of marker works best for marking an appliqué design on background fabric. The same tools and fabric do not behave the same way for everyone, so I recommend taking a piece of *your* fabric and using *your* markers on it. Then you can decide which marking tools you like and which you don't. You can also launder the fabric in *your* washing machine and *your* dryer and determine the markers and methods that work best for you. In general, I recommend that people test all markers, fabrics, detergents, and other equipment in their own homes, because the only way to find out the results you'll get is to test things yourself.

Mimi Dietrich

Special Pleasures

❖ Photocopy ❖
Transfer for Inking Fabrics

It can be lots of fun to incorporate inking into your quilts, but the process can be a bit intimidating if you don't feel steady with a pen. Here's a neat technique that relies on a black-and-white photocopy to transfer the image so it's ready for you to ink. This photocopy transfer process is much easier and more successful than tracing a paper image through a background square. (You can find more information about inking fabrics in *Baltimore Beauties and Beyond,* Volume II, 1991, C&T Publishing.)

1. Make a black-and-white photocopy of the image you want to ink on your quilt. Keep in mind that the image you press onto the fabric will be a reverse image of the original. If you want to reproduce the original image, you can do that by first copying the image onto

a sheet of mylar and then making a photocopy of that.

2. Press freezer paper onto the back of your background square to straighten and stabilize it. The freezer paper also enables the fabric to take the heat of your iron better when you press the image onto it.

3. Place a wooden board on your ironing board. Fold both the background square and the photocopy into quarters to find the centers and then match them, right sides together, on the wooden board. The background square should be on the bottom and the photocopy on top, image side against the right side of the fabric.

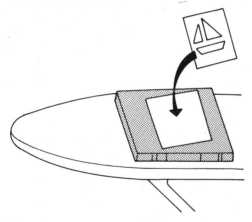

4. Use needles to pin one side of the photocopied image to your background square, within an inch of the image. Needles lie flatter than pins, and it's easier to iron over them without making indentations in the fabric.

5. Press the photocopy onto your background square using small circular

motions and pressing down hard with your iron. Gently pick up one side of the photocopy and peek at it to see if the image has "taken" well. If it hasn't, you may need to press harder with your iron or to move the control to a hotter setting.

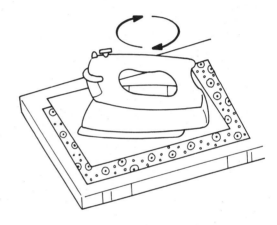

6. When the image is transferred to the fabric, remove the photocopy and let the fabric cool. Then go over the lines in Pigma permanent marker.

Elly Sienkiewicz

❖ Accessory for ❖
Appliqué on the Go

I like to see an appliqué block in its entirety before I start to stitch, so I like to cut out all of the pieces I need and put them on a piece of Pellon fleece, which holds them in place without pins. When I have the pieces arranged the way I want them in the finished block, I put slippery fabric, like a piece of drapery sheer, over the whole thing. That way, I can roll up the Pellon fleece and take it anywhere and the pieces stay put. To carry this idea even further, you can make a great portable appliqué sewing kit that looks similar to a loose-leaf binder made of fabric, with pockets in it for your sewing tools. You can fold it up easily for traveling and have your block ready to work on at a moment's notice, wherever you are.

Jeana Kimball

CHAPTER 10

Settings

Whether your blocks are 6 or 16 inches square, finding the right setting can change your quilt from "ho-hum ordinary" to "show-stopper stunning"! The set, or how the blocks are arranged together, deserves just as much attention as your choice of fabrics and design. There are lots of options from which to choose. Start by considering what kinds of quilts you like best. Do you like the look of blocks set side by side in a straight set, or blocks that alternate with secondary blocks to create a whole new design? What do you think of diagonally set quilts? How would bold sashing and corner squares look with your blocks? How about designing your own pieced sashing? Leaf through these pages for some inspiring ideas from expert quiltmakers on how to select sensational settings, plus tips and tricks on how to make them.

Sensational Quilt Sets

The Planning Stages

❖ Take Your Time ❖

When you're planning the setting for a quilt, a good starting point is to think about the look you want to create. Are you making a quick baby quilt for a friend? Maybe a straight, no-fuss block-to-block setting would be a good choice. Is your quilt a sturdy, durable bed covering for your child to take away to college? Perhaps you'd like the look of boldly colored sashing strips. Or are you making an elegant bed quilt for your master bedroom? This quilt could be complemented by blocks that are set diagonally, so they appear straight as the quilt is displayed on the bed.

Whatever kind of quilt you want to make, it can be helpful to look at lots of quilt photos in books and magazines to decide what kinds of sets you find most attractive. Bed-size quilts often look best if the design area covers the top surface of the bed, with the design continuing down the sides. And if your bed is often viewed from one side, think about having a diagonal set or about making each half of your quilt face toward the center. There are lots of decisions to make in assembling any quilt, large or small, so take your time in deciding exactly how you want to put your quilt together.

QNM Editors

PLEXIGLASS SAVES THE DAY

When you want to make sure that your blocks are the correct size before putting them into your setting, visit your local quilt shop and look for a quilter's plexiglass square ruler to help you view, measure, and true up the edges of your blocks. You'll probably find that there are several different kinds of plexiglass square rulers available. Some, such as the Quilter's Lap Board from Quilter's Rule, Inc., have both diagonal lines and straight lines at ½-inch intervals that you can use to place over your blocks to check whether the edges are square. Omnigrid square rulers are 15 inches square, with inches marked off in helpful, easy-to-see ⅛-inch increments. And occasionally you can find a kind of 12-inch "quilter's window" that is marked with lines like those of a Nine-Patch block. This works well if your blocks are 12 inches or smaller. Whatever your needs, you're sure to find a quilter's square ruler that you'll use again and again to true up the blocks in your quilts.

❖ Jane Townswick

❖ Sketch First, Stitch Later ❖

If you think you want to put sashing in a quilt, it can be helpful to sketch some setting ideas without drawing the actual quilt blocks. I don't include the blocks so that I can easily tell if I like the sashing "skeleton" of prints, solids, corner squares, striped fabrics, or pieced sashing. Use graph paper (with 8 grids per inch) to draw several setting possibilities. Then once you've narrowed down the number of settings you like, go back and put in a few or all of the blocks to see which sashing/setting idea creates the most interesting accent for your blocks. This is an easy way to discover the things you like before you cut fabrics and assemble the quilt.

Jane Townswick

❖ Polaroids Point the Way ❖

When you're trying to decide on an attractive setting for a sampler quilt, you can start by laying the blocks out on a floor. That allows you to walk around the blocks and analyze the balance of color in your arrangement from every angle and then decide how to balance the different types of blocks. Are there four star blocks that would make great anchors for the corners of your quilt? How many curved designs or floral appliqué blocks do you have? Combine the blocks in several different ways and take an instant film snapshot of each arrangement so you can compare them later and decide on a setting for your quilt.

QNM Editors

SETTING GOALS

When you start to think about the kind of setting you'd like to use for a quilt, try laying finished blocks out on a bed to see the variety of effects you can achieve. How would your blocks look on the bed if you used a diagonal set? Do any of the blocks need to be placed so that they appear right side up when the quilt is seen from across the room? What kind of look would it produce if you arranged the blocks so they faced toward the center of the bed in each quarter of the quilt? Try covering the bed with a solid fabric before you begin to lay out the blocks, to see whether sashing in that particular color would complement your blocks. Experimenting by working on an actual bed can reveal surprising and useful things that are often helpful in creating the perfect setting for your quilt.

❖ Jane Townswick

Straight Sets

❖ Side-by-Side Sets ❖

Play with your blocks until you find a layout that pleases you, with the blocks set next to each other in horizontal rows. Then follow these guidelines to help you assemble all the parts into a beautiful whole:

1. Make sure each block is the same size. If there are slight inconsistencies, you can trim the edges as necessary before you sew the blocks together into rows.

2. Press each block to make sure it lies smooth and flat.

3. Pin and sew two blocks of the first horizontal row together, matching seams and using an accurate ¼-inch seam allowance. Press the seam to one side.

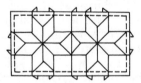

4. Continue sewing the remaining blocks in this row in the same way, pressing each seam in the same direction as you pressed the seam between the first two blocks.

5. Sew each horizontal row of your quilt in the same way, alternating the direction in which you press the seams between each row.

6. To join rows, start by pinning two rows together and matching seams.

The seams will fit together easily if the seams between blocks lie in alternating directions from row to row.

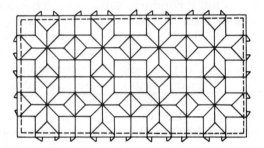

7. Press the seam between the horizontal rows to one side and continue adding horizontal rows until you've assembled the entire quilt top.

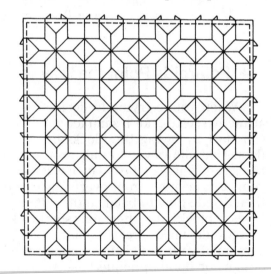

8. After you've sewn all of the rows together, press the entire quilt top to make sure that all seams lie smooth and flat.

QNM Editors

Solid Sashings

❖ Sizing Solid Sashings ❖

Sashing consists of strips of fabric between blocks and between the rows of a quilt. Colorful solid sashes (meaning those that are not pieced) can enhance patchwork designs or create an effective framework for appliqué blocks, and you can also use them effectively to enlarge your quilt. Here are handy pointers for determining the correct sizes for solid sashing strips:

♦ Determine the number and size of sashing strips you'll need for your quilt by drawing a sketch of your quilt on paper. (Graph paper can be particularly helpful for this step.) Count the number of short sashes between blocks and the number of long sashes between the horizontal rows of your quilt (including the outer ones at the top and bottom), as well as the two long outer vertical sashes.

♦ Sashes can be any width you like, most often from about 1 inch up to 6 inches. Whatever width you choose, the short sashing strips between the blocks of the quilt must be as long as the block measurement plus a ¼-inch seam allowance at each end.

♦ Here's a handy formula for figuring the length of a sash that goes between two horizontal rows:

Finished size of block
× number of blocks across = _____
Finished width of sashing
× number of sashes across = _____
(This is 1 less than number
of blocks across.)
¼-inch seam allowance on
each end of sashing strip = ½ inch
ADD THREE NUMBERS TO
GET TOTAL LENGTH OF
ONE HORIZONTAL SASH = _____

♦ To determine the length of the two outer vertical sashes, use this formula:

Finished size of block
× number of blocks down = _____
Finished width of sashing
× number of sashes down = _____
(This is 1 more than number
of blocks down.)
¼-inch seam allowance on
each end of sashing strip = ½ inch
ADD THREE NUMBERS TO
GET TOTAL LENGTH OF
ONE OUTER VERTICAL
SASH = _____

QNM Editors

❖ Set on the Bed ❖

When you plan to set blocks side by side, it can be helpful, whether they're identical or alternating blocks, to lay them all out on a bed before you sew them into rows. That way, you'll be able to see whether you're getting the effect you want in your quilt.

QNM Editors

❖ On a Grain, off a Grain ❖

Sashings and borders offer two alternatives in placement of fabric grain. One way is to cut all of your sashing and borders on the lengthwise grain, for consistent stability and strength with a minimum amount of stretch. This means that your fabrics must be long enough to accommodate the length of your longest sashing and border strips.

The other school of thought is to make the grain lines consistent throughout all of the sashing strips and borders in your quilt, which means that you'll cut the long sashing strips on the cross grain and the short sashing strips on the length of grain. For this method, the side borders would be cut on the length of grain and the top and bottom borders on the cross grain. This means that if your top and bottom borders are longer than 43 inches, you'll need to piece them.

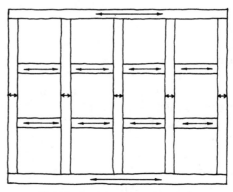

Sashing cut on crosswise grain

Sashing strips and borders cut by either method will stabilize your quilt blocks, so you can use either combination of grain lines to make your quilts lie straight and true.

QNM Editors

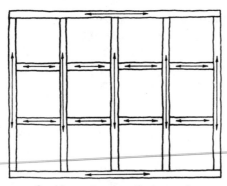

Sashing cut on lengthwise grain

❖ Making the First Cut ❖

It's a good idea to cut any long sashing strips before you cut the short ones for your quilt. That way, you can be sure you won't later have to piece to get the length you need for the long sashing strips.

QNM Editors

❖ The Merits of Marking ❖

Marking the long sashing strips before attaching them makes it easy to fit the strips to all portions of the quilt evenly, without distorting or stretching the sashing out of shape. To mark the sashing strips to match the horizontal rows of your quilt, you can use a pencil, a fabric marker, or a hera (a palm-size, hard plastic marker) with good results. (If you use a hera, you can mark lines on your fabric and remove them completely by pressing them with an iron.) Begin at the left end of one horizontal sashing strip and mark the ¼-inch seam allowance. Next, mark a second line to indicate the length of your quilt block. Follow that by marking a line at the finished width of your sashing, and continue this process until you reach the other end of the strip. You can mark outer vertical sashing strips in the same way, marking lines to indicate all block and sashing measurements.

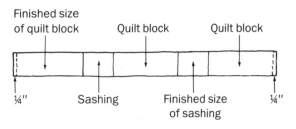

QNM Editors

❖ Quilt Assembly ❖ with Solid Sashings

It's not hard to put your quilt together in a set with solid sashing strips. Here are seven easy steps to help you add the pieces together in the proper order. Remember that before you start, you should mark all matching lines on your long sashing strips for a smooth fit.

The Step-by-Step for Solid Sashings

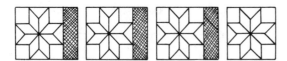

Step 1: *Beginning with the first horizontal row of your quilt, sew a short sashing strip to the right side of each block, except the last. Press each seam toward the sashing.*

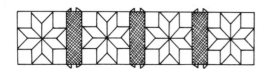

Step 2: *Sew the blocks together into a horizontal row, pressing seams toward the sashing strips. Complete your remaining horizontal rows in the same way.*

Step 4: *Add a long horizontal sashing strip to the bottom edge of each remaining horizontal row, except the last one. Press the seams toward the sashing strips.*

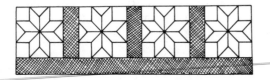

Step 3: *Sew a long sashing strip to the bottom edge of your top horizontal row, matching the marked lines on the sashing strip to the lines of your blocks and short sashing strips. Press this seam toward the long sashing strip.*

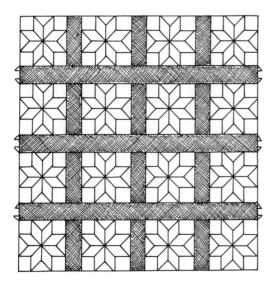

Step 5: *Sew the rows of blocks together with ¼-inch seam allowances, pressing these seams toward the sashing strips.*

Step 7: *If you plan to miter the outer corners of your sashing, sew the top and bottom sashing strips to your horizontal rows, beginning and ending each seam ¼ inch in from each end. Do the same for the two long outer vertical strips. Then you can miter the corner seams. (For more details on mitering, see "Miter Magic" on page 185.)*

QNM Editors

Step 6: *If you plan to make straight seams at the corners of your outer sashing, sew a long sashing strip to the top and bottom of the quilt. Then sew the two long vertical sashing strips to the outer edges.*

❖ Using Setting Squares ❖

If you like the look of solid sashing but want to break up long expanses of solid color in your quilt, setting squares may be just the touch you need. These squares appear interspersed among the horizontal sashing strips that run between rows of blocks. Once you've pieced together the long sashing strips with the setting squares, assembling the quilt is very similar to assembling one with solid sashing.

The Step-by-Step for Sashings with Setting Squares

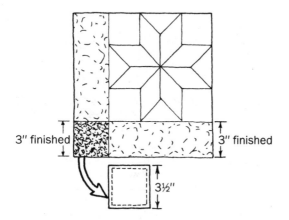

3" finished   3" finished

3½"

Step 1: *To determine the number and size of your sashing strips and setting squares, it's helpful to draw your quilt layout. The width you choose for your sashing strips will determine the size of your setting squares. For example, if your finished sashes are 3 inches wide, then your finished setting squares will be 3 inches × 3 inches. To allow for ¼-inch seam allowances on all sides, you'll need to cut setting squares that are 3½ inches × 3½ inches.*

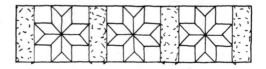

Step 2: *Sew together a horizontal row of blocks with sashing strips between them. Add sashing at the outer edges, as well. Press the seams toward the sashing strips. Repeat this for each row of blocks in your quilt.*

Step 3: *Sew a long row of sashing strips and setting squares, pressing the seams toward the sashing strips.*

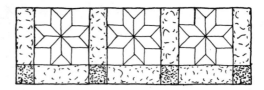

Step 4: *Sew a long row of sashing strips and setting squares to a horizontal row of blocks, pressing the seam toward the long row of sashing strips.*

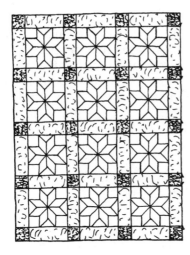

Step 5: *Continue assembling the rows of blocks and sashing strips/setting squares in this way until your entire quilt is completed, pressing each seam toward the long rows of sashing strips and setting squares.*

QNM Editors

Peerless Pieced Settings

❖ It's Simply Amazing ❖

The Garden Maze pattern is beautiful enough to be a quilt in itself. It's sometimes known by other names, such as Tangled Garter or Tirzah's Treasure. Used as a quilt set, it also makes a wonderful complement to the soft curves and fluid shapes in floral appliqué blocks. The Garden Maze is easy to make and well worth the effort. If you like the look of pieced sashing, follow these steps to plant a beautiful pieced maze in your own floral garden quilt.

Garden Maze Pieced Setting

1. Garden Maze sashing strips consist of three pieces of contrasting fabrics, usually with a lighter center strip that is twice as wide as the two outer

strips. The narrowest workable width for the outer strips is 1 inch finished. In this example, the finished center strip is 3 inches wide and the finished outer strips are 1½ inches wide each. That means that the finished pieced sashing strips will be 6 inches wide × the length of your block and that the finished setting squares will be 6 inches × 6 inches. The strips within the setting squares will always be the same width as the outer strips of the sashing.

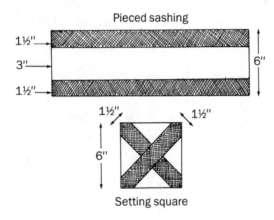

Pieced sashing

1½″ — 3″ — 1½″ — 6″

1½″   1½″

6″

Setting square

2. For a 25-inch block, cut the two darker outer fabric strips 2 inches wide × 25½ inches long (the ½ inch accounts for seam allowances), and cut the lighter center strip 3½ inches wide × 25½ inches long.

3. To make pattern pieces for your pieced setting squares, draw an accurate 6-inch square on graph paper. Then draw lines at 1½-inch intervals (or intervals to match the width of the outside strips on your sashing) diagonally through this square. Label the parts of the block for which you'll need to make templates with an A, B, and C. Trace these shapes onto template plastic and add ¼-inch seam allowances on all sides.

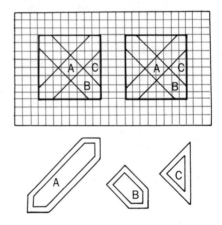

4. Sketch your entire quilt on graph paper to determine the number of fabric strips you'll need in each color for the pieced sashing, as well as the number of pieces you'll need of each A, B, and C shape for your setting squares. Cut your strips and pattern pieces out of fabric.

5. To piece each sashing strip, sew together the three fabric strips with ¼-inch seam allowances. Make enough of these pieced sashing strips for your entire quilt.

6. Piece each setting square by sewing together two BCB corner units and joining these units to the center A piece. Make the number of setting squares you need for your quilt.

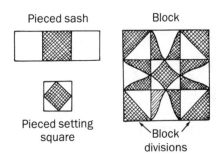

Pieced sash Block

Pieced setting square

Block divisions

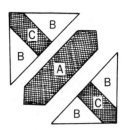

7. Assemble your quilt blocks, Garden Maze sashing strips, and setting squares as described in "Using Setting Squares" on page 164.

QNM Editors

❖ Sets by Design ❖

If you want to add your own touch to a quilt, why not design a pieced sashing to complement your blocks? You can start by using the basic divisions of your block in creating new and unusual pieced accents for your design. Here are a few ideas to get your creative juices flowing!

Overall design with blocks, pieced sashes, and pieced setting squares

Pieced sashes

Pieced setting squares

Pieced sashes and pieced setting squares

QNM Editors

Diagonal and Specialized Sets

❖ Diagonally Speaking ❖

It's just as easy to set your blocks on the diagonal as it is to set them horizontally. The only difference in a diagonal set is that you need four quarter-square triangles to complete each corner of your quilt and enough half-square triangles to fill in the side edges. Use these guidelines to investigate the details of diagonal sets.

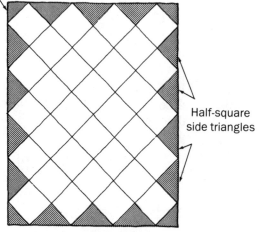

Quarter-square corner triangle

Half-square side triangles

Diagonal Block Setting

◆ It's a good idea to cut the quarter- and half-square triangles so that their outside edges are on the lengthwise or crosswise straight of grain. This avoids having bias edges that can stretch out of shape along the outside of your quilt.

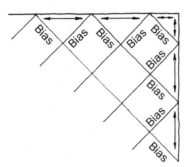

♦ The quarter-square triangles need to have two edges on the straight of grain, to keep the corners of your quilt from distorting. Use the cutting plan shown in the diagram below for your corner triangles.

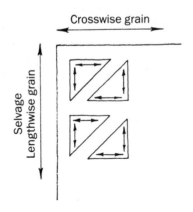

♦ The half-square side-setting triangles should be cut and positioned so that the straight grain runs along each side of the quilt. This helps the edges of your quilt stay true. The two bias edges on these triangles are stabilized by the edges of your quilt blocks. For these pieces, use a cutting plan like the one shown in the diagram below.

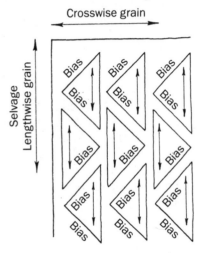

♦ When you sew the blocks together, sew them in rows diagonally, beginning with one block that has a half-square side-setting triangle on each side. Continue to sew the remaining rows of blocks in the same way, beginning and ending each row with a half-square side-setting triangle. The exception will be the one row that needs two quarter-square triangles for the corners of your quilt.

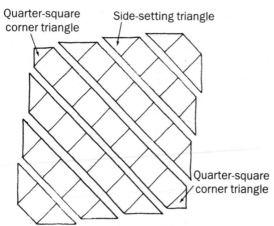

Quarter-square corner triangle

Side-setting triangle

Quarter-square corner triangle

Sewing rows with corner and side-setting triangles

◆ When you've completed all the diagonal rows for your quilt, sew the rows of blocks together, just as you would sew horizontal rows of blocks, and add a quarter-square corner triangle at the remaining two corners of your quilt.

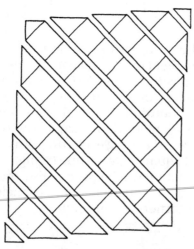

Join rows, adding two corner triangles.

QNM Editors

❖ Side and Corner Shortcuts ❖

For any diagonally set quilt, you'll need four quarter-square triangles for the corners and as many half-square triangles as it takes to complete the sides of the quilt. You can determine the exact size of each kind of triangle by drawing a square the same size as your finished blocks on a piece of graph paper. Divide the square in half diagonally to create the half-square triangle for the sides of your quilt, and add a ¼-inch seam allowance to each side. Then divide the other half of the drawn square diagonally to create the quarter-square corner triangle, and add a ¼-inch seam allowance to each side.

QNM Editors

❖ Going 'Round the Bend ❖

Special beds sometimes need special quilts. If you have an antique four-poster bed, you can make a T-shaped quilt to fit it to perfection, with careful planning. This kind of setting will allow your quilt to lie flat and round the corner posts smoothly. Look at the diagrams on pages 171 and 172 for some creative ways to approach this kind of special quilt set.

Settings for T-Shaped Quilts

 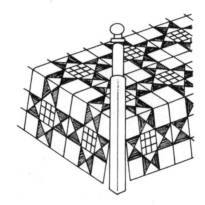

A T-shaped quilt has the two lower corners cut out so that the quilt will lie smoothly on either side of the footpost. The design area on both of these drops should match, so that the eye moves smoothly from one to the other. When you plan a quilt for this kind of bed, think about how the blocks will come together at these corners. One idea is to make blocks that are the same size as the length of the drop.

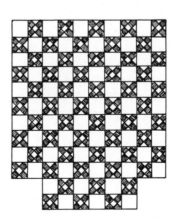 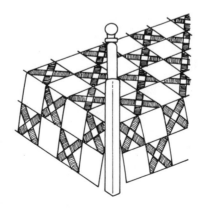

Another possibility for a T-shaped quilt is to plan a drop that's the width of two blocks.

Consider planning a border that is the same width as the quilt drop.

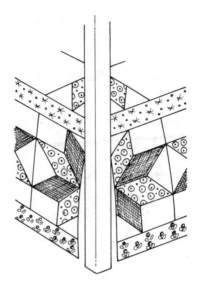

Placing a half motif at each corner can create an unexpected but pleasing effect.

QNM Editors

CHAPTER 11

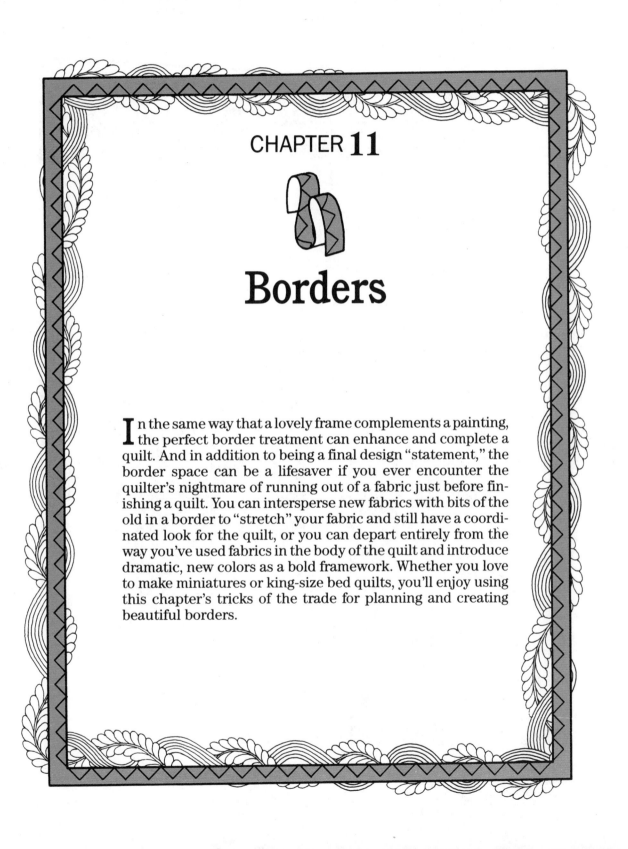

Borders

In the same way that a lovely frame complements a painting, the perfect border treatment can enhance and complete a quilt. And in addition to being a final design "statement," the border space can be a lifesaver if you ever encounter the quilter's nightmare of running out of a fabric just before finishing a quilt. You can intersperse new fabrics with bits of the old in a border to "stretch" your fabric and still have a coordinated look for the quilt, or you can depart entirely from the way you've used fabrics in the body of the quilt and introduce dramatic, new colors as a bold framework. Whether you love to make miniatures or king-size bed quilts, you'll enjoy using this chapter's tricks of the trade for planning and creating beautiful borders.

Basic Border Styles

Patchwork Borders

❖ The Final Flourish ❖

A great border that echoes some of the elements in the quilt can enhance the whole design and give the quilt a feeling of harmony. Use these ideas for complementary patchwork borders as a starting point for sketching your own border ideas on graph paper.

Ideas for Creative Patchwork Borders

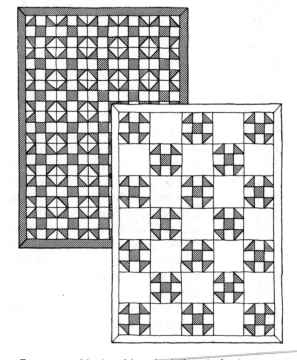

Repeat patchwork shapes in a positive/negative color combination.

Frame your blocks with a single band of color.

Add multiple borders to your quilt top. This quilt benefits from a narrow inner border and a wider outer border, made from two different fabrics.

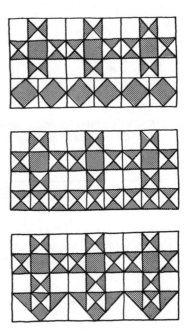

Regroup some of the center patchwork shapes to create a new border unit. Here are three examples of how portions of the star block can be repeated and recombined for striking effects.

Bring elements from a center medallion into the borders. Here, the modified fan and flower shapes from the center are echoed in the outer pieced border.

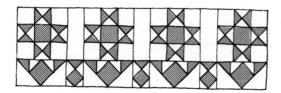

For a quilt with sashing, match a border unit to each block and another to each sashing strip.

Ideas for Creative Corners

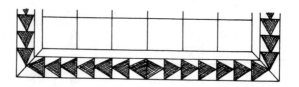

Reverse a directional motif at the center of the border, so that the corners meet symmetrically.

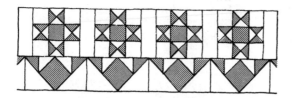

Make border units that meet at the midpoint of each sashing strip.

QNM Editors

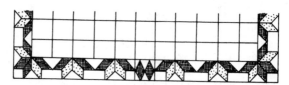

Plan a central unit that's larger or smaller than others in the border. The two diamonds shown here form a unit that is narrower than the other pieced half stars in the border.

❖ Motifs for Turning a Corner ❖

Perfectly matched corners make a patchwork quilt look symmetrical and visually complete. If your quilt is square, it's easy to work out one corner that you like and repeat it at the other three corners. For a rectangular quilt, it's easy to create the perfect corners for almost any design, with a bit of careful planning. Here are some creative alternatives for the corners of a patchwork quilt.

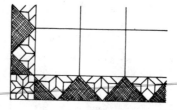

Introduce a separate unit at the corners of the border.

Planning Appliqué Borders

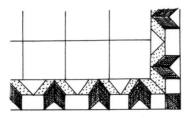

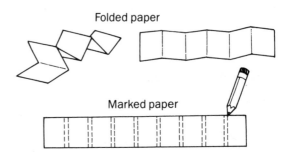

Folded paper

Marked paper

Put complementary shapes at a mitered corner. On this quilt, the triangles, when mitered together, form dark and light squares that enhance the positive/negative shapes formed by the other elements in the border.

Cut a piece of freezer paper or shelf paper the same length as your finished border and mark or fold it into equal segments that match the intersections of the blocks.

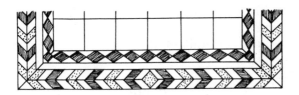

Add a solid border strip between two pieced borders to set them apart.

QNM Editors

Single motif

Double motif

Appliqué Borders

❖ Six Tips for Single Motifs ❖

Use single motifs and groups of motifs to adorn the borders of your appliqué quilts and perhaps to echo some of the elements in the central appliqué design. To plan your borders, try using full-size templates and these guidelines for working out design possibilities.

To plan the way you want to fill each segment of the border, mark or draw the shape of a single unit on another piece of paper. Try placing a single motif in this border segment. If a single motif seems too small, try putting repeated shapes in the border segment.

Try making miniature motifs to fill a border space.

QNM Editors

Another idea to play with is using reversed motifs to fill the space.

Connecting repeated motifs with a vine or a curved swag is an elegant design element.

❖ Creative Border Treatments ❖

You can use multiple motifs in a border to create new configurations of appliqué shapes that become interesting accents to the body of a quilt. Here are some hints on how to put motifs together to enhance your next quilt.

A Quartet of Border Ideas

If the motifs are shaped symmetrically, you can put them in a border that has either an even or odd number of segments.

If your motif is a bit too small, consider whether you can add another shape to fill the space in the segment.

If the border motifs are not symmetrical, you'll need to place the motifs in a way that pleases you. For an odd number of border segments, try planning one center border motif and placing the others on either side in opposite directions out to the corners.

❖ Graceful Corners ❖ for Appliqué Borders

Creating attractive corners for an appliqué quilt can be easy with the design leeway that appliqué offers. You can elongate a shape, put in an extra motif, or add an extra inch or two to a corner swag. Put some of the following ideas to work for you in planning your next appliqué border.

The Step-by-Step for Appliqué Corners

Step 1: *Start by drawing a full-size corner square on a piece of freezer paper or shelf paper. Draw a diagonal line through it and one full-size border motif on either side of this corner square to guide your placement of corner motifs. In this example, only half a heart was drawn on each side of the corner, since the other half will fall on the adjacent border strip.*

For a border with an even number of segments, try reversing the placement of alternate motifs.

You can also reverse directions of motifs in each half of the border, as long as there is an equal number of segments in each half of the border.

QNM Editors

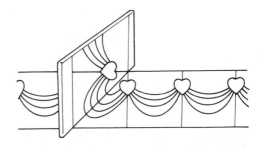

Step 2: *Place a mirror at a 45 degree diagonal through one of the border segments to find out how it would look as a corner motif for your border.*

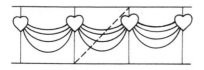

Step 3: *With a pencil, lightly mark a dotted line next to the mirror.*

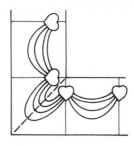

Step 4: *Use tracing paper and reverse the image to fill the corner square, checking to make sure that the corner motifs meet the border motifs symmetrically on each side.*

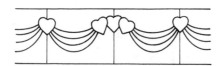

Step 5: *If your quilt is square, each of the four borders will be identical. If the quilt is rectangular, you may need to make adjustments to the two longer borders by elongating swags or adding extra motifs as fillers.*

QNM Editors

❖ Scalloped ❖ Borders by Design

Scalloped edges can be an integral part of a quilt, as in the Double Wedding Ring, or a delicate finishing touch, perhaps to the softly curved shapes of a floral appliqué quilt. If you want to plan a scalloped border for your next quilt, here are some helpful hints for creating symmetrically shaped curves and corners.

The Step-by-Step for Scalloped Borders

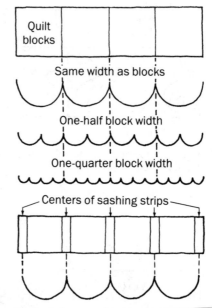

Scallops from sashing to sashing strip

Step 1: *Look at your quilt to decide how wide you'd like to make your scallops. Your quilt often suggests natural divisions, such as the width of one block, or even smaller, such as one-half or one-quarter block widths. If your quilt has sashing strips, you could space scallops between midpoints of the sashes.*

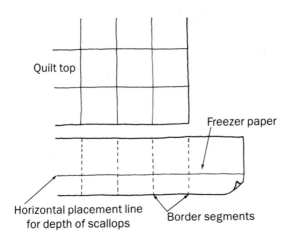

Quilt top

Freezer paper

Horizontal placement line for depth of scallops

Border segments

Use freezer paper to determine scallop placement.

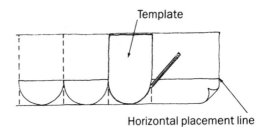

Template

Horizontal placement line

Step 4: *Use this template to mark the curve of each scallop on the piece of border-size freezer paper. This creates a full-size pattern to use for your border.*

Step 2: *When you've decided how wide and deep you want your scallops to be, cut a piece of freezer paper that will accommodate the depth of your border and add at least 2 extra feet in length. Lay the paper border next to the quilt and mark lines for the border segments to match the blocks in the quilt (or whatever divisions you've chosen), allowing enough extra length at each end to work out the corners. You can use the width and depth of one border segment to work out the curve of the scallops for the quilt. Mark a horizontal lengthwise line through the border where you want the inner points of the scallops to lie.*

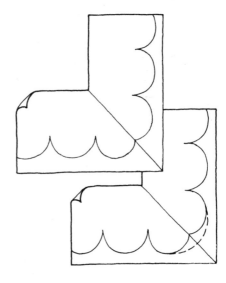

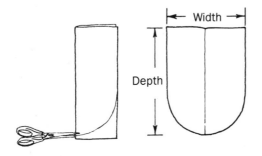

Width

Depth

Step 3: *Cut a new piece of freezer paper the same size as one of the border segments and fold it in half to mark and cut out a symmetrical curve shape to create a template for your scallops.*

Step 5: *To create a corner for your scalloped border, place two pieces of the freezer paper border together as if they were mitered, and draw lines where the curves of two scallops come together at that point. You may like the look of a slight indentation where the two scallops meet, or you might decide to round off the scallops slightly to create a continuous curve at the corner.*

QNM Editors

Tips and Tricks for Terrific Borders

Fitting Borders

❖ Rounded Corners ❖

If the edges of your quilt will fall to the floor when it's displayed on a bed, you can design your quilt to adjust for the excess fullness at the corners by rounding the edges.

1. Measure the length of the drop from the top edge of the bed to the floor.

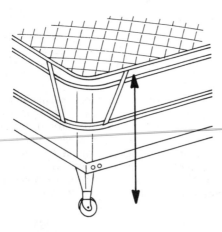

2. Cut a piece of paper that's large enough to draw a square that has sides the same length as the drop. With a string and a pencil (or a compass, if you have one large enough), draw a curve from one corner to the opposite corner of the square. This will become the template for the corner curve.

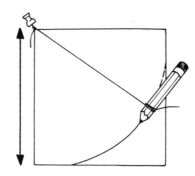

3. Use the corner curve template to plan that part of the quilt border. A curved corner is a good place for a twining vine with appliquéd flowers or for partial patchwork shapes from a pieced block.

QNM Editors

❖ Cut to Fit ❖

When you're sewing straight corners on the borders of a quilt, it can be very helpful to take the measurements of the sides and of the top and bottom edges of the quilt after you've finished the body of the quilt. If the sides differ by less than an inch, it's easy to use a compromise measurement between the two for figuring out the correct length for the borders. After you've determined this compromise measurement, you can ease the borders onto the sides of the quilt and be assured that the quilt will lie flat and the edges will be straight and the corners true. When you take the measurements for the top and bottom edges, you can make the same kind of compromise, if necessary. Remember to add the width of the attached side bor-

ders in determining how long to cut the top and bottom borders.

QNM Editors

❖ Stay Centered ❖

To sew borders to the sides of your quilt, find the center of each edge and place a pin at each of those points. Fold each of your border strips in half and mark those center points with pins. Measure out in both directions from the center pin on each border strip and put a pin at the correct distance for the end point of your quilt. Pin the border strip to one edge of your quilt, matching center pins and end points and spacing pins evenly between them. If your quilt has straight corners, sew borders to the sides first and then to the top and bottom. Stitch all the way to the outside edges.

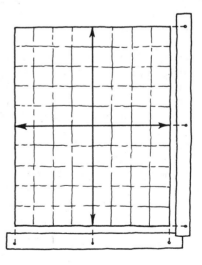

If you're going to miter the corner seams of the border, sew the borders to all sides of the quilt, beginning and ending each seam ¼ inch in from each edge of the quilt.

QNM Editors

HELP! I'M OUT OF FABRIC!

One of the best things that can happen to you in making a quilt is to run out of a fabric and *have* to choose something else. This can be very scary when it happens, but it also offers you a very inspiring and motivating opportunity. When you are forced to come up with a creative solution to this kind of fabric dilemma, what can be done? Can you bring a new fabric into your border that blends with the others in your quilt? Or maybe introduce even more than one new print? Can you stretch the amount of fabric you already have by using it sparingly, perhaps in small shapes, in your borders? You may find that you'll surprise yourself with your own creativity!

❖ Margaret Miller

❖ Sew Easy ❖

When I pin a border on a quilt top, I find the center of that border and the center of one side of my quilt and pin those points together. I also pin the border and quilt together along the edges and in the corners. I like to have the quilt and border flat, either on a table or on the floor, while I work. When I sew the border seam, I sew with the border on top and the quilt on the bottom, so that the sewing machine feed dogs will help me ease any extra fullness.

Diana McClun

❖ The Notch System ❖

I like to use what I call a "notch" system of marking sashing strips and borders to match them easily to the edges of a quilt. Here's how you can use this system to sew your quilt top and borders together quickly, efficiently, and perfectly.

Marking to Match Sashes and Borders

Wrong side

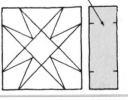

On the wrong side of the sashing strip, mark a light pencil "notch" at intervals that will match the seams in the adjoining patchwork block.

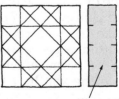

Wrong side

For plain blocks up to 12 inches, mark the midpoint of both the block and the sashing strip on the wrong side.

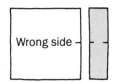

Miter Magic

❖ Fold-and-Press Miters ❖

One easy way to miter a corner seam, which works especially well for borders made from striped or other directional fabrics that you want to match, calls for a quick pressing and some handstitching.

The Step-by-Step for Mitered Corners

For plain blocks larger than 12 inches, mark the block and the sashing strip in thirds on the wrong side.

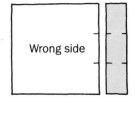

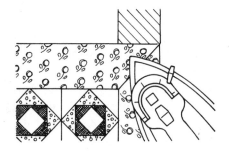

Step 1: *Place the quilt on your ironing board right side up, with the seams pressed toward the borders. At one corner, fold the top border up at a 45 degree angle over the lower border and press this fold.*

Mark the wrong side of a border at intervals the same width of each block.

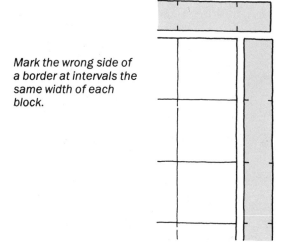

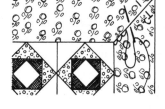

Step 2: *Pin the folded border piece in place and handstitch the fold from the top with a blind stitch, creating a perfect mitered seam.*

Janet Elwin

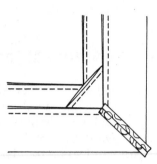

Step 3: *After you've completed this seam, trim the excess fabric from the wrong side and press the seam open.*

QNM Editors

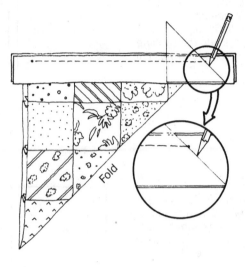

❖ Fold-and-Stitch Miters ❖

Another easy technique for perfectly mitered corner seams calls for folding your whole quilt and using a triangle to mark the sewing lines.

Step 2: *Use a 45 degree plexiglass quilter's triangle, or fold a piece of paper in half diagonally to create a perfect 45 degree angle, and place the triangle or the paper angle on the border, aligning it with the end of your stitching line. With a pencil or fabric marker, mark the miter line from the end of your stitching to the outer edge of the border.*

The Step-by-Step for Mitered Corners

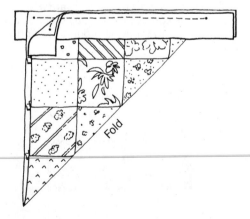

Step 1: *Fold your quilt diagonally, wrong sides together, placing adjoining borders exactly on top of each other.*

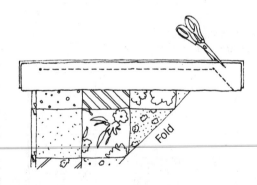

Step 3: *Stitch on your marked line, beginning this seam exactly at the point where the border seam ended. Check the miter from the right side of your quilt and trim the excess fabric to a ¼-inch seam allowance.*

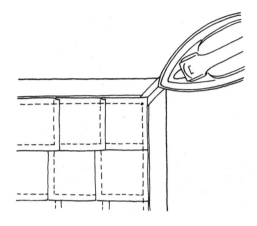

Step 4: *Press the seam open.*

QNM Editors

❖ Tricks with ❖
Lights and Mirrors

When you're debating whether to have mitered corners on a quilt, the first thing to determine is what the corners will look like in the finished quilt. You can use a mirror at a 45 degree angle on any piece of fabric to see what it would look like if it were mitered at that point. When you find a part of the fabric that gives you the look you want, cut your border so that this part of the fabric occurs at the corners of your quilt.

Eleanor Burns

❖ Press-and-Pin Miters ❖

I prefer to miter corners at the ironing board by placing one strip out flat and putting the second strip on top. Then I fold under the top strip at a 45 degree angle so that it matches the fabric in the first strip and press it. Then I fold the strips so their right sides are together and pin the two borders together accurately along the top strip. I then use the pressed line as my guide as I stitch the miter by machine, sewing from the inner corner to the outer edge of the mitered border.

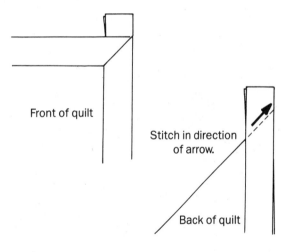

Front of quilt

Stitch in direction of arrow.

Back of quilt

Use pressed line as guide for machine stitching.

Eleanor Burns

❖ Hera's a Great Idea! ❖

You can use a Japanese hera to mark perfect 45 degree angles for mitering the seams at the corners of your borders. It's a small piece of plastic with a curved edge that puts a knifelike score in fabric. It won't leave any markings or chemicals on your fabric, and you can see the lines it makes on almost any fabric. When you press the seam, the lines will go completely away. Look for this handy tool at your local quilt shop or in quilting or sewing notions catalogs.

Carol Doak

Handy Border Bits

❖ It All Adds Up ❖

If you're working out a design for a very narrow border, especially for an appliqué quilt, try drawing out your design on adding machine tape! It's an inexpensive, great source of paper that you can just lay next to the body of your quilt and see the effect your design creates before you cut fabric and start constructing the border.

QNM Editors

ROLLING BORDERS

With a piece of freezer paper and a Graphic Wizard Roller Ruler, you can make your borders as creative as you like and ensure the accuracy of mitered corner seams and pieced border designs at the same time. This ruler actually locks in position every quarter inch, which can help in adding accurate seam allowances to pattern pieces. Here are some of the other ways a rolling ruler can help to create a perfect, precise border for a quilt:

❋ You can draw vertical lines to mark individual sections on a piece of freezer paper cut the same size as a finished border.

❋ You can draw angles, diamond patterns, or cross-hatching marks on the freezer paper border and trace them onto the fabric for quilting.

❋ You can draw French curves, arcs, and scallops to mark the border of an appliqué quilt with the position of flowing vines, scallops, or other curved shapes.

Look for this ruler in art or architectural supply stores, or for more information, contact Supa Roller Ruler, P.O. Box 1, Massapequa Park, NY 11762; 1-800-428-8208.

❖ Jane Townswick

❖ Cut Borders ❖ and Binding First

It's a good idea to cut all of the borders, binding, and large pieces from your fabric before you start to cut the small pieces for your quilt. That way, your borders will be seamless and you'll be sure to have enough continuous yardage for your binding.

QNM Editors

❖ Do Not Fold, ❖ Spindle, or Hang

Until you put the borders on your quilt and actually layer the quilt sandwich, treat your quilt as something very fragile. Sometimes people keep their quilt tops hanging up on design boards until they finish making the borders, and that can easily stretch a quilt out of shape.

Diana McClun

❖ A Border Balancing Act ❖

When you plan quilting designs for borders, it's a good idea to put as much quilting there as you do in the center part of your quilt. If the amount of quilting is balanced from the body of your quilt to the borders, your work will have a more even appearance. If the body of a quilt is more heavily quilted than the borders, they can sometimes appear bulky and large in comparison to the rest of the quilt.

Judy Mathieson

CHAPTER 12

Quilting Designs

Choosing the quilting designs for a quilt is a very personal matter, because the patterns and motifs you select will make your quilt as individual and unique as your signature. Do you like the traditional look of quilting a quarter inch from each seam in a patchwork quilt? Maybe you're attracted to whole-cloth quilts with elaborate feathered circles and scrolls, leafy floral vines, and diagonal cross-hatching. What about the idea of putting a recurring motif in each quilt you make, as your unique "logo"? Would you enjoy making a quilt with an unrelated quilting design that marches exuberantly over the top of every block? This chapter will give you lots of fresh and fun ideas for quilting designs, along with an array of today's best methods for marking them on your quilts. You'll also find useful ideas on custom fitting them to your own patchwork and appliqué creations.

Designing and Drafting Quilting Designs

❖ Quilting Quiz ❖

There are four basic points to consider when planning your quilting designs. Give yourself this "quiz" to help determine how you want to quilt your quilts:

♦ How prominent do you want the quilting to be in your finished quilt? Will it be an integral part of the design, or will it be less important than your patchwork or appliqué?

♦ How formal or casual is your quilt? Is it an informal design that would be best suited by an allover quilting pattern like the Clamshell shown in the diagram below? Or does your quilt have a more formal feel that would be enhanced by elegant feathered motifs and symmetrical cross-hatching?

♦ Is your quilt traditional or contemporary? Contemporary quilts may call out for the innovative, the unique—something completely unlike traditional quilting patterns.

♦ How much do you enjoy the actual quilting process? If all of the other facets of quiltmaking are more enjoyable for you than this part, it's a good idea to take that into account when you're planning the quilting designs.

Gwen Marston

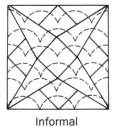
Informal

Formal

❖ "Quilt As Desired" ❖

If you're a beginning quilter and you see those words in a quilt pattern, does your heart sink? How are you supposed to *know* what kind of quilting you desire? Selecting quilting designs comes up each time you make a quilt, so you need to become aware of all your choices and then use some guidelines to pick the best quilting designs for your newest creation. Here's a list to help you figure out how to "quilt as desired":

♦ The most effective designs are balanced within the spaces they occupy, enhancing those spaces and creating interesting texture and dimension.

♦ Quilting around floral appliqué shapes will make them look three-dimensional.

♦ Try quilting around appliqué shapes and bringing the same motif into a quilted border. Add some straight lines of quilting to lead the eye diagonally through Nine-Patch blocks.

♦ Quilt ¼ inch inside the seams of any areas you want to visually recede. Quilting inside patches will make them appear flatter, like these dark background triangles, which are not

as puffed out as the lighter, unquilted Flying Geese triangles.

♦ Quilt patchwork motifs, omitting the surrounding areas. You can lead the eye in circular patterns, create depth where you want it, and create regularity in your quilt by quilting each patchwork motif in the same way, as in this Kaleidoscope pattern.

♦ Repeat lines, curves, or angles that appear elsewhere in your quilt. Here, quilted points were added to an Eight-Pointed Star.

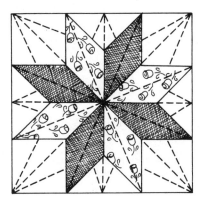

♦ Use alternate blocks to showcase more intricate designs, such as a feathered circle with a background grid of squares and straight lines.

♦ Add a design "statement," such as quilted rays of sunlight streaming gently from the corners of an Attic Window block.

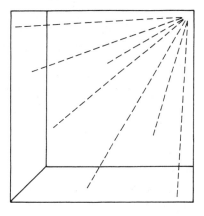

QNM Editors

❖ Alternately Speaking ❖

Plain blocks offer a built-in showcase for beautiful quilting stitches, so you may want to design something special for areas like these. Get out some quilt books and look at several quilts that have alternate plain blocks. Then make a few rough sketches of ideas that appeal to you, writing down page numbers so you can refer to those designs again, if necessary. When you've chosen a quilting design that pleases you, cut a piece of paper the same size as your finished block and use it to draw your own original design. Starting with the largest shapes, block out a very rough sketch of the design you like. For example, if you like a floral design that has one large rose, a stem, and several leaves, start by sketching just an outline of the rose shape, add the stem, and fill in the rest of the space with leaves. The key to this process is *not to quit*–just keep on sketching until you fill the space with shapes you really like, and then you can refine your design by tracing it onto another piece of paper.

Gwen Marston

❖ A Background in Quilting ❖

If your quilt has a substantial amount of open background area, there are lots of ways to fill that space beautifully with quilting. For some ideas on creating a stunningly quilted background, look over the following diagrams and captions. Remember that in selecting the final quilting design, the most important thing is to please yourself and your sense of what is right for your quilt.

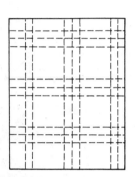 

Combining lines at different intervals and angles produces interesting background textures.

Allover patterns, like this Clamshell, can add richness and depth to background areas.

Ideas for Quilted Backgrounds

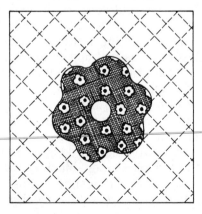

Simple diagonal grids can be very effective, especially behind the curves of floral appliqué shapes.

Quilting lines that run parallel to the edges of an appliqué shape create a wavelike "echo" effect.

The denseness of stipple quilting can make an area appear flatter than surrounding areas.

QNM Editors

❖ Going in Circles ❖

When you draft feathered circle quilting designs, it's helpful to remember a formula from geometry class for finding the circumference of a circle. The circumference of any circle equals 3.14159 times its diameter. This means that a circle with a 10-inch diameter has a circumference of 31.42 inches (round off the results so you're only dealing with two numbers after the decimal point). For practical purposes, you can round this number to 31½ inches. Here are two ways to use this information for drafting a feathered circle quilting design:

♦ *Single Feather Approach:* Draw one "feather" shape and decide how you want to place a series of these shapes along your circle. Measure the space the feather will take up on the circle and divide 31½ inches (or the circumference of your particular circle) by this number to determine how many feathers will fit around the circle. If necessary, you can make slight adjustments to the angle of your feathers to space them evenly when you mark the feather shapes around the circle.

Measure this space.

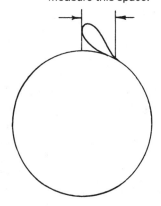

◆ *Multiple Feather Approach:* Decide how many feathers you want to have around the circle and divide that number into the 31½-inch circumference (or whatever the measurement of your circle is) to determine the size to draw the individual feather shape. For most feathered circle quilting designs, there will be more feathers on the outside of the circle than on the inside.

QNM Editors

❖ Flower Power ❖

If you think you can't draw a straight line, drafting floral quilting designs is for you! It's a simple matter of tracing a picture of a flower you like from a seed catalog, encyclopedia, or garden book. Then you can eliminate a few details, size your drawing to fit your quilt, and you're ready to

play with arranging the motifs in a pleasing quilting pattern. Have fun using these guidelines for drafting your own floral quilting designs.

The Step-by-Step for Drafting Floral Designs

Step 1: *Select an uncluttered photo of a flower you like that has asymmetrical shapes and pleasing curves.*

Step 2: *Trace the picture, simplifying the lines to make them easier to quilt. Enlarge the motif you've drawn, using a photocopy machine to make it the size you want in your finished quilt. Copy the motif onto a sheet of tracing paper.*

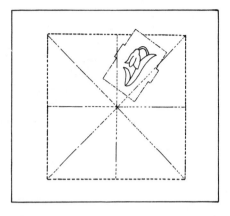
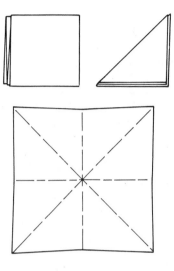

Step 3: *Cut a square of tracing paper the size of your finished block or border section and fold it in half, then in fourths, and then diagonally into eight sections.*

Step 5: *Place a large sheet of tracing paper over the motif and mark straight lines to indicate the eight sections. Trace the flower motif in one section onto the large sheet of tracing paper.*

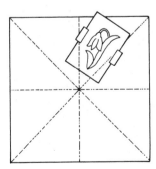

Step 4: *Tape the traced flower motif over one section of the paper, so that it fills one wedge without overlapping the section on either side. You can vary the position of the motif within the wedge to create different angles.*

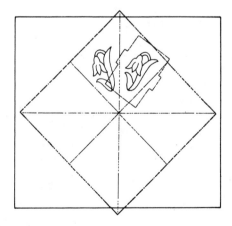

Step 6: *Rotate the large sheet of tracing paper, aligning the section marks, and trace the motif onto the remaining seven wedge-shaped sections.*

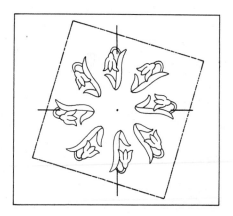

Step 7: *Remove the completed drawing. If your drawn design looks crooked, it's easy to mark new block alignment lines on another piece of tracing paper and trace your design at an angle you like better.*

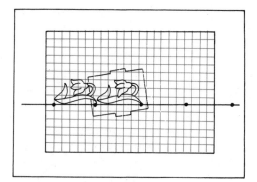

Step 8: *For borders, you can tape a single tracing paper motif on a sheet of graph paper and position it against the border to find the angle you like. Then place the border over the graph paper and trace each flower motif onto the border segments.*

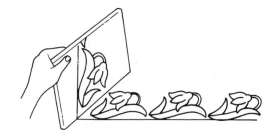

Step 9: *To create a graceful border corner, experiment with angles and placement of motifs by placing a mirror over one of your motifs to determine the angle you like best.*

Judy Martin

❖ Border Tactics ❖

Carefully planning the quilting for borders will help you space motifs evenly and turn the corners to perfection. The easiest way to plan border quilting designs is to cut a piece of freezer paper the exact width and length of the border. If the quilt is square, you'll need to plan only one border, since the three others on the quilt will be identical to this. If the quilt is rectangular, you'll need to make two border plans, one for both the sides and another one for the top and bottom. Fold each freezer paper border in half lengthwise to guide your placement of designs.

Then fold it into as many horizontal sections as you want the border to have and begin to work out your quilting designs. Try out a few of the following ideas, or use them as starting points to create your own unique designs.

Designs with gentle curves are easy to stitch and great for quilting in one direction if you work at a floor frame.

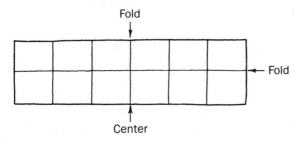

Fold

Fold

Center

Make freezer paper guide to plan border quilting.

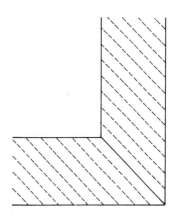

Hints for Creating Quilted Borders

Diagonal lines are beautiful and easy to quilt, and you can mark the spaces between them easily with masking tape.

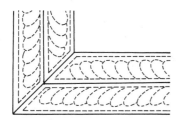

Some designs let you avoid quilting through seams. In this example, each line of feathers is defined by an outline of stitching that parallels but doesn't cross the mitered seam of the border.

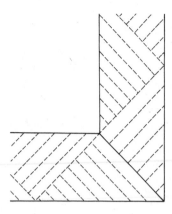

Try an alternating pattern of diagonal lines for an even richer texture.

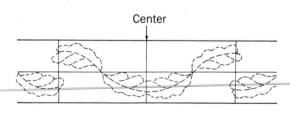

Create a quilting design by grouping several motifs that echo appliqué shapes in your quilt.

Reverse a motif at the center of a border.

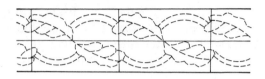

Add lines of quilting to connect disjointed motifs.

QNM Editors

❖ Customizing Corners ❖

Armed with a roll of freezer paper, scissors, and tape, you'll quickly see how easy it is to design a perfect corner for your quilted borders.

1. To work out how two borders will come together at the corner, cut two pieces of freezer paper the width of the borders and tape them together at right angles to actually form the corner in paper.

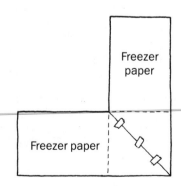

2. Fill in the border segments on each side of the corner with the motifs that will be joined to form the corner. Once those are drawn, you can begin to work out your corner motif.

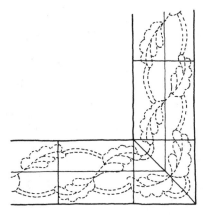

3. There are lots of possibilities for pleasing corner designs. You may like corners with reversed motifs that meet at a mitered corner seam, with lines of quilting that connect them to the borders, or perhaps you like the look of a corner design that interrupts your borders completely. Experiment to develop a corner that pleases you, by adding or subtracting parts of motifs, adding new motifs, or spacing designs differently to fill the corner.

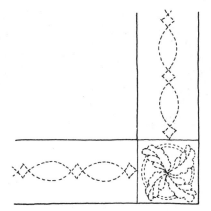

QNM Editors

A WORLD OF DESIGNS

Working out your own quilting patterns is a great way to express yourself, and it's practical, too, because commercial stencils don't usually fit the areas you want to quilt. For inspirational ideas to help you start drafting your own quilting designs, try looking through books and studying the quilting motifs and patterns in antique quilts. Many wonderful quilts from the eighteenth and nineteenth centuries contained incredibly interesting, original quilting, and if our great-great-grandmothers could come up with such innovative designs, we can, too! You may also find inspiring ideas in the shapes of flowers and leaves on the wallpaper in your own home, or in the curled scrolls of a piece of silver flatware, or in the asymmetrical floral patterns in an antique silver service. Take a close look at crewel tapestries, rug designs, tin ceilings, and architectural moldings, too—the world around us is full of shapes, lines, and curves that would make beautiful quilting designs.

❖ Gwen Marston

❖ Carry a Sketch ❖ Pad at All Times!

You can collect ideas for wonderful quilting designs if you carry a small sketchbook with you whenever you attend a quilt show. Keeping paper and pencil at-the-ready will allow you to jot down your thoughts and make quick sketches and drawings to spark your imagination and creativity in the future. You might look at your drawings later and be happily surprised at the quilting designs that emerge from them. Can you combine elements from two or more designs that appeal to you, or eliminate a motif here or there to simplify a design for easier quilting? Can you suit the shapes you like to the spaces in your quilt by enlarging or reducing them or by grouping them in clusters? Inspiration is all around you, so keep paper and pencil within easy reach whenever you travel!

QNM Editors

Marking Quilting Designs

❖ Chalk Full of Designs ❖

For marking machine quilting designs, I like to use chalk markers, especially in small one-block areas. Chalk marks stay in place long enough to allow you to quilt the design (be careful using chalk in larger areas, since it can rub off before you've finished quilting). I also like the EZ brand wash-out chalk pencils in blue, red, or white, which are made to be washed out after you're finished quilting.

Anne Colvin

❖ Hera Today, Gone Tomorrow ❖

I think the Japanese hera is an unbeatable tool for marking quilting designs. It's a small, white piece of plastic that scores visible, accurate lines on almost any fabric. Place the curved edge on the fabric and press firmly, pulling it toward you to score an easy-to-see indented line in the fabric. You'll get the most defined lines if you place the fabric on a rotary-cutting mat or another surface that will hold the fabric firmly in place while you mark. If you make a mistake in marking, just spritz your marks with water—they'll vanish instantly before your eyes! You can put a quilt hoop over marks made by a hera, and the lines will stay visible indefinitely.

You can mark each area of your quilt when you're ready to work on it, through all three layers of the quilt sandwich. If you use a quilter's ruler with the hera, you can mark lines ¼ inch away from every seam in your quilt, without ever having to use a single fabric marker, pencil, or piece of masking tape. The hera works well for marking curved lines, too! The only time a hera does not work well is on a very "busy" or large-scale print. For all other fabrics, it's wonderful. And when your quilt is finished, no one will be able to tell how you marked your quilting designs.

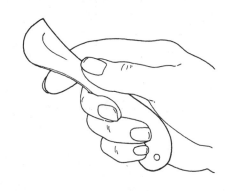

Carol Doak

❖ A Good Backup Plan ❖

When I mark quilting lines with a hera, I like to put my 6 × 24-inch ruler in position to mark a line and then back the ruler up approximately ⅛ inch. That way, the hera is positioned to mark accurately. I hold the hera in the palm of my hand, put my finger at the tip, and press down, pulling it toward me as I mark each line.

Eleanor Burns

❖ Pencil Dependability ❖

Regular lead pencils were used more than anything else in the past for marking quilting designs. I think pencils are very effective for marking if you choose hard lead like No. 3 or No. 4, which won't smudge as easily as No. 2 lead, and if you mark very lightly on your fabrics. Keeping a very sharp point also helps to maintain fine lines as you mark. With harder lead pencils like these, your lines will be fine enough that your quilting stitches can cover them up almost completely.

Gwen Marston

❖ Super Spray Starch ❖

Before I mark any machine quilting lines in blue water-soluble marker, I like to apply spray starch to the fabric. I've found that the starch makes it much easier to remove the blue markings later. Spray starch creates a kind of protective coating on the surface of the fabric and bonds with the marking substance, preventing it from being completely absorbed into the cotton fibers of the fabric. Another plus to starched fabric is that it stays smoother and is easier to work with than unstarched fabric.

Debra Wagner

A GREAT "T-RASER"

I like to use a piece of a white, 100 percent cotton T-shirt or bed sheet to erase pencil marks from a quilt. Rub the T-shirt fabric in the direction of the lengthwise or cross grain of the fabric in the quilt, never on the diagonal. The soft cotton erases graphite beautifully when you rub very gently, without disturbing the nap of the fabric in your quilt. If you don't have any old, soft T-shirts or bed sheets you want to cut up into smaller pieces, try looking for them in thrift shops. The older and softer they are, the better they'll be for erasing pencil marks on your quilt.

❖ Anne Oliver

❖ A Marvelous Marking Board ❖

I like to use a marking board when I mark a quilt with stencils. You can make one quite easily and inexpensively by covering an 18 × 24-inch piece of plywood with canvas. To use it, lay a section of your quilt over the marking board, where the canvas will hold your fabric firmly in place while you mark the quilting design. This board works well for marking borders, too, because you can slide it easily around the entire edge of your quilt.

Carol Doak

Marianne Fons

❖ Is There a ❖ Doctor in the House?

It's helpful to work out quilting designs on a piece of paper that's exactly the same size as the space you want to quilt, especially feathered quilting designs. A large-size pad of high-quality tracing paper is an excellent investment, because it's easier to fold and see through than freezer paper. It's sometimes easier to erase lines on tracing paper than on freezer paper, too, so I recommend it highly for drafting quilting designs. You can get good tracing paper at any art supply store. A visit to your doctor's office may send you home with a suitable large-scale substitute for tracing paper. Ask if the office is willing to sell you one of the large rolls of acid-free paper used for covering examining tables, which works just as well as artist's tracing paper.

❖ Viva Vellum! ❖

Try using vellum tracing paper for tracing large quilting designs. It's available at any art supply store on large rolls in widths of 18, 24, and 36 inches. It's also made in a 45-inch width, with grids of 8 squares to an inch, which can sometimes be a real time-saver because you don't need a ruler or a T square to take measurements or to find right angles.

Sue Rodgers

❖ A Corner on Freezer Paper ❖

When you're using freezer paper to plan quilting designs for corners, make a mitered corner by folding the paper at a 90 degree angle. This gives you perfect corners for your quilting designs. And if you ever need to design something for a very large space, you can even splice freezer paper by ironing the edge of one piece to another.

Anne Oliver

❖ A Good Contact to Know ❖

Contact paper makes great quilting templates that can be used again and again. Just draw your quilting design on the contact paper with a permanent pen, cut it out, and place it wherever you want to quilt that motif. Quilt around the edges and remove the contact paper when you're finished.

QNM Editors

❖ Marked Improvements ❖

When you find a quilting design you like, trace it onto a sheet of tracing paper and place it over your quilt to see how it fits and whether you like it there. Investigate photocopy machines if you need to enlarge or reduce a design to custom fit your quilt. If the fabric in your quilt is light, you can darken your quilting design with a permanent pen and lay your quilt over that to trace the design onto your quilt. For dark fabric, you may want to place your quilting design on a light box or a window to trace it onto your quilt.

Marianne Fons

❖ Fresh Tape Is the Best Tape ❖

Masking tape is a wonderful way to evenly space lines of quilting, but one bed-size quilt can easily take up to six rolls of tape. Besides quantity, there is the issue of age to consider, as well. Because old tape can be yellowed and leave a sticky residue on quilts, I like to go to a paint store and purchase a new, unopened box of masking tape. I also take out each roll of tape from the box and actually measure it, to make sure that it's exactly the right width. And finally, when I store masking tape at home, I keep it in plastic bags in a dark closet so that it stays fresh.

Anne Oliver

❖ Sizing Up the Situation ❖

A photocopy machine with the capacity to enlarge and reduce at variable percentages can put a whole world of quilting designs into your hands. If you've found an interesting cable, or any other kind of quilting design that appeals to you, try reducing or enlarging it at different percentages to custom fit it to your own quilt.

Sue Rodgers

❖ A Paper Doll Technique ❖

To work out a quilting design for a border, I cut a piece of freezer paper the exact width and length of the border and fold it into as many sections as I want for the border. Then I draw or trace a design onto one section, fold the paper sections together again, and cut out the entire border design at once, paper doll fashion. Then I press it onto the quilt border and quilt around it. Another option is to press it onto the fabric, trace around it, and remove the freezer paper before you start to quilt.

Anne Oliver

❖ On the Border Line ❖

When I mark diagonal grid lines in a border, I start by making the corner lines absolutely correct. Then I can work toward the middle of the border and make any adjustments I need to make in the long, straight area. It's very easy to stray from a perfect 45 degree angle when you mark diagonal lines, so I check my work by folding a piece of paper diagonally and comparing it to the angles of my lines about every 2 to 3 inches.

Anne Oliver

CHAPTER **13**

Hand Quilting

After you've assembled a quilt top and marked the quilting designs, adding the quilting stitches is the final part of expressing yourself in fabric. The process of hand quilting is slow and deliberate, which allows you to focus your attention on each stitch and to savor every moment it takes to unite the layers of fabric and batting into your finished quilt. You may find that you enjoy the contemplative aspect of sitting at a floor frame while you stitch, taking time to slow down in a world that seems to go faster and faster every day. Or maybe you like quilting in a hoop in the comfort of your living room, surrounded by members of your family. However you like to work, the practical bits of information and helpful hints you find here from some of the best quilters in the country are sure to find their way into your repertoire of favorite stitching tricks and techniques.

Learn about the Layers

Batting Basics

❖ The Right Stuff ❖

When you're faced with choosing a batting from the wide array now available, it can be difficult to know what kind of middle layer you want for a quilt. Use this quick review of the content and characteristics of today's most popular batts to help you make the right choice for your quilts:

◆ *Cotton batting* provides a ⅟₁₆- to ⅛-inch middle layer for a quilt, with no fiber migration, or "bearding," through fabric. It's warm in winter, cool in summer, and it works well for both hand and machine quilting. It shrinks approximately 5 percent when washed and becomes softer and more drapable with time. The fibers of cotton batting can shift, requiring quilting lines that are ½ inch to 2 inches apart. If you like compact quilting and the wrinkled look of antique quilts, Mountain Mist batting and Mountain Mist Blue Ribbon batting are some choices you have.

◆ *Cotton/polyester batting* is an 80 percent cotton/20 percent polyester combination batt with a loft of approximately ⅛ inch. Its long fibers allow you to quilt it at 3- to 4-inch intervals, and it works well for either hand or machine quilting. If the surface of the batt is bonded to retard bearding, as is the surface of Fairfield Cotton Classic, you can presoak the batt to break down the coating and make it easier to needle. If you select Hobbs Heirloom Cotton, you can choose either to presoak it for a smoother look or to use prewashed fabrics in your quilt and wait to wash the batting until you're finished with the quilt. It shrinks approximately 5 percent, which will give the quilt an antique, "crinkly" appearance.

◆ *Polyester batting* launders well with minimal or no shrinkage, and it requires quilting at generous 3- to 4-inch intervals. Bonding the surface of polyester batting reduces the tendency to beard, but this coating can sometimes make it harder to needle. Low-loft batts work well for creating a small amount of texture, and you can achieve tinier hand-quilting stitches on low-loft batts than on thicker batts. Needle-punched batting is made of densely packed, or "punched," fibers, making a compact batt that works well for projects that need body, shape retention, and support. Regular-loft batting works well for both hand and machine quilting, and it launders easily. High-loft polyester batts are wonderful for making fluffy, tied comforters that withstand vigorous use and frequent washings.

♦ *Silk batting* is actually many lightweight layers of silk "leaves" rather than a large sheet of batting. To use silk batting, you need to peel off the layers, pull the fibers apart to separate and fluff the strands, and pat them into place on a quilt backing in order to regulate the loft. Silk adheres to fabric easily, which creates minimal shifting. It needs to be quilted at 1½-inch intervals. If silk fibers beard through your fabric, it's better to clip them off than to pull them out, which can cause even more fiber migration. Silk is more expensive than other battings, but it's very drapable, which makes it a good choice for summer quilts or very fluid clothing. You can wash silk batting in cold water with mild soap and tumble dry it on the "air" setting.

♦ *Wool batting* is lightweight and warm, but its fibers tend to migrate easily through cotton fabrics. You can offset this bearding tendency by encasing a wool batt in layers of cheesecloth before basting a quilt. Wool is very easy to needle in both low and regular lofts. It needs to be quilted at about 2- to 4-inch intervals. High-loft wool batts are wonderful for tied quilts. You can launder wool batts by soaking them gently in tepid, soapy water and spinning and rinsing them several times in clear water in a washing machine. If wool is subjected to agitation or very hot water, it can felt or shrink dramatically. Wool batting can be dry-cleaned successfully, but it's

helpful to make the dry cleaner aware of the wool content.

QNM Editors

❖ Handy Batt "Cheat Sheet" ❖

To streamline your decision making when it comes to selecting a batt for your quilt, ask yourself the four questions listed in the chart on the opposite page. How you answer can help you pinpoint the best batt for your project.

QNM Editors

❖ Beating the Bearding Blues ❖

Fiber migration, or bearding, happens when bits of batting work through the fabric of a quilt. It's a concern with all but 100 percent cotton batts. To enjoy using cotton/poly combination or polyester batts and keep bearding to a minimum, it's helpful to pay attention to the quality of everything you use to make a quilt, from high-thread-count cotton fabrics to small needles to high-quality threads. Look closely at the labeling on each package of batting you see in a store and buy the best "branded-fiber" batts you can find, those that indicate the actual brand names of the polyester fibers used in them. Rather than just the word "polyester," look for such brand names as Dacron and Astrofil, which are fibers unblended with any other polyester products. Spending the time and effort to find the best supplies available will pay off in producing a quilt that's less likely to beard.

Mary Reddick

Batting Selection Guide

Use this handy table to take the guesswork out of choosing batting for your quilting projects. In the batting column, a symbol indicates the batting's appropriateness for the answer you have selected for each of the questions below.

Questions to Guide Your Selection	Cotton — 100% Cotton	Cotton — Needle-Punched "Natural"	Cotton/Polyester — 80% Cotton, 20% Polyester	Polyester — Low Loft	Polyester — Needle-Punched	Polyester — Regular Loft	Polyester — High Loft	Silk	Wool — Low-Regular Loft	Wool — High Loft
1. How do you plan to hold the three layers together?										
a. Hand quilting.	❖	❖	❖	❖	❖	❖		❖	❖	
b. Machine quilting.	❖	❖	❖	❖	❖	❖		❖	❖	
c. Tying.		❖	❖	❖	❖	❖	❖		❖	❖
2. How do you want your completed quilt to look?										
a. Old-fashioned, rather flat; it will show off my fine quilting stitches.	❖	❖	❖	❖				❖	❖	
b. Some texture and loft, some quilting motifs will show along with quilting that outlines my beautiful fabric patches.			❖		❖	❖		❖	❖	
c. Puffy and cozy.							❖	❖		❖
3. How much time do you plan to spend quilting this piece?										
a. As long as it takes; quilting is my favorite part.	❖		❖	❖		❖		❖	❖	
b. As much as I have to, but I'm anxious to start sewing the next top.		❖	❖		❖	❖		❖		
c. Minimal—just enough to hold it together!		❖								
4. How will your quilted piece be used?										
a. With care on a bed.	❖	❖	❖	❖		❖	❖	❖	❖	❖
b. As a piece of clothing.	❖	❖	❖	❖				❖	❖	
c. As a wall hanging.		❖	❖	❖	❖	❖		❖		
d. Over the back of the couch, to throw over someone who is napping.	❖	❖	❖	❖		❖	❖		❖	❖
e. Carried around by a toddler with sticky fingers.		❖	❖	❖		❖	❖			
f. As an entry in a quilting competition.	❖	❖	❖	❖	❖	❖		❖	❖	

Types of Batting

❖ Throwing In the Towel ❖

To relax batting, unfold it and tumble it in a clothes dryer for a few minutes, either on "air dry" or the lowest heat setting. Putting in a slightly damp towel will add a bit of moisture, too, which helps take wrinkles out even more quickly.

Liz Porter

❖ Fabulous Flannel ❖

Cotton flannel gives an almost "no-loft" look to quilts and quilted garments. If you use cotton flannel in a quilt, it's a good idea to wash it at least twice in very hot water to preshrink it thoroughly and then lay it out flat on a table to dry.

QNM Editors

Choosing the Backing for a Quilt

❖ That Old Back Magic ❖

When you choose the backing for any quilt, look for a soft, firmly woven cotton fabric for ease in quilting. If you're a beginner, why not look for a pretty print that will enhance the back of the quilt, as well as camouflage your early stitching efforts? And if you're experienced enough to want to showcase tiny, delicate quilting stitches,

choose a solid fabric to give the backing the look of a whole-cloth quilt. Whatever backing fabric you choose, it should be at least 2 inches larger than the quilt on all four sides. If that means that the backing needs to be pieced, try to place seams vertically to add more strength along the length of the quilt. For any pieced backing, it's best to place the seams symmetrically, whether they're vertical or horizontal. The diagram below shows a few possibilities for seam placements.

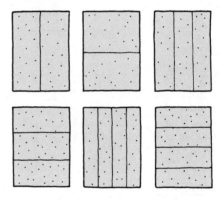

QNM Editors

❖ Count on Cotton ❖

Very high quality cotton bed sheets make beautiful, totally seamless quilt backings for almost any size quilt. And it's actually easier than you might think to quilt through a sheet that has a thread count of 200, as long as it is 100 percent cotton. In better department stores, you often can find beautiful cotton sheets in colors, as well as in white, in sizes that range from twin to king.

June Culvey

❖ Mad for Madras ❖

Why does the backing for a quilt necessarily have to match the fabrics in the quilt top? I like to use unrelated fabrics, such as madras plaids, for quilt backings. Madras is inexpensive, colorful, and easy to quilt through. You should always prewash it and check for colorfastness, however, because it often contains colors that bleed. Whenever it's on sale, I like to buy 6 to 9 yards, which is enough to back almost any size quilt.

Liz Porter

❖ A Real Cutup ❖

You can make a great backing for a quilt from other projects that didn't work out, by cutting them into pieces and sewing them together randomly to create an entirely new piece of fabric. This creative piecing can make the back of a quilt more interesting and help you make good use of fabrics you might not otherwise use.

Margaret Miller

❖ Looking for Loft ❖ in All the Wrong Places?

If your quilt guild plans to make a group quilt, it can be worthwhile to test several kinds of batting, because the batting affects both the ease of quilting and the look of the finished product. Try making up several "sample quilts" using the same fabrics and different batts and ask participating members to make comparisons. After the test quilts are finished, it's helpful to wash them to check for bunching or bearding and to compare them for drapability before selecting the batt for a group project.

QNM Editors

❖ Shh . . . My Batt's Asleep ❖

Any kind of batting can be compressed from being rolled and stored in its plastic bag for a long period of time. It's a good idea to unroll and unfold a batt a day or two before you layer a quilt, to let the creases and folds even out a bit. If your schedule will not permit that much "resting" time, take a few extra minutes when you layer the quilt sandwich to gently smooth out the creases in the batting.

QNM Editors

❖ The Lights in Baltimore ❖

If you're making a floral appliqué quilt with a very light-colored fabric in the background, it's important to choose a very light-colored fabric for the backing, too, because darker fabrics can sometimes "shadow," or show through, the front of a quilt.

Lynn Lewis Young

Layering a Quilt Sandwich

❖ Thread Basting 101 ❖

When you thread baste the layers of a quilt together, choose white thread to avoid getting the tiny spots of color on the quilt that darker thread might leave behind. To assemble a quilt sandwich for thread basting, follow these steps:

1. Press the seam or seams in the backing open and spread the backing out, wrong side *up*, on a clean work surface, such as a table, bed, or floor.

2. Open the batting and, if necessary, trim it so that an extra 2 inches extends beyond each edge of the quilt top. After trimming, roll the batt into a loose tube. Place it in the center of the backing and unroll it, smoothing it out gently and evenly as you work toward each edge of the backing.

3. Place the quilt top over the batting, right side up, checking to make sure that the three layers of backing, batting, and quilt top lie smooth and flat.

4. With a friend, pull the backing fabric taut from each end and carefully lift the batting and top over the backing seams to check to see that these seams are straight. Place a few pins through the quilt to secure the layers in spots for basting.

5. Cut a very long strand of white thread and tie a knot in the end of it. Beginning at the center and working out toward each edge, or starting at one edge and working toward the opposite edge, baste the layers of the quilt with a simple running stitch of about 2 inches on top of the quilt and approximately ½ inch underneath the quilt. You can "meander" your lines of basting to avoid seams or areas that you plan to quilt, while creating a grid of vertical and horizontal basting lines about 6 inches apart. As you stitch, you may want to gently roll up the quilt to make it easier to reach the next basting area. When you're finished basting the entire quilt, you're ready to begin quilting.

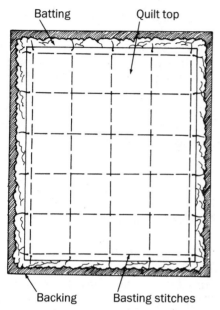

Batting   Quilt top

Backing   Basting stitches

QNM Editors

surface will allow you to keep the pins in a quilt for a long time without discoloring the fabric. Space the pins at the same 6-inch intervals you use when basting with thread.

QNM Editors

❖ A Pin Collection ❖

I may have the world's largest safety pin collection because I ask friends and family to save the safety pins that come with clothes returned from the dry cleaner. These rustproof pins are perfect for pin basting, and best of all, they're free!

Suzanne Nelson

❖ A Basting Wall ❖

If you have a vertical design board, you can baste the layers of a small quilt together on the wall and not have to experience the back strain of bending over a table. Just pin the top edge of the backing up on your design wall, wrong side facing you, and add the layer of batting, pinning it in place along the top edge. Smooth it out over the backing, and the cotton fabric will "hug" the batting, helping to hold it in place while you work. Pin the quilt top over the batting along the top edge. It's easy to make sure that everything is smooth and flat when the layers are hanging vertically, and the basting wall allows you to stand or sit in front of the quilt as you join the layers together with thread or pins.

Doreen Speckmann

❖ The Finer ❖ Points of Pin Basting

Basting with safety pins makes a good alternative to thread basting quilt layers together. To prepare a quilt for pin basting, follow the procedure outlined in Steps 1 through 4 in "Thread Basting 101" on the opposite page. Some people prefer pin basting because it's so much faster than using thread. If you like this idea, look for quilter's rustproof, nickel-plated brass safety pins in either size 0 or 1. They are short and their shaft diameters are narrow, which means they will be less likely to slide in and out of the quilt, leaving large holes in the fabric. And the rustproof, nickel-plated

❖ Borrow a Tailor's Trick ❖

Basting a quilt in diagonal rows can lead to distorted corners, so I prefer to baste in either a vertical or horizontal grid, using a stitch that's actually called the "diagonal baste." This stitch is used to hold layers of fabric together in tailoring, and it works very well on a quilt, too. To do diagonal basting, start by making one horizontal stitch. Then bring the thread down diagonally and make another horizontal stitch. The spaces between horizontal stitches can be up to 1½ inches long, so the basting process goes very quickly. Another bonus is that this stitching is more secure than other basting methods.

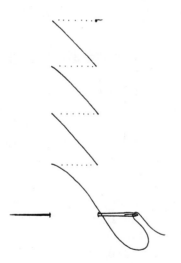

Diana McClun

❖ Darn It All! ❖

I like to use size 7 cotton darning needles for basting a quilt together because they're long and thin. This type of needle is easy to hold as you insert it repeatedly in and out of the quilt, which means your fingers won't ache as much as they might with a shorter needle.

Carol Doak

❖ Come Spoon with Me ❖

If you like to use a slightly curved needle for basting the layers of a quilt together, an old teaspoon is wonderful for catching and lifting the point of the needle on the top of the quilt after you take each stitch. It works especially well if you're using thick batting. The advantage of "spoon" basting is that it's easy to work with both hands on top of the quilt.

QNM Editors

Mastering Hand Quilting

Hand-Quilting Essentials

❖ The Basics ❖ of the Running Stitch

Quilting by hand is nothing more than a simple running stitch that binds the three layers of backing, batting, and top into a finished quilt. When you learn to quilt, it's important to strive for evenness, and the size of your stitches will become smaller as you gain more experience. If you want to try your hand at quilting, here is the step-by-step for the basic running stitch. Enjoy your first efforts at quilting, and be sure to keep the very first stitches you try, so you can measure your progress as your mastery increases.

Supplies

- ◆ High-quality, 100 percent cotton quilting thread
- ◆ Quilting needles, called "betweens," in size 9, 10, or 12
- ◆ Small scissors for snipping threads
- ◆ Thimble to fit the finger pushing the needle
- ◆ Quilt frame or hoop to put even tension on the quilt

The Step-by-Step for Hand Quilting

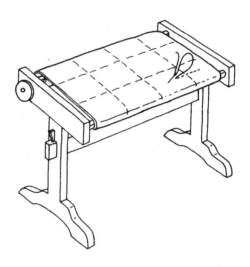

Step 1: *With your quilt in a frame or a hoop, start the first line of quilting from right to left (reverse this if you are left-handed). Thread a quilting needle with a strand of quilting thread approximately 20 to 24 inches long and tie a knot at the end.*

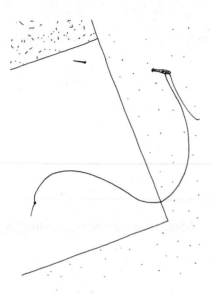

Step 2: *To begin the first quilting stitch, bury the knot by inserting the needle into the quilt top and layer of batting about 1 inch away from the starting point.*

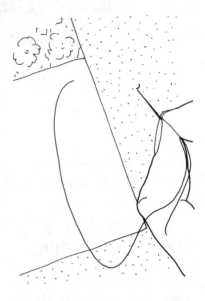

Step 4: *You may need to use the needle to work the very end of the thread into the layer of batting. (Working in this tail of thread instead of clipping it avoids any devastating, accidental snips into the surface of the quilt.)*

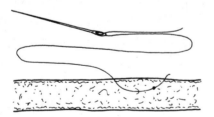

Step 3: *Tug gently on the thread to "pop" the knot through the quilt top. The goal is to lodge the knot inside the layer of batting.*

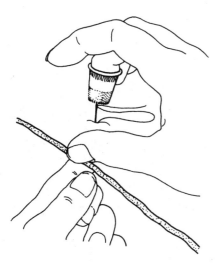

on the top of the needle. Push the thumb on top down just in front of the needle to steady the quilt. Continue making one stitch at a time, inserting the needle and pushing it back up, until you're comfortable with the "rocking" motion of your upper hand. Then use the same motions to put two stitches at a time on the needle, matching the length of those stitches, as well as the spaces between the stitches. When that seems natural, you can increase the number of stitches you make at one time to three or four. Practice will tell you the number of stitches that seems most comfortable to take on the needle at one time.

Step 5: *Wear a thimble on the finger with which you will push the needle and place your other hand underneath the quilt to guide the needle as you stitch. Begin the first stitch by holding the needle perpendicular to the top of the quilt and inserting it completely through the three layers, until you feel the tip of the needle with the finger underneath.*

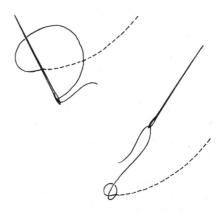

Step 7: *To end a line of quilting, bring the needle to the top of the quilt just past the last stitch. Make a knot at the surface of the fabric by bringing the needle under the thread where it comes out of the fabric and up through the loop of thread it creates.*

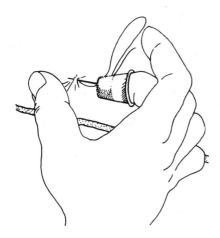

Step 6: *Use the underneath finger to gently guide the tip of the needle back up through the quilt, and use the top finger with the thimble to push down*

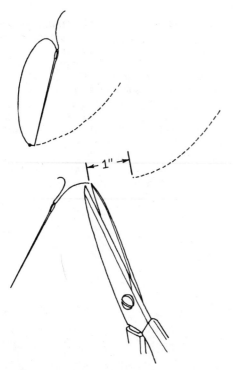

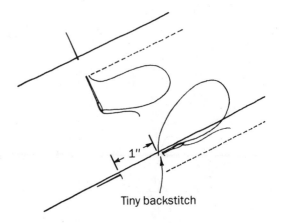

Tiny backstitch

Step 8: *Repeat this knot and insert the needle into the hole where the thread comes out of the surface. Run the needle inside the batting layer for about an inch and bring it back to the surface. Tug gently on the thread, and the knot will pop through to the layer of batting. Check to make sure the thread doesn't go through to the back of the quilt and then clip the thread close to the top surface of the quilt.*

Step 9: *An alternate way to end a line of stitching is with a backstitch instead of a knot. For this method, the last stitch you take must be within an inch of a seam. Simply insert the needle into the batting layer and bring it back up exactly on the nearest seam line. Take a very tiny backstitch in the seam where it won't show, then run the needle inside the batting layer about an inch and clip the thread.*

QNM Editors

❖ Why Knot? ❖

Follow these four easy steps to make a quick and almost effortless knot at the end of the thread before you begin to quilt.

***The Step-by-Step
for a Quick Quilter's Knot***

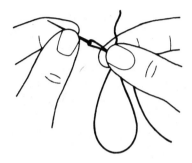

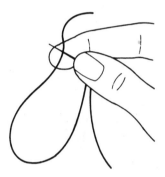

Step 1: *Start by holding the needle and the end of the thread against the forefinger of your right hand.*

Step 3: *Pull the wound thread down the length of the needle, between your thumb and forefinger.*

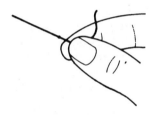

Step 4: *Gently work the wound thread down the entire length of the thread so that it forms a tiny knot at the very end.*

QNM Editors

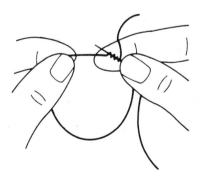

Step 2: *Wind the thread three or four times around the needle.*

❖ Thumb Quilting ❖

There are three good reasons to learn to quilt with your thumb (substituting your thumb for the finger you normally use to push the needle on the top side of the quilt). One is that it enables you to quilt in any direction you want without having to turn the quilt. Another is that you'll no longer need to rely on one finger for all quilting, which reduces the stress on your hand by 50 percent. That alone can be helpful for anyone who suffers from muscle tension or carpal tunnel syndrome. The third advantage is the fact that your thumb is larger and stronger than other fingers, which allows you to put more stitches on a needle at one time.

When you're learning how to do thumb quilting, wear a thimble on your thumb and try putting just two stitches on a needle at a time, using your thumb just as you would any other quilting finger. It's much easier to match a pair of stitches than to try to make sure several individual consecutive stitches look alike. When you're comfortable with making two stitches, add a third stitch, and then a fourth. I recommend practicing this technique on a quilt that can be donated to a local hospital or charitable organization. That way, you can perfect your stitching technique and at the same time make something for someone to really use and cherish. By the time you finish quilting one quilt, thumb quilting will seem like second nature.

Carol Doak

❖ Two-Finger Exercise ❖

I like to wear a tailor's thimble on my thumb or index finger when I quilt. (I prefer not to wear a thimble on the middle finger at all.) The open top of the thimble allows your fingernail to be comfortable while you stitch, and the deep dimples on the sides allow you to quilt with the side of your thumb or index finger. A well-fitting tailor's thimble should allow the top of your thumb or finger to be even with the top of the thimble. This kind of thimble makes it easy to quilt away from yourself with a pushing motion of the thumb, or toward yourself with a pulling motion of the index finger. This method works very well for quilting at a floor frame, as well as for hoop quilting, because you can quilt in any direction without turning the quilt.

Carol Doak

❖ Optical Illusion ❖

You can give the back of a quilt all the beauty of a whole-cloth quilt design by stopping short of hard-to-stitch areas like seams and seam allowances and going back to fill them in later. Pause and take a look at your quilt from the back when you're finished quilting. Any areas that need to be filled in will be easy to spot because they tend to "pooch" out, interrupting the smoothness of quilting lines. To make stitching lines look smooth and continuous on the back side of a quilt, fill in just a few stitches by stitching through the layers of backing and batting *only*. This will make the stitching lines continuous even over the seam lines and the seam allowance areas. When you've connected all of the stitching lines on the back side of your quilt, you can turn the quilt over and do the same thing from the front side, stitching through the layers of top and batting *only*. The finished quilt will look perfect from both sides.

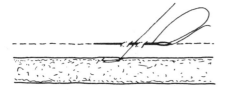

June Culvey

❖ Ties That Bind ❖

There are several good reasons to tie rather than hand quilt the layers of a quilt together. Tying a quilt produces a puffy, cloudlike look quite unlike that of hand quilting, and you can tie a quilt in a short amount of time. Tying is easy to do, which makes it a good choice for young quilt-makers starting out on their first projects. Even if you're an experienced quilter, you may like tying soft, cuddly baby quilts that look like miniature down comforters. Here are a few guidelines for tying a quilt:

♦ Select a durable, colorful, and attractive kind of material for tying, such as pearl cotton, embroidery floss, yarn, ribbon, or cording. It should be strong enough to withstand a good tugging, flexible enough to knot easily, thin enough to go through the three layers of a quilt, and washable.

♦ Use a crewel needle, which has a sharp point, with an eye large and long enough to hold specialty threads.

♦ Layer the quilt you want to tie on a flat working surface, such as a large table or open space on the floor.

♦ Decide where you want the ties to be placed on the quilt and mark each place with a pin. Avoid seams and seam allowances if possible.

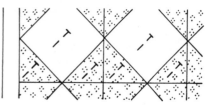

♦ Thread your needle with a 30-inch strand of thread and do not knot the end of it. Take a ⅛- to ¼-inch stitch at the first pin, pulling the thread through the layers of the quilt until there is a

3-inch tail. Leave the needle threaded and tie the ends securely in a square knot. Clip the thread ends to the length you desire.

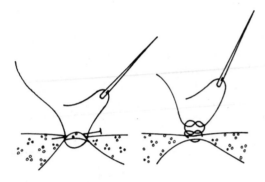

◆ If you wish, make a bow, rather than a knot, to tie the quilt.

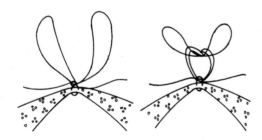

QNM Editors

❖ Fit-to-Be-Tied Kids' Quilts ❖

Try some of these creative ideas for tying a child's quilt. Always keep in mind the age of the child when considering these ideas; don't add any small, possibly removable embellishments that the child might be tempted to pull off and put in his or her mouth.

Clever Tricks for Tying

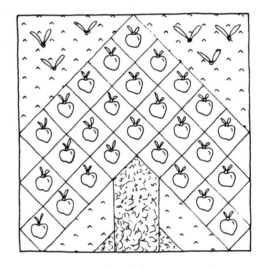

Many pieced tree blocks can have "apple" beads or charms tied on with green ribbon or pearl cotton. Perhaps one or two apples could rest on the ground under the tree. Add some flying birds in the sky with dark ties cut about ⅜ inch.

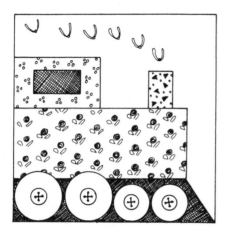

A choo-choo train for a child's quilt can have white puffs of tied steam coming out of the smokestack. For wheels that can really turn, make soft "buttons" (with or without batting) from circles of fabric and stitch a ¼-inch buttonhole in the center of each button wheel. Sew real buttons in place on top of the wheels, stitching through the buttonholes.

A curious cat with tied whiskers sniffs a prickly tied cactus while a butterfly flutters overhead. The butterfly's antennae are made with ties, with little knots at the ends. Use ties on the back side to fasten other areas of the block, or plan to quilt around the cat and the edges of the block.

QNM Editors

MEANDERING STITCHES

The simplicity and exuberance of folk art offers a chance to be creative in your approach to quilting designs, as well as to the appliqué. If you've created a quilt with a design of trees, birds, people, weather vanes, chickens, sunflowers, or other free-form folk art shapes, think about quilting your work without marking the lines before you stitch. Let your quilting take its shape from the edges of the appliqué patches, echoing the angles and curves and changing them slightly with each new line of stitches you make. Or quilt right over the top, without regard to the appliqué design itself. Free-form quilting can be delightful and ebullient, producing a feeling of playful abandon and individuality.

❖ Jane Townswick

Needle Tips and Stitching Tricks

❖ A Quilter's Warm-Up ❖

I think it's useful to take some time to practice quilting *before* you start stitching on an actual quilt. You use different hand muscles to quilt than you use for other parts of the quiltmaking process, so it is helpful to give yourself a "warm-up" period just as you would for any other kind of physical exercise. With a 5-inch square of fabric from your quilt top and pieces of the batting and the backing fabric, spend some time practicing the motions involved in quilting. As your fingers become more adept, it will be easier to make even, small stitches, and when you start working on the quilt, you'll be in top-notch quilting condition.

Mary Reddick

❖ Tip-Top Finger Protection ❖

If you like to feel the point of your needle as it comes through to the underside of the quilt when you make each stitch, try putting a very small piece of masking tape on the tip of your finger. It's thin enough to allow you to sense the needle, yet protective enough to keep your finger free of callouses.

Anne Oliver

❖ A Gripping Saga ❖

I like to wear a secretary's rubber finger on the index finger of my right hand when I quilt. It makes pulling a needle through several stitches easy, and it protects your finger from becoming sore after stitching for a long period of time.

Sharyn Squier Craig

❖ Take the Short Cot ❖

If you like the way surgical finger cots help pull a needle through several stitches at a time, but you find them constricting, you can shorten them. Cut off about an inch below the rolled edge, shortening the finger cot to about 2 inches long. It will be more comfortable to wear, and you'll still get all the traction you need to pull a needle through quilting stitches with ease.

Sue Rodgers

❖ By a Thread ❖

After you've taken three or four quilting stitches on a needle, pull the needle out just far enough so that you can grab the thread beneath the eye. Pull the stitches taut by grasping the thread rather than by tugging on the needle. This avoids weakening or breaking the thread where it goes through the eye of the needle.

Liz Porter

❖ Back Up Gently ❖

If you've pushed your needle too far out of the quilt and you want to pull it back, pull on the *eye* of the needle rather than push against the point of the needle with your thimble. A thimble is strong enough to withstand a great deal of pressure, but a needle will become dull after only a few pushes.

QNM Editors

❖ Needle Pointers ❖

I think it's helpful to experiment in deciding what kinds of quilting needles you like best. Try using different brands and sizes to see which ones feel good in your hand and what kinds of things appeal to you about each needle. Do a few lines of quilting with several needles and compare the results and your feelings about each of them. If your hands are small, perhaps you'll be comfortable immediately with a shorter needle, such as a #12 sharp. If you have long, slender fingers, maybe you'll like working with the longer length of a #10 sharp. For easier "threadability," a needle with a larger eye might be just what you like. I'm not sure it is always true that the smallest needle produces the smallest stitch. I think that the best results usually come from working with quilting tools and equipment that you really enjoy using.

June Culvey

❖ Needle Notes ❖

For hand quilting, I like to use Piecemakers #12 betweens because they don't bend easily and they retain their sharpness for a long time. The eyes on Piecemakers needles are large, which makes them easy to thread, and these #12 betweens are very short, which is helpful in making tiny stitches. If you can't find this brand at your local quilt shop, you can contact Piecemakers Country Store, 1720 Adams Avenue, Costa Mesa, CA 92626; (714) 641-3112.

Sharyn Squier Craig

A SPOONFUL OF STITCHES

I like to use a spoon to push the point of a needle back up through the layers of a quilt. By using a spoon to manipulate and guide the needle, you can make quilting stitches the same width as the edge of the spoon, so it's helpful to use a spoon with a sharp, narrow edge. Because the point of a needle tends to score and dull the surface of any spoon, sand the surface of the spoon with an emery board occasionally. You can buy inexpensive stainless spoons at most import shops like Pier I or discount stores, so they're easy to find and have on hand for quilting.

❖ Jinny Beyer

❖ The Whole Nine Yards ❖

I like to wax entire spools of cotton quilting thread. It's easy and quick to do, and it's nice not to have to wax individual strands each time you want to thread a quilting needle. Just set a clean, empty tuna can in a pan of hot water and melt a small amount of candle wax in the can. Unroll a few inches of thread and drop the spool into the melted wax, soaking it for approximately 5 minutes until it's completely coated. Blot the spool on a folded paper towel and allow it to dry completely, and the thread will be evenly coated and easy to use, with no knotting or tangling.

Peggy Beals

❖ Don't Come Unwound ❖

To keep thread from unwinding, slip a clean rubber band around the spool. It will keep the thread on the spool and still allow you to pull out a strand of thread easily, whenever you need one.

QNM Editors

❖ Up in Arms ❖

I like to use a short strand of thread for quilting—long enough to stitch for a while without having to rethread a needle, yet short enough to pull the thread in and out of the quilt without straining my arm or shoulder. That length varies from person to person, but a good, workable thread length is usually about 24 inches. To find the thread length you like to work with, try quilting with a piece of thread that's as long as the distance from your elbow to your hand and halfway back again.

Liz Porter

❖ A Quicker Clipper-Upper ❖

I like to put a slender seam ripper into the hole of the spool of quilting thread I'm using. That way, whenever I need to cut a new thread, I can pick up the spool, put the thread over the seam ripper, and clip the thread with a single quick tug. I put a

piece of masking tape over the bottom hole of the spool so the seam ripper doesn't accidentally slip out.

Sue Rodgers

❖ Residue Reduction ❖

Tape makes a great guide for quilting straight lines, and I like Scotch 230 drafting tape even better than masking tape. It has only half the stickiness of masking tape, which means that it's less likely to leave a residue on fabric or to cause batting to beard through the quilt. It's sticky enough to use again and again, however, and you can find this kind of tape at most art supply stores.

Sue Rodgers

❖ Set in Your Ways ❖

Quilters who use lap hoops sometimes complain of problems with uneven tension as they move the hoop from place to place across the surface of the quilt. I've found that first marking and quilting only the "skeleton" of the quilting designs across the quilt top "sets in" the lines of quilting and reduces tension problems later. For instance, with an intricately woven cable design, I mark and stitch just the basic outer shape, then go back and fill in the remaining lines later, when I'm ready to put that part of the quilt back into my hoop. This way, any puffiness or uneven parts will be contained within these lines that are already quilted in place. This results in a quilt that will lie flat and true, with no unevenness in tension.

Anne Oliver

❖ The Fudge Factor ❖

It's easier than you might think to make border quilting designs look symmetrically perfect. Almost everyone will eventually encounter the need to "fudge" in quilting, because fabric does not behave like paper. It moves, stretches, and sometimes causes distortions in quilting designs. I like to make corrections in areas where they're least likely to be noticed by the viewer, so I make sure that all corners are quilted as accurately as possible, making any adjustments gradually over a wide area of a border.

Anne Oliver

❖ The Finish Line ❖

I like to put a line of running stitches at the very edge of a quilt, without knotting or finishing off the ends of the thread. If you run several threads around the entire

quilt, you can adjust for any unevenness in the edges of the quilt by drawing in these threads to make the quilt lie straight and true. And you can leave these stitching lines in the quilt, because they'll be covered by the binding.

Anne Oliver

❖ Quilting Doubles ❖

When a quilting pattern has two or more parallel rows, you can ensure the evenness of your stitches by keeping a needle and thread going in each row at the same time and alternately stitching them to quilt the design evenly.

QNM Editors

❖ Three-Vein Feathers ❖

You can give a dramatic look and more stitch definition to feathered quilting designs by quilting three lines at the center veins. After you quilt the center vein, just "eyeball" the line on either side. Marking isn't necessary because the lines are so close together.

June Culvey

❖ Stippler's Advice ❖

I like the effect of stipple quilting on cotton batting, but the dense stitching can mat the batting down, making it lose loft. I recommend washing a quilt after you've finished stipple quilting it, to make the batting regain its loft and show off stipple quilting to its best advantage.

John Flynn

❖ Radiating Quadrants ❖

Dividing a quilt into sections helps both my marking and stitching. I start by marking diagonal lines from corner to corner in both directions across the quilt top, using a .07mm mechanical lead pencil. I also like to mark the quilt in half horizontally and vertically. These guidelines are a great aid for placing geometric quilting designs in mirrored places on the quilt. I start quilting at the very center of the quilt and complete all of the stitching from that point to the outer edge of the quilt, before returning to the middle and completing the second half. That way, all of the quilting motifs, borders, and edges are less likely to be uneven or rippled.

June Culvey

❖ Trapunto Trials ❖

I like to use pieces of polyester batting as the stuffing for trapunto work, even if the quilt batt is cotton. Adding enough cotton batting to make the stuffed areas look attractive can end up giving your quilt a stiff look. I find that polyester batting creates high relief, without producing a hard spot in the quilt that might wear easily. It can be helpful to experiment with batting to find the type and amount you like for stuffed work. A formula that works well for me is to double

the amount of batting in stuffed areas, because that amount seems to enhance the look of trapunto stitching.

John Flynn

❖ Crochet Magic ❖

When you need to take out a few quilting stitches, it's easy to snag the fabric in a quilt. I like to use a very fine steel crochet hook to pull out the stitches and leave the fabric intact. The rounded tip of a crochet hook slides under quilting stitches, and the hook will remove them easily, without catching threads in the fabric.

Anne Oliver

❖ Swabs to the Rescue ❖

If you remove some quilting stitches and you find that a tiny line of holes remains in the fabric, try dampening a cotton swab with warm water and rubbing it over the holes to make them disappear like magic.

QNM Editors

Quilt Hoops and Floor Frames

❖ Hooping It Up! ❖

I like to sit in a hard rocking chair with firm back support and quilt in a 14-inch hoop, no matter how large the quilt. I find that a hoop larger than 14 inches is more difficult to keep in my lap. I also like to turn my work often and to quilt toward myself for feathered quilting designs, which is impossible to do at a floor frame.

Marianne Fons

❖ Stitches by the Hoopful ❖

I use a 22-inch quilting hoop for all of my quilts, because it's portable and it allows me to quilt in comfort while sitting on a couch. It takes approximately two or three weeks to finish the amount of quilting I like to do in a 22-inch hoop. I leave the quilt in position in the hoop for that entire time, without removing the top hoop, and I've never had a problem with creases. When I stop quilting for the day, I like to leave a needle threaded and in progress somewhere in the hoop. If you know that everything's ready to pick up and stitch at a moment's notice, you can get an amazing amount of quilting done in very short periods of time.

Anne Oliver

❖ Tails from the Back Side ❖

When you're quilting in a hoop, which gives you the option of turning over your work, I think it's helpful to look at the back of the quilt now and then to see that all of the stitches are even, with no thread tails peeking through the backing. When you jump from one line of quilting to another, it can sometimes feel as if the needle is moving within the layer of batting when it has actually penetrated the backing layer of the quilt.

Anne Oliver

❖ That's a Wrap! ❖

To avoid the marks that can come from putting a quilt hoop over fabric that has a shiny finish, I wrap 2-inch-wide cross-grain strips of muslin around my quilt hoop. I secure the first strip on the outside of the larger hoop with tacks or staples and wrap the entire hoop with muslin strips, tacking, stapling, or sewing the final edge in place (always securing the strip ends on the outside). Then I wrap the smaller, inner hoop the same way, securing the strips on the inside of the hoop, where the quilt will never touch them. Wrapping a hoop in muslin also helps keep any fabric from slipping out of position while you quilt, and you can put new muslin strips on the hoop whenever the old ones become worn.

Sue Rodgers

❖ Do-It-Yourself D-Hoop ❖

If you like to quilt in a hoop and want to make sure the edges of the quilt will be even and flat when you're finished, try pinning or basting the edge of the quilt to a terry cloth towel when you're ready to quilt the border. A terry cloth towel usually has approximately the same thickness as a layered quilt, and it allows you to put the quilt into a hoop and quilt easily up to the very edge, with even tension on all parts of the border.

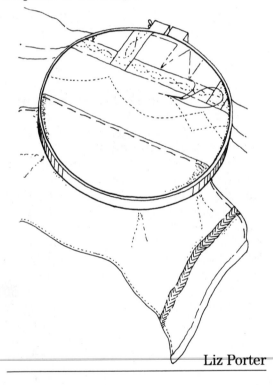

Liz Porter

❖ Two-Handed Quilting ❖

Learning to quilt at a floor frame can sometimes be awkward and frustrating, because your hands are making unfamiliar motions. But I think it offers a wonderful opportunity to become adept at quilting with both hands. If you try both right-handed and left-handed quilting at your floor frame from the very beginning, it will probably not be more awkward to use one hand than the other, and in the end, you'll be able to quilt equally well with both hands. I recommend practicing on a real quilt, too, rather than on a practice piece, using a backing fabric that's the same color as your quilting thread to camouflage any unevenness in your stitches.

Jinny Beyer

❖ A Great Cover-Up ❖

If you like to quilt at a floor frame, you can keep the fabric in the quilt bright and dust-free between quilting sessions by spreading a bed sheet over the entire quilt frame.

QNM Editors

❖ Card Table Trickery ❖

You can make a great portable quilting frame from an old card table! Just remove the tabletop and wind strips of upholstery-weight fabric around each of the four side bars. That way, you can simply lay a quilt over the top of the table, pin it securely to the upholstery fabric with T-pins or safety pins, and create whatever amount of tension you like for quilting.

QNM Editors

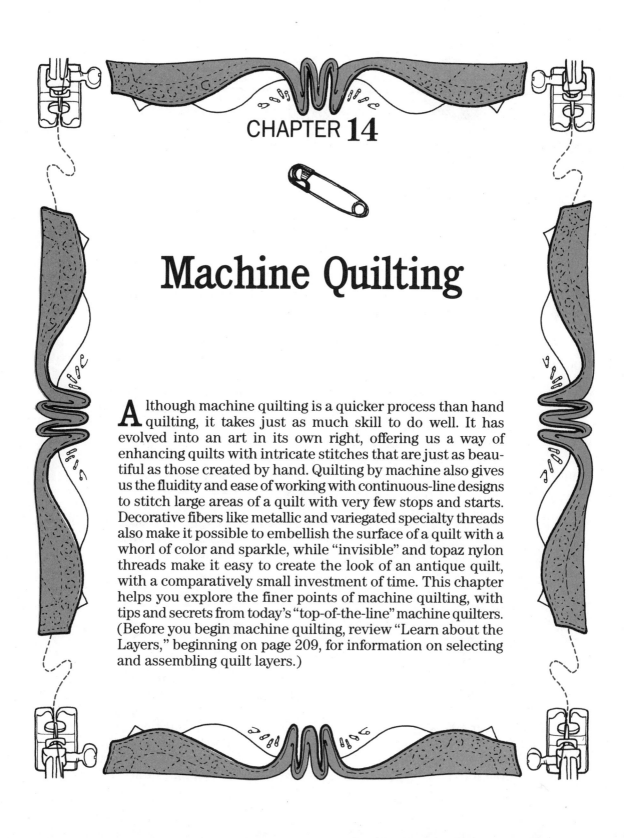

CHAPTER 14

Machine Quilting

Although machine quilting is a quicker process than hand quilting, it takes just as much skill to do well. It has evolved into an art in its own right, offering us a way of enhancing quilts with intricate stitches that are just as beautiful as those created by hand. Quilting by machine also gives us the fluidity and ease of working with continuous-line designs to stitch large areas of a quilt with very few stops and starts. Decorative fibers like metallic and variegated specialty threads also make it possible to embellish the surface of a quilt with a whorl of color and sparkle, while "invisible" and topaz nylon threads make it easy to create the look of an antique quilt, with a comparatively small investment of time. This chapter helps you explore the finer points of machine quilting, with tips and secrets from today's "top-of-the-line" machine quilters. (Before you begin machine quilting, review "Learn about the Layers," beginning on page 209, for information on selecting and assembling quilt layers.)

Mastering Machine Quilting

Tips on Techniques

❖ Straight-Line Quilting ❖

This is often the easiest machine quilting for beginners to tackle, since the motion of feeding the quilt through the machine is the same as in regular sewing. The combination of a walking foot and feed dogs makes all three layers of the quilt move evenly under the needle. Follow these guidelines to master basic straight-line quilting:

◆ Mark the quilting designs on the quilt and layer it as you would for hand quilting. (For information on quilt layering, see Steps 1 through 4 under "Thread Basting 101" on page 214.) Baste with quilter's rustproof safety pins. Pin basting is a better choice than thread basting because the pins will stay securely in place and keep the layers from shifting as you manipulate the quilt. (See "The Finer Points of Pin Basting" on page 215.)

◆ Attach a walking foot, or an even feed foot, to your sewing machine.

◆ Choose regular 100 percent cotton sewing thread for the bobbin and nylon thread or thread to match the fabric for the top.

◆ To start a line of stitching, first pull the bobbin thread up onto the top of the quilt. Insert the needle back in the hole where the bobbin thread comes up. Using the stitch length adjustment on your machine, make six very small stitches instead of a knot to anchor the stitching in place and then gradually return to your regular stitch length.

◆ When you come to a corner or a sharp turn in a quilting design, stop the machine with the needle inserted in the fabric, raise the foot, pivot the quilt, lower the foot, and continue stitching.

◆ To end a line of stitching, use the stitch length adjustment again to take about six very short stitches. Clip the threads close to the surface on top and bottom.

QNM Editors

❖ Free-Motion Quilting ❖

Quilting designs that are made of continuous lines are particularly wonderful for machine quilting because they allow you to quilt longer without having to stop, tie off threads, and begin a new line of stitching at other points on the design. To quilt continuous lines, you need to use free-motion machine quilting. In this technique, you lower the feed dogs and slide the fabric backward, forward, and side to side, to "draw" the quilting design with the needle. The trick to free-motion quilting is learning how to coordinate the speed of the needle moving up and down with how fast you move the fabric under the needle. Here are some pointers on mastering free-motion quilting:

♦ Mark the quilting designs on the quilt and layer it as you would for hand quilting. (For information on quilt layering, see Steps 1 through 4 under "Thread Basting 101" on page 214.) Baste with quilter's rustproof safety pins. Pin basting is more effective than thread basting at holding the layers together and keeping them from shifting. (See "The Finer Points of Pin Basting" on page 215.)

♦ Disengage the feed dogs on your sewing machine so that you can move the quilt freely under the needle as you work.

♦ Replace the regular machine presser foot with a darning foot or a machine embroidery foot, which will hold the fabric in place while the needle moves.

♦ Choose regular 100 percent cotton sewing thread for the bobbin and nylon thread or thread to match the fabric for the top.

♦ To start a line of stitching, first pull the bobbin thread up onto the top of the quilt. Insert the needle back in the hole where the bobbin thread comes up. Using the stitch length adjustment on your machine, make six very small stitches (which anchor the stitching, in place of a knot) and then build up to your regular stitch length.

♦ Use both hands to guide the marked design under the machine needle, working the quilt evenly and at a medium speed.

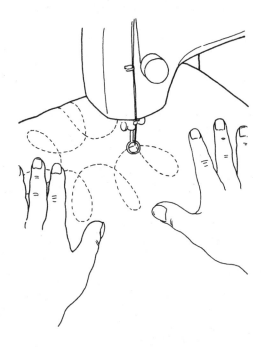

♦ When you come to a point, hesitate in place to lay down a few small stitches, then continue stitching along the design.

♦ To end a line of stitching, use the stitch length adjustment again to take about six very short stitches. Clip the threads on top and bottom.

QNM Editors

❖ A Never-Ending Story ❖

You can use single motifs to create your own continuous-line quilting designs.

Try these simple ideas for using Tulip Loop and Daisy Chain floral designs to create continuous-line designs, and then work with motifs of your own choosing to develop even more-interesting configurations.

Clever Design Variations

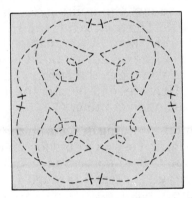

Quilt four Tulip Loop motifs facing inward on the diagonals of a block, connecting the small spaces between motifs with smooth curves.

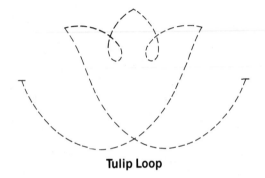

Tulip Loop

Quilt four Tulip Loop motifs facing outward, connecting the outer curved lines at the point of each diagonal in a block.

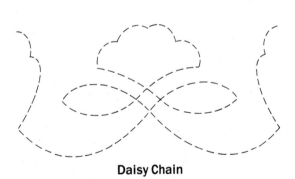

Daisy Chain

Quilt Tulip Loop motifs along a border, turning alternate motifs upside down.

Quilt four Daisy Chain motifs facing the center of a block, connecting motifs at the corners.

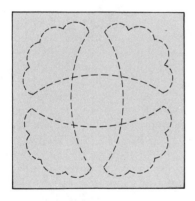

Quilt a portion of the Daisy Chain motif facing outward at each corner in a block, connecting motifs at the center.

Quilt the flower part of the Daisy Chain motif in a border, connecting motifs at the bottoms of the flowers.

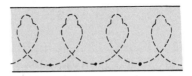

Use the outer leaf portion of the Daisy Chain motif to create a border quilting design, connecting the lines at the bottom of each leaf.

Quilt the entire Daisy Chain and leaf combination in a border, connecting motifs with curved lines.

QNM Editors

❖ Practice ❖
Makes Perfect Sense

It can be helpful to practice machine quilting on a sample block before starting a larger project like a bed-size quilt. I often make a small pillow or another quick project to practice starting and stopping, pivoting, and turning. For example, this kind of practicing has taught me that when I start and stop, I like to bring the bobbin thread up to the top surface of my quilt. That allows me to cut it from the top later, without having to reach underneath the quilt or turn the quilt over to cut the thread.

Lynn Lewis Young

❖ Ten-Digit Mastery ❖

Before I start machine quilting, I like to coat my fingertips with rubber cement and wait for it to dry. The rubber cement makes it easier to grip the fabric and manipulate the quilt as it goes through the sewing machine.

John Flynn

❖ Driving Home ❖ a Quilting Design

When I teach a class on free-motion machine quilting, I ask my students to visualize driving a car and learn to look ahead of them, never at the needle or inside the presser foot. If you looked at the hood ornament while you were driving a car, it would be difficult to operate the car effectively, and it's the same thing in machine quilting. If you look approximately ½ inch ahead, rather than directly at the needle, you'll be able to see where you're going with the line of stitches.

Harriet Hargrave

CREATIVE "THREADPLAY"

It can be mentally freeing and creatively productive to allow yourself time to simply "play" with threads and different kinds of stitches at your sewing machine. Try layering 2 yards of muslin and 1 yard of batting as a practice piece. Put your sewing table in front of the television, find a good movie, and spend a couple of hours machine quilting circles and curves, with no particular purpose in mind other than to see what happens. As you work, notice what kinds of patterns you're creating when your hands make certain motions. You may discover something you never thought would happen. And remember to give yourself permission to "fail" once in a while—if everything turns out well, you're probably not allowing yourself enough freedom to experiment. Playing is a valuable exercise that will allow you to discover the well of creativity that's inside you.

❖ Caryl Bryer Fallert

❖ Seated in High Places ❖

For machine quilting, it's most effective and comfortable to sit at a height that allows you to look down over your work. It's easier to manipulate a quilt from above, without having to look up at your work from a chair that's too low. You may even find it helpful to move your sewing machine around to determine what angle works best for you.

Anne Colvin

❖ Even-Steven ❖

For machine quilting, I like to keep the surface of my sewing machine level with the cabinet or table I'm working on. If your entire sewing surface is flat and even, it's much easier to manipulate a quilt through a sewing machine.

Eleanor Burns

❖ Wrists Up! ❖

The easiest, most joint-friendly way to machine quilt is by holding your hands as though you were playing a piano. That way, you'll cause less physical stress to your hands and wrists, and it will be easier to make the quilt go through the sewing machine.

QNM Editors

❖ The Battle of the Bulk ❖

A bed-size quilt poses a logistical problem when you machine quilt—where do you put all the bulky fabric while you're working with it on the relatively small area of your sewing machine? Probably the best way to solve the problem is to keep trying different options for handling the bulkiness until you find one that works best for you. Here are some ideas for you to try:

♦ Keep the whole quilt up and off the floor. Any portion that drags over the edge of your sewing table will make it harder to maneuver the portion that's under the needle. Place a card table behind your sewing table to provide extra surface to support the quilt.

♦ Some quilters swear by rolling up the quilt and holding the roll together with bicycle clips. Others fold the portion of the quilt that's between the needle and the body of the sewing machine into loose, accordian-like pleats.

♦ Instead of sitting with a giant mound of quilt in your lap, see if you can roll it and "wear" it over your shoulder.

Suzanne Nelson

❖ Great Grids ❖

A large quilt with sashing in it can be stabilized with a "gridwork" of quilting lines before you add the rest of the quilting designs. Starting at one side of the quilt, quilt from top to bottom in the ditch along the entire right side of the first long sashing strip. Working toward the other side of the quilt, skip to the next sashing strip and do the same thing, without turning the quilt sideways. When you've quilted on the right side of each long sashing strip, turn the quilt one quarter turn to your left and quilt on the right sides of the sashing strips that are perpendicular to the first sashing strips. After you've stabilized the right side of each sashing strip in the entire quilt, you can go back and quilt on the left side of each sashing strip. This grid of quilting stabilizes the quilt so that you can go back and fill in smaller quilting areas later in any order you like, without puckers, gathers, or pleats.

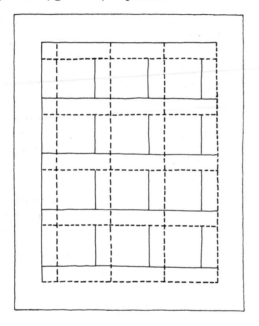

Anne Colvin

❖ Taut for the Day ❖

Pin basting is the usual way to prepare projects for machine quilting. You can eliminate puckers on the back of a quilt by clamping the backing to a table when you layer the quilt sandwich for basting. If the backing is stretched taut while you pin the layers of the quilt together, there will be no excess fabric to cause puckering.

Harriet Hargrave

❖ Water and Waves ❖

A quilt that's loaded with machine quilting in the borders can sometimes suffer from "wavy" edges. You can contain the rippling effects of the quilting by placing the quilt on the floor and spritzing it with water. Pat the edges in place to block them, and allow the fabric to dry flat. When you bind the quilt, use lengthwise or cross-grain binding, rather than bias binding, to control stretching and further tame the tendency toward waves.

Anne Colvin

❖ Backfield in Motion ❖

For a dark-colored quilt on which the quilting designs don't show up very clearly, try using a light-colored fabric for the backing and marking the designs on the back of the quilt. Then quilt from the "wrong" side, using nylon thread in the bobbin and regular cotton sewing thread on the top.

Liz Porter

❖ Paper Patter ❖

If it is difficult to see marks on my quilt because the fabrics are large-scale prints or dark, I like to draw my quilting designs on tissue paper and pin them in place on the quilt. I machine quilt right through the tissue paper, which is very easy to remove when I'm finished quilting.

Liz Porter

Tools and Accessories

❖ Cotton to This ❖

I'm a firm advocate of making quilts to use, not to tuck away on closet shelves. And if you're going to use them and wash them all the time, polyester batting just doesn't hold up. I recommend cotton batting, which not only holds up better with repeated washing but also is easier to work with. Cotton batting makes the layers of a quilt stick together beautifully, eliminating any tendency for them to separate or slide around the work surface.

Harriet Hargrave

❖ Avoid Unsightly Rolls ❖

One of the best things you can do in quilting is to buy the very best supplies you can find. If you're looking for batting, avoid buying the kind that is sold in large sheets on a roll, which is not as high-quality as the finer, packaged batting you can find at quilt shops or fabric stores.

Harriet Hargrave

❖ Wonderful ❖ Weighty Woolens

When I want to make sure a machine-quilted quilt will hang absolutely straight and square, I use a wool blanket as the middle layer. I particularly like the kinds of wool blankets you can buy at Army & Navy surplus stores, because they're very heavy and dense. The weight of the wool pulls on the fabric in a quilt and helps it to hang straighter. I also prefer wool over polyester, because it allows me to use a steam iron when I'm blocking the quilt.

Caryl Bryer Fallert

❖ Kwik, Klip It! ❖

If you love quilting gadgets that really work, try the Kwik Klip for closing safety pins when you layer a quilt for basting. This handy little tool looks a bit like a screwdriver, but there are ridges on the brass head that will hold the point of a pin up from the surface of a quilt, so you can flip the pin shut quickly and effortlessly. If you can't find this tool at your local quilt shop, contact Paula Jean Creations, 1601 Fulton Avenue, Sacramento, CA 95825; (916) 488-3480.

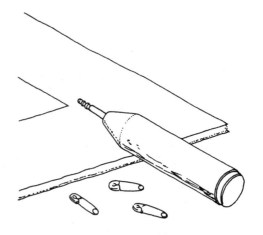

Harriet Hargrave

FLEXIBLE FINGERS

An office supply or stationery store may not seem like an obvious shopping destination for a quilter. But if you're having trouble keeping a good hold on your quilt as you move it through the sewing machine, you might want to pay a visit to the nearest store of this kind. Ask for secretarial rubber "filing" fingers, the kind that have tiny tentacle-like knobs on them. These really grip the fabric, allowing you to use a much lighter touch when you manipulate a quilt through the sewing machine.

❖ QNM Editors

❖ The Subject Is Closed ❖

When you pin baste a quilt with safety pins, try using a grapefruit spoon to close the pins and save yourself sore fingers. Use the ridges in the grapefruit spoon to catch the tip of each pin and flip it closed easily.

Eleanor Burns

❖ Fancy Footwork ❖

I like to use a darning foot in my sewing machine for free-motion quilting, because I can move a quilt freely in every direction under it and I can easily stitch over several layers of fabric. For quilting in the ditch or on a pencil line, I like to use an open-toed embroidery foot, which lets me see exactly where the needle will go.

Caryl Bryer Fallert

❖ Try Big Foot on for Size ❖

If your machine doesn't come with a darning foot attachment for free-motion quilting, you might want to try the Big Foot, which comes in different sizes to fit different models of low- and high-shank sewing machines. Big Foot is available from Little Foot Ltd., 605 Bledsoe NW, Albuquerque, NM 87107; (505) 345-7647.

Suzanne Nelson

❖ It's in the Cards ❖

The feed dogs on my particular sewing machine can't be dropped, so when I want to do free-motion quilting, I take an old business card (a section of index card would work just as well) and tape it down over the feed dogs. This allows the fabric to move smoothly over the feed dogs.

Suzanne Nelson

❖ Think Electronic! ❖

When you're shopping for the perfect sewing machine to use for machine quilting, one of the best features to look for is an electronic foot control, which will stay cool indefinitely. A thermal foot control gets very hot if you sew for a long period of time, which means that you might possibly burn out the foot control on your machine. You can't tell from its appearance whether a foot control is electronic or thermal; the only way to know for sure is to ask the dealer.

Debra Wagner

❖ Pogo Stitching Pleasures ❖

I like to use a spring needle for machine quilting. It actually sits inside a small wire spring, which holds the fabric flat while the needle goes in and out of the fabric. You can find a spring needle to fit almost any kind of sewing machine in fabric stores or machine dealerships that stock sewing machine needles.

Eleanor Burns

❖ Your Machine ❖ Knows the Difference

High-quality needles are important for getting the best results in machine quilting. Even if your machine is top of the line, a poor-quality needle can make it perform badly and destroy a whole project. I recommend using a size 12 needle or smaller for machine quilting, nothing larger. And in the bobbin, the best results come from using a 50-weight, 3-ply, 100 percent cotton sewing thread.

Harriet Hargrave

❖ Nylon Naturals ❖

One of the two threads I recommend for machine quilting is Sew Art International nylon .004 thread, in both clear and smoke, which is sold in most quilt shops and fabric stores. The other thread is YLI Wonder Thread .004, which you also can buy in both clear and smoke colors and is available from Harriet's Treadle Arts, 6390 W. 44th Avenue, Wheat Ridge, CO 80033; fax (303) 424-1290. Either of these threads will give your machine quilts the soft and fluid look of hand quilting, while stiffer threads tend to lie flat on the fabric, creating much less stitch definition.

Harriet Hargrave

❖ Shining Lights ❖

Madeira or Sulky rayon variegated machine embroidery thread is my choice for machine quilting, especially on scrap quilts that have many different fabrics in them. These threads have a bit of shine, which is a decorative look I like, especially in the medium to dark variegated tones. Look for these threads in your local sewing or quilting store or in specialty quilting catalogs.

Liz Porter

❖ A Clip in Time ❖

On some brands of nylon thread, the thread is meant to feed from the top of the spool, not from the side as most cotton sewing threads do. This can cause tension problems for machine quilting. You can offset such tension problems by taping a paper clip near the wheel of your sewing machine and running a strand of nylon thread through the paper clip before threading it through the machine.

Anne Colvin

❖ Untightening ❖ Tension Troubles

If you're having tension trouble with nylon thread, try placing the spool on a metal spool holder that you can stand behind your machine. The spool holder allows the thread to feed off the top of the spool, which can alleviate problems with tension tightening up.

Suzanne Nelson

❖ A Bicycle Built for Quilts ❖

I like the oval bicycle clips for machine quilting rather than the round ones, because the oval ones will actually stay on a quilt while the round clips can spring off easily. Cottage Tools makes oval clips that are the perfect size to use on a quilt. If you can't find them at your local quilt shop, contact Harriet's Treadle Arts, 6390 W. 44th Avenue, Wheat Ridge, CO 80033; fax (303) 424-1290.

Harriet Hargrave

❖ Shedding Light ❖ on the Subject

It's important to have a well-lighted work area for machine quilting, so I keep a floor lamp at my left side and another at my right, positioned to cast a good amount of light on my quilt. If you like decorative lamps, look for an antique lamp with a swivel arm that will allow you to place the light bulb exactly where you want it. Or if you like contemporary lighting, investigate the useful lamps that you can clip onto a hard surface near your workspace. I think that the ideal lighting for quilt-making would include one lamp placed very close to your work and another light source that shines down over your work, to avoid glare. And if you can put your sewing machine near a large window, it's an advantage to be able to sew in natural light.

Anne Colvin

❖ Slip-Sliding Away ❖

If the table you work on for machine quilting is made of wood, try polishing the surface with furniture polish. The table will become slippery enough to make your quilt feel as if it's almost "dancing" under your fingers as you sew.

Eleanor Burns

CHAPTER **15**

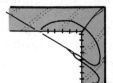

Finishing

T he final step in making a quilt is "going over the edge," or
encasing the raw edges of the quilt top, batting, and backing. A quilt itself can sometimes tell you what kind of edge
finish would be most attractive or dictate the grain of fabric
you choose for cutting the binding strips. Does your quilt
have straight edges? Binding strips cut along the straight of
grain can "contain" the edges of a quilt, making it hang straight
and true. Does your quilt have curved edges? Bias binding
strips offer the greatest amount of stretch, which makes finishing curved edges a breeze. There are some other, more
unusual binding treatments for you to consider as well, options
such as covered cording or lined binding strips made from a
deliciously soft shade of silk. In this chapter, finishing means
more than just putting the final stitches into the binding.
Labeling a quilt, so that people know as much about your
work as possible, is every bit as important as mitering perfect
corners on the binding. And you'll find clever and useful
suggestions for signing your quilts so you can create the
perfect finishing touch.

Finishing Edges

Binding Basics

❖ How Wide Is Wide Enough? ❖

Deciding on the proper width to cut binding strips depends on the look you want to create, as well as on the method you plan to use for binding the quilt. Both ½- and ⅜-inch bindings are commonly used for bed-size quilts, while ¼-inch bindings are often more attractive for smaller quilts. The choice between single-fold or double-fold binding comes down to individual preference, because each offers advantages. Single-fold binding takes less fabric and offers greater ease in mitering corners. Double-fold binding provides more layers of fabric encasing the edges of a quilt, which creates greater strength and durability. Whatever width or type of binding you choose, use these helpful guidelines for deciding exactly how wide to cut the binding strips:

♦ For a single-fold binding, the strips should be cut four times the width of the finished binding. For example, if you want to make a single-fold ½-inch finished binding, each strip should be cut 2 inches wide, which allows for a ½-inch width on both the front and the back of the quilt. You may want to add an extra ¼ inch to the width of each strip if the batting you're using has a very high loft.

♦ Because a double-fold binding is actually two layers of fabric applied to the quilt, each strip should be cut six times the width of the finished binding. This means that for a ½-inch finished binding, each strip should be cut 3 inches wide, to allow for the width of the seam allowances and bringing the fabric to the back side of the quilt.

QNM Editors

❖ Lengthwise-Grain ❖ Binding Strips

Cutting binding strips on the lengthwise fabric grain creates a binding with the least amount of stretch, and it's a nice option if you're working with a length of fabric that's several inches longer than the longest side of the quilt. That way, you can cut four length-of-grain strips and make a binding with the fewest number of seams possible. To make a cutting plan on paper, start by deciding how wide and how long you want to cut each binding strip. Then draw a rectangle to represent your fabric and label the width and the length on the drawing. Sketch in along the length of the fabric the binding strips you want to cut, and determine how much fabric you'll have left when you've cut them out. Trim the selvages and cut the strips parallel to that edge. Then cut the other patches for your quilt from the remaining fabric.

QNM Editors

❖ Cross-Grain Binding Strips ❖

To determine the amount of fabric you'll need for cutting cross-grain binding strips, follow these steps:

1. Determine the distance in inches around the entire quilt.
2. Divide that number by the width of your fabric. For most cotton fabrics, use 42 as the number for the width, which allows for possible shrinkage. This division gives you the number of binding strips you'll need *in any width* to bind your quilt. If this number is not a whole one, round it off to the next highest number of strips.
3. Multiply this number by the width you want to cut each binding strip, which tells you how many inches of fabric you'll need to make binding for your quilt. Divide this number by 36 inches to determine the actual fabric yardage. You may want to add a few extra inches to this number to allow for shrinkage and for possible cutting errors.

QNM Editors

❖ A "Math-Magical" ❖ Formula for Bias Binding Strips

Calculating the amount of fabric you'll need for cutting bias binding strips is easy when you follow these steps. All you need to have on hand is a tape measure, a quilt to be measured, and a calculator with a square root function.

1. Measure the number of inches around the edges of the quilt.
2. Multiply that number by the width you wish to cut the binding strips.
3. Calculate the square root of this number by pushing the square root key on the calculator. This number tells you what size fabric square will give you bias strips in the width you want.
4. Add 2 or 3 inches to this number, to allow for the amount of fabric that will be taken up by seam allowances. Then cut a square of fabric this size from which you can prepare the bias binding strips for the quilt.

Doreen Speckmann

❖ Quick-Cut ❖ Continuous Bias Strips

After you've calculated and cut the size square of fabric that will give you the amount of bias binding needed for a quilt, the next step is to cut all the strips. This quick-cutting method lets you make one long continuous strip of binding, instead of having to cut individual strips and piece them together one at a time.

The Step-by-Step
for Continuous Bias Strips

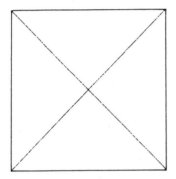

Step 1: *Fold the square in half diagonally in each direction and press a crease in each of the folds.*

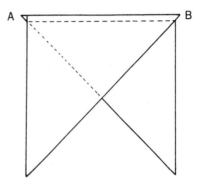

Step 3: *Sew the two halves of the square from point A to point B, right sides together, with a ³⁄₁₆-inch seam. Press this seam open.*

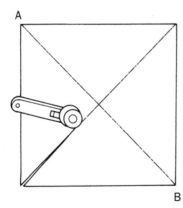

Step 2: *Open the square of fabric and cut it apart along one diagonal crease.*

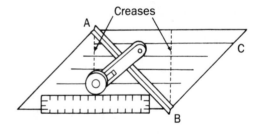

Step 4: *With a rotary cutter and a plexiglass quilter's ruler, cut slits at right angles to the original crease lines. Beginning at point C, the first cut you make should go from the very edge of the fabric to within 1 inch of the opposite side. Each cut you make after the first one should stop within 1 inch of both sides. The distance between each slit should be the width you desire for the cut binding strip.*

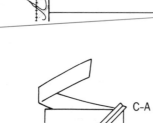

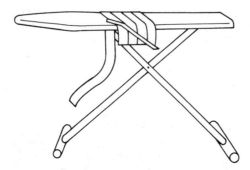

Step 5: *With right sides together and using a ³⁄₁₆-inch seam allowance, sew the fabric into a "tube," so that point A meets point C and the previously cut slits are in alignment.*

Step 6: *Place the tube of fabric over an ironing board and press the seam open. Mark straight lines to connect the slits and cut them open with scissors to form the completed length of continuous bias binding.*

Valda Whitman and the QNM Editors

❖ Cylindrically Speaking ❖

Have you ever wrestled with a tube of fabric from which you were trying to cut a continuous bias strip? To make it easier to cut the tube apart, try placing a large wooden cutting board or a piece of ply-

wood under a rotary-cutting mat at the narrow end of your ironing board (the wood gives the "floppy" cutting mat stability and support). Then slip the tube of continuous bias over the end of the ironing board. This makes it simple to slide the fabric around while you use the rotary cutter to slice the fabric tube into one long bias strip.

Carol Doak

❖ Fold-and-Cut Bias Strips ❖

Binding a large quilt means that you'll need to cut a lot of bias strips. Here's an easy method for cutting 3-inch bias strips quickly and accurately for a quilt that's up to 90 inches square:

1. Cut a 36-inch-square piece of fabric and fold it at a 45 degree angle, on the true bias.

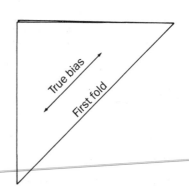

2. Fold the fabric again by bringing the bottom corner up to meet the top corner. Mark a line parallel to this second fold that is just half the desired

width of the binding strips. Mark lines parallel to the first line at the full width of the binding strips and use a rotary cutter and ruler or a pair of shears to cut the fabric into strips along these lines.

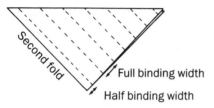

Second fold

Full binding width

Half binding width

Doreen Speckmann

❖ Longer Strips ❖
Seam Shorter

Here's a handy way to create a bias binding that has the fewest possible seams in it. Cut the strips diagonally across the width of the 44-inch fabric, rather than from a smaller square of fabric. The resulting bias strips will be approximately 60 inches long, and the remaining fabric can be used to cut the other patches for the quilt. This method can require more fabric, but it results in a binding that has fewer seams.

QNM Editors

❖ Wear-Dated Threads ❖

On a binding made from the lengthwise or cross grain of the fabric, a single worn thread can cause the binding to split apart all along the edges of a quilt. That usually means you need to replace the entire binding, rather than try to repair it. The threads in a bias binding intersect at 45 degree angles, which means that bias binding is likely to wear much longer than straight-grain binding. If you're concerned about the longevity of your quilts, consider that bias binding has more staying power.

Doreen Speckmann

❖ A Grain of Thought ❖

I prefer not to straighten the fabric grain for cutting binding strips, because in a lengthwise-grain or cross-grain binding, a single thread lies at the very edge of the binding. If this single thread becomes worn, frayed, or cut, the entire binding can split apart along the thread. Instead, I cut the binding strips across the width of the fabric as it comes from the bolt, which is almost always slightly off grain. This gives me the best of both worlds, because the strips have enough "give" to make applying the binding easier, yet enough strength and durability to help make the edges of the quilt hang straight and true.

Harriet Hargrave

❖ Making Ends Meet ❖

Here's a quick method for applying double-fold binding to a quilt with straight edges, whether you use lengthwise-grain, cross-grain, or bias strips.

The Step-by-Step for Double-Fold Binding

Note: *Art adapted from* Heirloom Machine Quilting, *by Harriet Hargrave, with permission of C & T Publishing.*

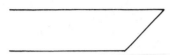

Step 1: *When you calculate the entire length you'll need for the binding on a quilt, allow 12 inches extra for the binding seams and overlapping the ends of the binding. If your binding strips are cut on the lengthwise or cross grain of the fabric, cut off the ends of each strip at a 45 degree angle.*

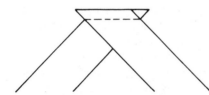

Step 2: *Sew the binding strips together with ¼-inch diagonal seams and press the seams open. Fold the entire binding in half lengthwise with wrong sides together and press a crease at the folded edge.*

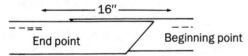

Step 3: *Position the binding so that the raw edges align with the edges of the quilt top. Beginning at a point away from a corner of the quilt, leave approximately 8 inches of binding free and sew the binding around the entire quilt with a ¼-inch seam, mitering the corners as described in "Mastering the Miter" on the opposite page. Stop about 16 inches from the point where you began, backstitch, and remove the quilt from the sewing machine. Place the binding on the left over the binding on the right, keeping the strips folded.*

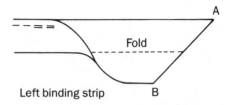

Step 4: *Open up the left binding strip and label points A and B.*

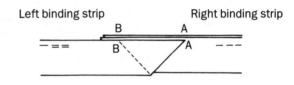

Step 5: *Fold the left binding strip up again and place it over the right binding strip. Mark matching points A and B on the right binding strip.*

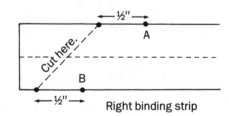

Step 6: *Open up the right binding strip and use a ruler to mark a line ½ inch to the left of points A and B. This ½-inch measurement allows for the seam joining the two binding strips.*

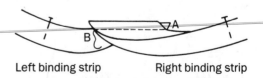

Step 7: *Open up the other binding strip and sew the strips right sides together, with a ¼-inch seam allowance.*

Step 8: *Press this seam open and refold the binding strips. Sew the remaining, unattached portion of the binding to the quilt. Bring the binding around to the back of the quilt and handstitch it in place.*

Harriet Hargrave

❖ Mastering the Miter ❖

Neatly mitered corners on a binding are a nice finishing touch. The trick in mastering miters is getting the 45 degree angle of the mitered binding to align with the corner of the quilt. Follow these five steps to see how easy it can be to make perfectly mitered corners on a binding.

The Step-by-Step for Mitered Binding

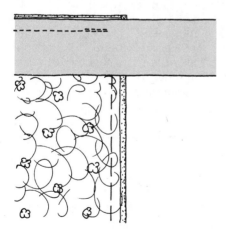

Step 1: *As you approach a corner of the quilt, stop sewing exactly ¼ inch from the edge of the quilt and backstitch.*

Step 2: *Raise the presser foot, clip the thread, and remove the quilt from the machine. Turn the quilt 90 degrees and fold the binding up at a 45 degree angle to create the first part of the mitered corner.*

Step 3: *Fold the binding back down so that the top fold is aligned with the top edge of the quilt, and the right edge is lined up with the quilt, ready to be sewn along the next side. Start ¼ inch from the top edge and sew the binding to the side of the quilt. Follow the same steps to miter each corner.*

Front of quilt

Step 4: *As you bring the corner of the binding up over the edge of the quilt from front to back, a diagonal fold will form at the mitered corner.*

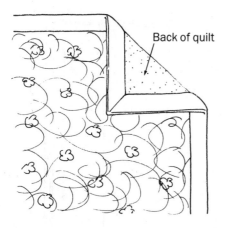

Back of quilt

Step 5: *When you handstitch the corner of the binding to the back of the quilt, the folded miter on the back should match the one on the front of the quilt.*

QNM Editors

RELIEVE QUILTER'S GUILT!

What quilter doesn't at some point get the "guilts" from too many "not-quite-finished" projects lurking in the dark recesses of her personal sewing closet? If you've learned all you can from some of your unfinished past projects and you're absolutely certain that you have no more interest in completing them, why not search out places to send them where someone else could have the chance to enjoy them? Take time to go through the projects you haven't finished in at least a year and decide which ones you won't want to spend time on in the future. Then donate those projects to a school, church, or senior citizens' center and let other people share freely in the pleasures of your quiltmaking. That way, you'll be "free" and ready to move on to your next quilting venture, with no nagging guilt to hinder your progress, and you'll benefit others at the same time.

❖ Mary Mashuta

❖ Angled Edges? ❖ No Problem!

Not every quilt top follows the straight and narrow. Some quilt designs, like Tumbling Blocks, Country Crossroads, and Endless Chain, have angled edges that require a special binding treatment. The best binding approach is to leave the edges as they are—don't trim them off to straighten the sides of the quilt, or you'll ruin the overall effect of the design. This binding method requires that you calculate the yardage carefully, by measuring one angle, then multiplying that by the total number of angles along the sides of the quilt. This gives you the total length in inches of bias binding required. Along with figuring the numbers, you also must be willing to stitch the many "ins and outs" by hand. Here are a few pointers on how to finish those angled edges:

1. Trim the batting and backing even with the edges of the quilt top and pin about 6 inches of the binding to the quilt at a time. With a single strand of thread, work from the top side and sew a ¼-inch seam through all three layers with a running stitch, backstitching occasionally and pivoting the stitching at each inner and outer corner.

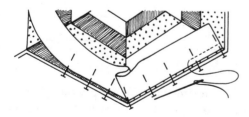

2. Fold the binding to the back of the quilt and blindstitch it in place, form-

ing tucks at each inner corner and slight miters at each outer point.

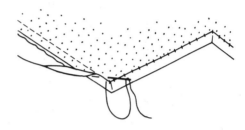

QNM Editors

❖ When No Binding Is Best ❖

Quilts with scalloped, curved, or even deeply angled edges may be good candidates for the no-binding treatment. In this approach, you blindstitch the edges of the quilt together. This finishing technique requires handstitching, but it's an easy and precise way to handle the challenges of curves and angles. This kind of edge finish shows wear more easily than bound edges do, so you may wish to save this technique for a quilt that won't receive hard use over the years.

1. Quilt to within ⅝ inch of the edges of the quilt.
2. Trim the batting so that it lies ¼ inch inside the edges of the quilt top. This will allow the batting to reach completely to the edges of the quilt after you've finished sewing.
3. Trim the backing even with the edges of the quilt top.

4. Turn under the ¼-inch seam allowances of both the quilt top and the backing, encasing the batting inside one of the seam allowances as you work. Blindstitch all around the edges of the quilt.

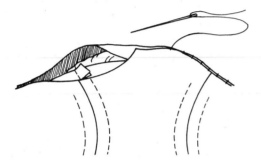

5. Finally, do enough quilting at the edges of the quilt to secure the batting in place.

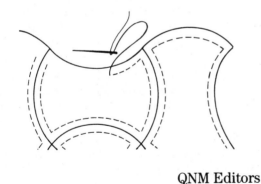

QNM Editors

❖ Time for a Trim ❖

Some patterns simply cannot be bound with anything but a straight binding, so it's perfectly valid to trim away portions of patches at the edges to create a quilt with straight edges. The Clamshell pattern shown in the diagram below is a good example, with its awkward convex and concave edges creating too many sharp points and curves to bind easily. Why not trim the edges, add straight borders, and bind with straight binding?

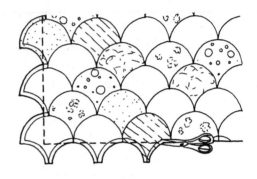

Sometimes a quilt simply has too many angles and points. One solution is to trim away enough of the points to make finishing the edges of the quilt more manageable. The hexagons on a Grandmother's Flower Garden pattern are being trimmed just enough to allow the binding to be attached easily, as shown in the diagram below.

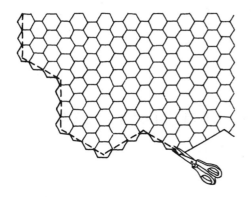

QNM Editors

❖ Appliqué Saves the Day ❖

Sometimes the only way to retain the shape of uneven patches is to appliqué the edges of the quilt to a coordinating straight-edged border. This may be just the technique you need if you like patterns with large motifs, like Baby Blocks or Double Wedding Ring, but you want the quilt to have straight edges. This technique is actually part of constructing the quilt top, so it's done before you start quilting.

1. Measure the width and length of the center portion of the quilt top and determine how wide and how long to cut border strips so that the quilt top will overlap them by at least 1 inch. Miter the corner seams of the border and press them open. (For help with mitering, see the tips under "Miter Magic," beginning on page 185.)

2. Lay the border on a flat surface and center the quilt top on top of it. Check to make sure that the edges of the quilt top overlap the inner edges of the border by at least 1 inch.

3. Baste a line of stitches ⅝ inch inside the edges of the quilt top, taking care not to stretch the quilt top out of shape.

4. Turn under a ¼-inch seam allowance and blindstitch the edges of the quilt top to the border. Trim the excess border fabric from the wrong side, after you've completed the appliqué. Layer and baste the quilt, finish the quilting, and bind the edges with straight binding strips.

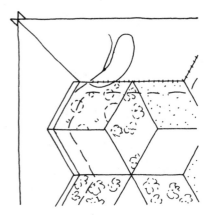

QNM Editors

Tips and Tricks for Fabulous Finishes

❖ I'll Be Seaming You in ❖ All the Old Familiar Places

Before I apply the binding, I like to sew the three layers of a quilt together ⅛ inch from the edges. This "edge" seam unites the three layers into one, which is much easier to handle than three separate layers when you're binding a quilt. The extra line of stitching will lie inside the binding, so no one will ever see it.

Mimi Dietrich

❖ Filled to the Rim ❖

Binding looks fuller and feels firmer if you trim the backing and batting layers so that they extend a little bit outside the edges of the quilt top. This creates a filled binding that is more attractive than if you had trimmed the backing and batting exactly even with the quilt top. And to make sure you trim evenly, you can wait to trim the backing and batting until after you've sewn the first edge of the binding on the quilt top.

Marianne Fons

❖ Stretching the Truth ❖

I like to bind quilts with bias binding because it helps to control waviness in the edges of a quilt. To contain rippled edges, I place straight pins at the uneven portions of the quilt, so that as I attach bias binding, I can stretch the binding a bit more in those areas to help ease in any distortions.

Doreen Speckmann

❖ A Dog-Feed-Dog World ❖

As you attach the binding, the border of a quilt can tend to creep and drag a little bit, causing puckers and wrinkles, because the feed dogs of the sewing machine are moving opposite the presser foot. If your machine has a walking foot (also called an even feed foot), you can easily eliminate problems with puckers. This attachment works *with* the motion of the feed dogs, not against it, so the border and the binding move evenly through the machine.

Liz Porter

❖ Binding Ties In ❖

For binding a Double Wedding Ring quilt, which has a lot of inner mitered corners, I use bias strips. At the exact point of each inner corner, I stop and pivot, turning the quilt to continue sewing along the next angle. Then I clip a tiny V in the seam allowance almost to the seam line at each corner, which creates a tiny bit of extra "space" for the binding fabric to lodge. In sewing the binding to the back of the quilt, I take one little "anchoring" stitch to tie the binding fabric to the seam allowance at each inner corner to make it stay in place and form a smooth corner fold, without distorting the edge of the quilt.

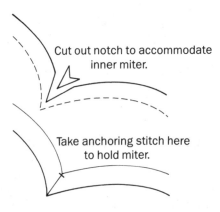

Cut out notch to accommodate inner miter.

Take anchoring stitch here to hold miter.

John Flynn

❖ Crossing over the Line ❖

When you sew the binding strips to the front of a quilt by machine, try using a bobbin thread that is a shade or two different in color from the quilt backing. That way, when you turn the binding over to stitch it to the back, you'll be able to see the slightly different color thread and bring the binding down to cover it more easily.

QNM Editors

❖ The Longest Yard ❖

One of the worst experiences you can have in quiltmaking is to finish a quilt and realize that you don't have enough of the right fabric left for the binding. If that ever happens to you, it will probably happen only once! I make it a rule to buy an *extra* yard of whatever fabric I plan to use to bind a bed-size quilt. And if the quilt is king-size, I suggest purchasing an extra 1¼ yards of the fabric from which the binding will be cut.

Mimi Dietrich

A HAIR-RAISING TALE

There's something even better than straight pins for holding the binding in place while you stitch it to the back of a quilt. The next time you visit your local drugstore or pharmacy, pick up some "snap-shut" hair clips! You can just clamp them over a quilt binding to keep it securely in position for blind stitching, using several clips at a time and moving them along the binding as you stitch.

❖ QNM Editors

❖ Binding Novelties ❖

What rule says that a binding has to be made from only one fabric? There are lots of quilts in which multiple fabrics make a better binding. To spark your imagination and create your own unique bindings, glance through these ideas on piecing bindings for striking effects:

♦ Piece lengthwise-grain strips of fabric together and cut them across the grain to create an evenly pieced "patchwork" look for the binding.

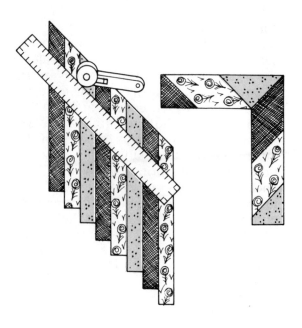

QNM Editors

❖ Look for a Silver Lining ❖

You can use even delicate fabrics like silk to bind a quilt, by lining them with a coordinating cotton fabric first. Start by cutting strips of the lining fabric the same width as the outer binding strips, remembering to match the fabric grain of the lining strips to the grain of the binding strips. If the outer binding strips are made of a slippery fabric like silk or satin, it's helpful to baste the two fabric layers together at the very edges, so that the threads won't need to be removed. You can attach a lined binding to a quilt as you would any binding.

QNM Editors

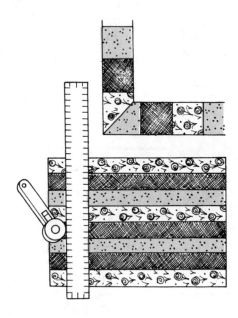

♦ Sew fabric strips together in stair-step fashion to create a parallelogram. Cut them apart at an angle to create a "candy stripe" binding.

❖ Cording Splendor ❖

My favorite method of binding a quilt is to use very narrow (⅛ inch) cable cording and cover it with bias strips wide enough to hold the cord. I stitch the fabric-covered cording to the edges of the quilt top with a ¼-inch seam. When I've finished quilting, I turn in the edges of the backing and batting, fold under the edges of the quilt top to meet them, and blind-stitch them together by hand from the back of the quilt. This leaves the cording along the very edge of the quilt, for a nice, neat finish.

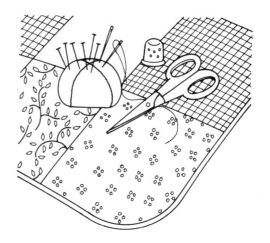

Judy Mathieson

Signing and Dating Quilts

❖ Put It in Writing ❖

Signing and dating your quilts is vital for making sure that accurate information about your work is available in the future. You might not think that anyone will care about the background of your quilts, but think about how you feel when you see an anonymous antique quilt, wishing you could know something about the quilt-maker and how and why he or she came to make that particular quilt. To keep future generations well informed about your quilts, consider including the following information somewhere on each quilt:

♦ *Sign your entire name as the quilt-maker.* The most important piece of information to include in signing a quilt is your name in its entirety.

Initials can be misleading; there could be many B. Joneses at any point in time. If you use a married name, include your maiden name, as well. Quilts that are handed down through families can be more easily traced if they're signed with both names of the quiltmaker.

♦ *Include names of other people who participated in making the quilt.* Perhaps you constructed the quilt top and someone else did the quilting; credit any and all persons who helped to complete the quilt.

♦ *Record the entire date of the quilt's completion.* Naming the year alone is adequate, but it's a delight to see a quilt with more specific information. The date given on the quilt should indicate the completion of the entire quilt, not just the quilt top. Seeing the date "April 12, 1907" on a quilt can enable an avid quilt detective to check the newspapers published on that date for interesting events happening at the time the quilt was made. You could even add a note describing the importance of a personal, national, or global event at the time you made the quilt.

♦ *Indicate where the quilt was made.* Future family members and quilt historians will thank you for opening further doors to investigation.

♦ *Note the occasion that inspired making the quilt.* Researchers love finding evidence of special events like birthdays, christenings, engagements, weddings, anniversaries, or retirements connected to the making of a quilt.

QNM Editors

❖ What's in a Name? ❖

The most beautifully documented quilts are those in which names and dates are incorporated into the design of the quilt top, leaving no doubt about the quilt's origin and authenticity. There are lots of ways to be creative in signing your quilts for posterity, however. Consider some of these guidelines for preparing your signature for your next quilt:

♦ Chain stitching can lend a touch of elegance to a quilt signature, whether you stitch on the actual surface of the quilt or make a separate label to appliqué on the back of the quilt. Start by signing your name in permanent pen on a piece of plain white tissue paper and baste the tissue paper signature to the surface of the quilt or to a piece of background fabric.

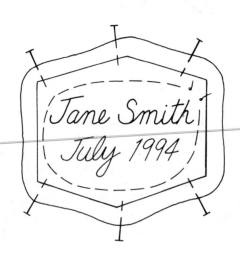

◆ Use embroidery floss to chain stitch your name and remove the tissue paper with your fingers or tweezers when you're finished stitching. If you're making a separate label, trim the background fabric to whatever size and shape you like and appliqué it in place on back of the quilt.

◆ You can quilt your signature into the quilt itself, using light thread to make a message seem almost invisible on a light background or a darker thread to enhance the inscription.

◆ Cross-stitching is another way of making a permanent signature for a quilt. You can stitch through waste canvas on the quilt top before you start quilting, or you can make a separate label to attach to the backing. After you finish stitching, dissolve the starch in the waste canvas by wetting the quilt back (only that portion with the waste canvas) or by putting the label in water. You'll be able to remove the threads of the waste canvas effortlessly.

QNM Editors

❖ The Elegance of Script ❖

In the nineteenth century, women used indelible ink to label linens and sign their fine handwork, including quilts. With today's choice of tools and array of techniques for writing on fabrics, you can re-create all of the elegance of those delicately designed inscriptions in signature labels for your own quilts. Here are some pointers for writing on fabric:

1. Choose a 100 percent cotton fabric that is light enough to allow ink to show well. Prewash the fabric to eliminate the sizing, which can act as a barrier to absorbing the ink.

2. Use either a Pigma XSDK or a Niji Stylist II permanent pen for inscrib-

ing your message on a label for a quilt. These pens are available in point sizes from .01, which is very fine, to .05, which makes a thicker line. The Pigma pens come in a variety of ink colors, and the brown and black pens are perfect for re-creating the sepia look of faded ink on old quilts.

3. Always test a pen on the fabric you plan to use, to determine exactly the look you like. Pens can react differently to different fabrics, sometimes bleeding or washing out more easily on one fabric than another.

4. Iron the wrong side of your fabric onto the shiny side of a piece of freezer paper to stabilize it and make writing on the fabric easier.

5. If you decide to re-create the ornate swirls and curling designs often seen on antique quilts, remember that practice makes perfect. Start by outlining the shape of a heart, circle, square, or oval medallion lightly in pencil on the fabric.

7. Add leaves to the vines by resting the pen on the fabric momentarily or by drawing small dots. This will suggest leaves. Combine them in matching pairs on each side of the vine, or alternate the position of each successive leaf.

8. Use dots, small or large, to suggest tiny flowers or grapes. Clusters of three or five dots can suggest a flower, while six dots resemble a bunch of grapes. Use a single dot to suggest a flower bud. Space the motifs close to one another or far apart, symmetrically or asymmetrically.

6. Draw vines around the shape, using simple S curves. Make them whatever size you like, and don't worry about making them match.

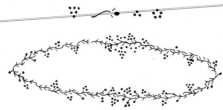

9. Place delicate grapevine tendrils randomly around the shape. Make "squiggles" with the pen in a series of e shapes. Using a very light touch, lift the pen from the wreath in an outward direction, ending with the pen in the air.

and between flowers with randomly spaced tiny dots.

10. Add your signature or other message, and shade the area around the wreath

11. Peel off the freezer paper before stitching the label to your quilt.

Susan McKelvey

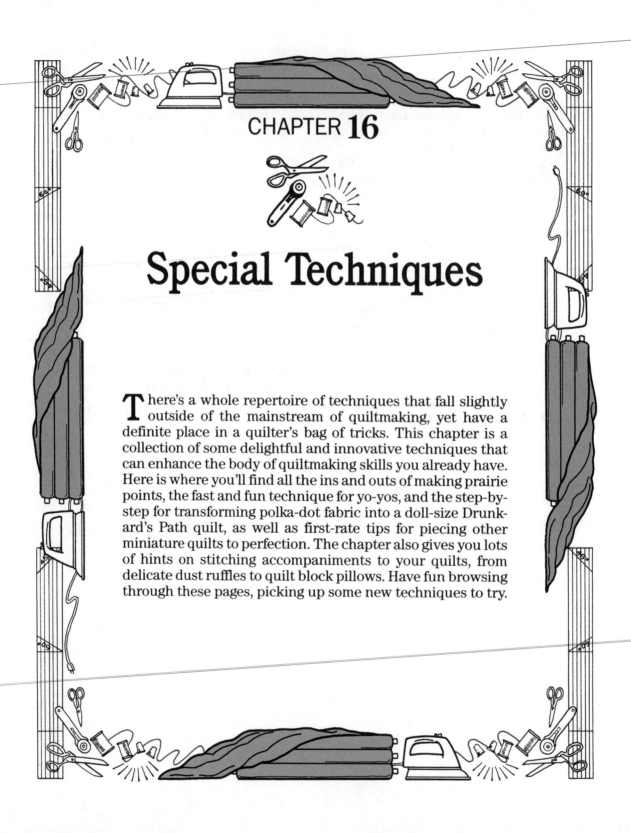

CHAPTER 16

Special Techniques

There's a whole repertoire of techniques that fall slightly outside of the mainstream of quiltmaking, yet have a definite place in a quilter's bag of tricks. This chapter is a collection of some delightful and innovative techniques that can enhance the body of quiltmaking skills you already have. Here is where you'll find all the ins and outs of making prairie points, the fast and fun technique for yo-yos, and the step-by-step for transforming polka-dot fabric into a doll-size Drunkard's Path quilt, as well as first-rate tips for piecing other miniature quilts to perfection. The chapter also gives you lots of hints on stitching accompaniments to your quilts, from delicate dust ruffles to quilt block pillows. Have fun browsing through these pages, picking up some new techniques to try.

Special Touches for Quilt Edges

❖ Ruffled Edges ❖

A gathered ruffle that matches one of the fabrics in a quilt often makes a perfect final touch to a child's comforter or a frilly and feminine young girl's quilt. Figuring out how much fabric to buy is easy if you follow the directions and the table below, and making ruffles is fast when you use a rotary cutter to cut the strips of fabric. (The step-by-step directions for attaching the ruffle appear in "The How-To for Quilt Ruffles" below.)

1. To figure out the total length of a quilt ruffle, first measure around the edges of the quilt and add 12 inches to allow for extra fullness at the corners of the bed. Multiply this number by 2 to determine the total length.

2. Decide how wide you would like the finished ruffle to be and multiply that measurement by 2, to allow for folding the ruffle. Add 1¼ inches to this number to allow for two ⅝-inch seam allowances.

3. To calculate how many strips you can cut from 44-inch cotton fabric, use the number 42 rather than 44 in your calculations, to allow for possible shrinkage in the width of the fabric and removal of the selvages. Divide 42 by the width of your ruffle (the final number you determined in Step 2) to find out how many strips you can cut

from the fabric width. Then divide the total length needed for the ruffle by this number of strips to find out how much fabric to buy (this figure will be the total in inches). Divide this figure by 36 to determine the number of yards you'll need to buy. To help you plan a ruffle and figure out yardages quickly, use the "Easy Ruffle Yardage Table" on page 268.

QNM Editors

❖ The How-To ❖ for Quilt Ruffles

Quick cutting, pin marking, and a few quick spins along the ruffle with gathering stitches are all it takes to prepare a ruffle to attach to the edges of your quilt. Once you've figured out how much fabric you need, with the help of the information in "Ruffled Edges" above, you're ready to get started with preparing and attaching the ruffle.

1. Remove both selvages from the fabric, then use a rotary cutter to cut whatever number of fabric strips you need from the lengthwise grain of the fabric. Place the short ends of the strips right sides together, join them with ¼-inch seams into a continuous loop, and press the seams open. Fold the entire

Easy Ruffle Yardage Table

Ruffle Width		Ruffle Length					
Finished Size (in.)	Cut Size (in.)	300 in.	400 in.	500 in.	600 in.	700 in.	800 in.
1½	(4¼)	1 yd.	1⅜ yds.	1⅝ yds.	2 yds.	2¼ yds.	2⅝ yds.
3	(7¼)	1¾ yds.	2⅜ yds.	2⅞ yds.	3½ yds.	4 yds.	4⅝ yds.
4½	(10¼)	2¼ yds.	2⅞ yds.	3⅝ yds.	4⅜ yds.	5 yds.	5¾ yds.
6	(13¼)	2⅞ yds.	3⅞ yds.	4¾ yds.	5¾ yds.	6⅝ yds.	7⅝ yds.

ruffle in half lengthwise, with wrong sides together, and press the long folded edge. Press the short fold at each end to crease the midpoints of the ruffle. Then place those creased folds together and press another crease at the end of the ruffle to mark the quarter points. Instead of pressing, you could insert pins to mark the midpoints and quarter points.

2. With a stitch length of about 6 stitches per inch, sew a line of gathering stitches along the raw edges in each of the four segments of the ruffle, leaving a 6-inch tail of thread at the beginning and end of each line. Sew another line of gathering stitches ¼ inch from each of the first lines.

3. Place a pin at the midpoint of each side of the quilt and match the pressed creases or pins in the ruffle to those points. Pin the ruffle to the quilt, raw edges together, and pull up the lines of gathering stitches to distribute the fullness of the ruffle evenly around the quilt. If the quilt has square corners, allow a bit of extra fullness in the ruffle to go around each corner.

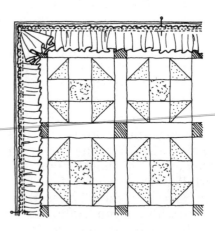

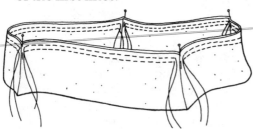

4. One way to attach a ruffle to a quilt is to sew the raw edges of the ruffle to the edges of the quilt through both the top and batting layers. Then place the quilt backing over the batting and blindstitch the backing to the ruffle from the back side of the quilt.

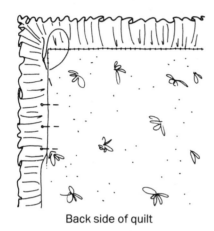

Back side of quilt

5. Another way to complete the edges of a quilt with a ruffle is to use thread to baste the ruffle in place along the edges of the quilt top, and then place the layers on top of each other in the following order: first the batting, then the quilt backing, face *up*, and then the quilt top, face *down*. This sandwiches the ruffle between the quilt top and the backing. Sew around the edges of the quilt with a ⅝-inch seam, backstitching at the beginning and the end of the seam and leaving approximately 14 inches unstitched. Turn the quilt right side out and sew the opening closed by hand with a blind stitch. When the ruffle is attached

to the quilt, the quilt is ready for quilting or tying.

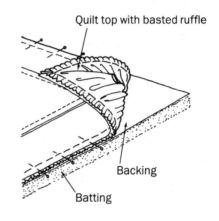

Quilt top with basted ruffle

Backing

Batting

QNM Editors

❖ Prairie Pointers ❖

Folding small squares of fabric into triangles has been a favorite edge-finishing technique among quilters for the past hundred years. Jean DuBois coined the name "prairie points" for these triangles. You can tuck prairie points into the borders to create an interesting edge finish, or you can incorporate them into the body of a quilt, where they become an unusual design element. Use the helpful hints that follow to transform squares into triangles that will add pizzazz to any quilt:

◆ One way to make a prairie point is to fold a small square of fabric diagonally, wrong sides together, then fold it a second time to create the finished triangle.

Diagonally folded prairie point

♦ Another way is to fold a square of fabric from side to side with wrong sides together and make two diagonal folds from the midpoint, creating a finished triangle with a vertical fold that can become an interesting design feature in a quilt.

Vertically folded prairie point

♦ When you're deciding how large to make the prairie points for a quilt, a helpful thing to remember is that the raw edge of the finished triangle will be the same length as the side of the square you cut. Also, the ¼-inch seam that attaches the prairie point to the quilt takes out approximately ½ inch of that length. For example, if you cut a 3-inch square of fabric, the finished prairie point will be approximately 2½ inches at the bottom when it is attached to the quilt.

♦ To finish the edges of a quilt with prairie points, you can overlap the triangles just a little bit, quite a lot, or combine different size triangles to create an unusual edge finish. The diagrams below provide examples of these three looks.

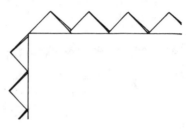

Prairie points with slight overlap

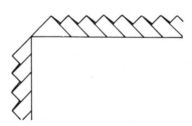

Prairie points with deep overlap

Different size prairie points combine for interesting effect.

♦ To attach prairie points to a quilt, position the triangles so that the folds face the same direction and pin or baste them in place along the edges of the quilt. Make sure that the long edges of the triangles are even with the edges of the quilt top. Sew them with a ¼-inch seam, through both the quilt top and the batting layers. (Keep the backing pinned out of the way while you stitch.)

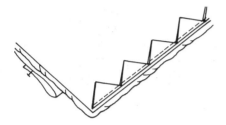

♦ To encase the prairie points in the outer edges of the quilt, turn the triangles away from the quilt and bring the backing up over the batting, turning it under ¼ inch and pinning it

to cover the bottom edges of the triangles. Blindstitch the backing in place.

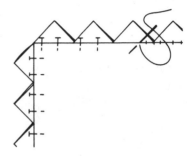

Jean DuBois and the QNM Editors

Specialty Techniques for Special Quilts

❖ Play with Yo-Yos ❖

When you feel like sewing something fun and making use of some of your smaller scraps of fabric at the same time, try playing with a yo-yo quilt! One of the most popular "nonquilt" quilts, yo-yos are a great portable project for car trips or vacations.

1. With a removable fabric marker or pencil, mark a circle around a cup, jar

lid, saucer, or other small round object on a piece of fabric and cut out the circle. You can also use a compass to draw a circle in whatever size you like. No matter what size circle you draw, the finished yo-yo will be half the size of this initial circle.

2. Holding the fabric circle with the wrong side facing you, turn under ¼ inch and use quilting thread to sew

short running stitches. Begin with a knot at the end of the thread, and after you've made the final stitch, bring the needle through to the other side of the yo-yo.

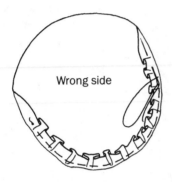

3. Pull the thread tightly to gather the edges of the circle and pull it into a smaller circle. Make a couple of "tacking" stitches to knot the thread. Make as many of these circles as you need to complete the size quilt you want to make.

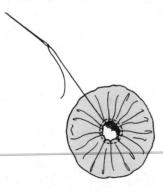

4. To join yo-yos, place two finished circles flat sides together and tack them firmly through the folded edges

with three or four whipstitches. Take a small stitch to secure the thread before you clip it.

5. Open up the two joined yo-yos to make sure they lie flat.

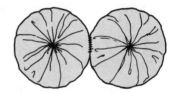

6. Continue adding yo-yos to make a quilt in whatever size you like.

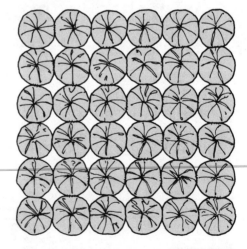

QNM Editors

PICTURE THIS!

Transferring photographs, poetry, and line drawings to fabric offers a number of interesting and creative options for quilt-makers. You can incorporate the likenesses of friends or family members into quilt blocks or make a label with a favorite verse dedicated to the person receiving the quilt. You can even create an album quilt with photographic images celebrating special occasions and events. Fabric Fotos has patented a direct printing process that allows any image that can be photocopied to be reproduced on RocLon bleached or unbleached muslin, provided by Fabric Fotos. The resulting image becomes permanent with chemical treatment or is removable if it remains untreated, and the muslin stays soft and supple, without hardness in the area of the image. This direct printing process works for any image that will fit on a piece of fabric up to 11 inches × 17 inches. For more information about the process, contact Charlene Dodson, Fabric Fotos, 3801 Olson, #3, Amarillo, TX 79109; (806) 359-8241.

❖ Susan McKelvey

❖ Polka-Dot Pleasures ❖

Making a miniature Drunkard's Path quilt is a challenge for almost any quilter. If you don't feel like tackling those tiny curved seams, you can use fabric with printed polka dots to make a miniquilt with the look of any Drunkard's Path variation you can dream up.

The Step-by-Step for a Miniature Drunkard's Path

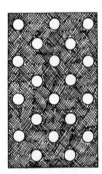

Step 1: *You need two polka-dot fabrics in the same two colors, one light with dark dots and one dark with light dots. The dots must be exactly the same size. It's possible to make a quilt using polka dots as small as ¾ inch or as large as 1¾ inches in diameter. If you're planning to go "dot" shopping, late summer and early fall are usually the best seasons for stocking up on polka dots, which are often in demand for Halloween costumes. For a quilt approximately 12 inches × 15 inches, you'll need to purchase at least ¼ yard of each fabric.*

Step 2: *Make a template from your fabric by marking the exact center of one dot. Then use a plexiglass quilter's ruler to draw two perpendicular lines through the marked center point. This outlines the square edges of the basic quarter-circle portion of the Drunkard's Path block.*

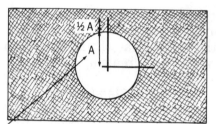

Distance from midpoint to outside of circle

Step 3: *Extend each of these lines into the background to a point beyond the dot that's half as long as the distance from the midpoint to the outside of the circle. Each of these lines must be exactly the same length when measured from the midpoint of the circle.*

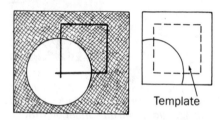

Template

Step 4: *Draw two more lines at right angles to these lines to create a square. This shape forms the basis of the other, "square" portion of the Drunkard's Path block. Depending on the size dots you're working with, add a ⅛- or ¼-inch seam allowance to each side of the square. Trace this square onto a piece of template plastic and then place the plastic over the polka dot to trace the curve of the quarter circle.*

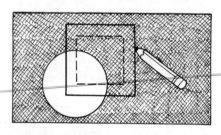

Step 5: *Use the template to line up, mark, and cut the polka dots and the background fabric into the correct size patches for the Drunkard's Path block.*

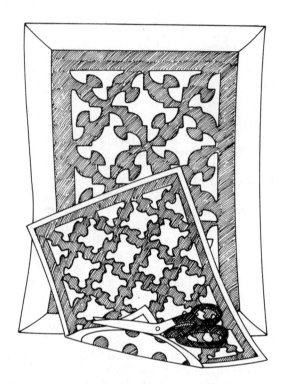

Step 6: *Cut half of the total number of blocks in your Drunkard's Path variation from dark fabric and half of them from light fabric. Arrange the blocks in the Drunkard's Path pattern of your choice and sew the blocks together. Add borders, and a backing, and your mini-Drunkard's Path quilt is ready to be layered and quilted or tied. (It can be fun to use the original polka-dot fabric for the backing.)*

Barbara Brackman

❖ Miniature Magic ❖

Webster's dictionary defines a miniature as "anything that is smaller than the original." I like to make a miniature quilt as accurate in proportion to and as complete a representation of the larger original quilt as possible, which means attending to the smallest details in every phase of the construction of the quilt. Here are some guidelines and principles that I've found helpful for making heirloom miniature quilts go together easily and precisely:

♦ Choose a pattern for a miniature that you've already enjoyed making as a large quilt.

♦ Use construction techniques that you've employed successfully in making a large quilt.

♦ Use the highest quality, most accurate tools and equipment you can afford for drafting patterns and marking fabrics. Your investment will pay off when the pieces of a miniature quilt fit together with precision. When you shop, look for graph paper with accurate grids, permanent markers such as the Pilot brand, utility knives, and rulers at engineering supply, art supply, or high-quality stationery stores.

♦ For piecing a miniature quilt, use a standard quilter's ¼-inch seam allowance and trim the allowances only at places where multiple seams come together, such as at the midpoint of a star. The width of a ¼-inch seam allowance gives stability and strength to a miniature quilt.

♦ For hand appliqué, use a turn-under allowance of ⅛ or ³⁄₁₆ inch. It's easy to stitch around acute angles with a smaller turn-under, using a blind hem stitch or a small whipstitch. It's helpful to test-stitch any appliqué fabric to determine whether it will fray easily before using it in a quilt.

♦ It's a good idea to press each seam in a miniature quilt to one side after you sew it.

♦ To make a miniquilt drape gracefully over the edges of a doll bed, use a thin

polyester batting in the portion of the quilt that will lie on top of the bed. Leave the side and bottom portions of the quilt without batting, which eliminates bulk from the overhang.

♦ Another effective way to make a miniature quilt hang nicely on a bed is to quilt the sides, either diagonally or vertically.

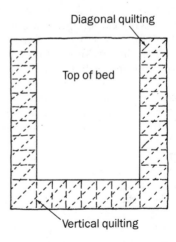

♦ For binding a miniature quilt, try cutting bias strips ¾ inch wide and applying the unfolded strips with a

⅛-inch seam allowance. It's helpful to baste the binding to the front of the quilt before you sew it by machine. This binding is ¼ inch wide when it's finished.

Tina Gravatt

BEADS, BAUBLES, AND BANGLES

It has taken me a while to "loosen up" in my approach to quiltmaking, to allow myself to add three-dimensional objects to the surface of my quilts. But once I began playing around with ribbons, beads, buttons, and other treasures, I realized how much fun it can be to add embellishments to the fabric. Now, just about anything is fair game! On a quilt I recently finished for my younger daughter, I stitched on the tiny satin ribbon rosettes I used to put in her hair when she was a baby. I scour local flea markets and antique shops for costume jewelry that has interesting baubles and bangles to stitch onto quilts. Antique buttons have become very popular as embellishments, and consequently much harder to find. But you can look for strips of beading clipped from vintage garments; often there are enough beads or surface area to work into a quilt block. Found objects can add that unexpected twist that lifts a quilt from the ordinary to the extraordinary.

❖ Suzanne Nelson

❖ Keep Yourself in Stitches ❖

Crazy quilts offer the perfect opportunity to expand your creative stitching horizons and explore the use of some of today's most interesting specialty threads. Play with pearl cotton, embroidery floss, or even acrylic yarns with metallic filaments, and express yourself in embroidery on your next crazy quilt. Try some of the stitches shown in the diagram below to cover the seams between different fabrics, and think about embroidering your name or initials and the date in the middle of one patch, as a decorative signature for the front of the quilt.

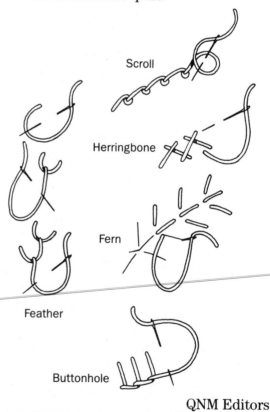

Scroll

Herringbone

Fern

Feather

Buttonhole

QNM Editors

Accompaniments to a Quilt

❖ How Much ❖
"Ruff" Makes a Ruffle?

Dust ruffles are easy to make, and they create a colorful frame around the edges of a quilt. Solids are wonderful for contrasting with a multicolored patchwork quilt, and prints offer the perfect way to make one of the fabrics in a quilt figure more prominently in your decor. Read the points that follow for some general guidelines on figuring the yardage for a dust ruffle to fit your bed. (The steps for making a nice, full-looking dust ruffle appear in "Making a Dust Ruffle" on page 278.)

1. A dust ruffle is attached to a piece of fabric that lies between the mattress and the box spring. This center fabric is not visible when the mattress is on the bed, so you can use either a fitted sheet or a flat sheet cut to fit the top of the bed. To determine the measurements for cutting a sheet for this center piece, measure from one end of the box spring to the other, referring to line A on the diagram above, and add ½ inch to each end for seam allowances. Measure from side to side on the box spring along line B to find the correct width for the center piece, and add ½ inch to each end for seam allowances.

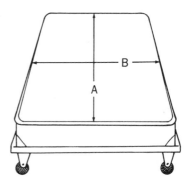

2. When you've cut the sheet to the correct measurements, turn under the top edge ¼ inch and stitch it in place. Then turn under another ¼ inch on the same edge and sew another ¼-inch seam, creating a finished hem at the top. Lay the finished edge of this center piece at the top of the bed and trim each of the corners to round them off a bit and make them fit the contours of the box spring.

3. To determine the depth for the dust ruffle, measure from the top edge of the box spring to the floor, referring to line C in the diagram on page 278. Add 4 inches to this measurement to allow for a hem and another ½ inch for a seam allowance at the top. To determine how long a dust ruffle it will take to go around the bed, measure around

277

the box spring following line D, starting and ending 5 inches in from each corner of the headboard. These 5-inch measurements allow for enough fabric in the dust ruffle to overlap the top corners of the bed. Multiply the measurement of D by 2½ to find the total number of inches it will take to make the finished dust ruffle. Divide this number by 36 inches to determine how many yards of ruffled fabric it will take to fit the bed. If you buy 45-inch-wide fabric, you should be able to get two ruffle lengths by splitting it down the middle lengthwise; in this case, you can divide the yardage for the dust ruffle in half to determine how much fabric to purchase.

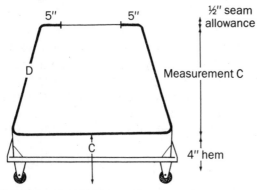

Use C to determine depth; use D to determine length and yardage needed.

and stitch the lengths together to create a one-of-a-kind dust ruffle that is the fitting finish to a bed covered by one of your quilts.

1. Wash and press the fabric and remove the selvages. Then cut it in half lengthwise to create two lengths for the ruffle.

2. Join the two pieces at one end with a French seam. Place the short ends of the two pieces of fabric *wrong* sides together and sew them with a ¼-inch seam. Press the seam to one side.

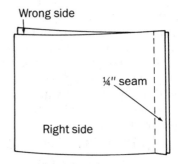

3. Bring the right sides of the pieces of fabric together and sew a ⅜-inch seam that encases the previous seam. Press this seam to one side.

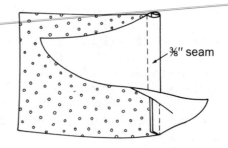

QNM Editors

❖ Making a Dust Ruffle ❖

Once you've figured out how much fabric you need, it's a simple matter to cut

4. Hem one long edge of the fabric by turning under 2 inches twice and stitching the fold down by hand or machine. At the two short ends of the dust ruffle, turn under ¼ inch twice and hem the edge by hand or machine.

5. Place the short ends of the fabric together to fold the fabric in half. Then fold it into quarters and press creases at the midpoint and the quarter points. Set the sewing machine at about 6 stitches per inch. Leaving a 6-inch tail of thread free at the beginning and end, sew a line of gathering stitches ¼ inch from the raw edge of the fabric, from one short end of the fabric to the first crease. Sew another line of gathering stitches ¼ inch from the first line of stitches, ending at the first crease. Make two rows of gathering stitches in each of the four quarters of the dust ruffle.

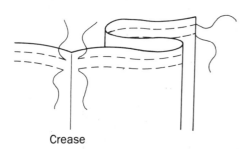

Crease

6. Lay the center fabric piece over the box spring, with the hemmed edge at the top of the bed. Divide the total distance that the dust ruffle will occupy (from 5 inches in from the top corner around the entire bed to the final point 5 inches in from the other top corner) by 4. Measure this number of

inches from the first point and mark it with a pin on the side of the center piece. Measure this distance again and mark that point with a pin (this should be at the center of the bottom of the bed), and mark the final distance with a pin on the other side of the bed.

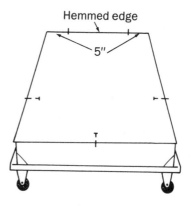

Hemmed edge

5″

7. Align the raw edges of the dust ruffle with the raw edges of the center piece (the bottom edge of the dust ruffle will be lying on top of the bed, facing toward the middle) and match the crease marks on the dust ruffle to the pins on the center piece. Pull up the gathering threads to distribute the fullness of the dust ruffle evenly within each of the four sections, pinning the ruffle in place as you work. Sew the dust ruffle to the center piece with a ½-inch seam, and stitch a second seam ¼ inch from the first seam for added strength.

8. Place the center piece with attached dust ruffle over the box spring (flipping the ruffle down so the seam is

covered) and set the mattress on top. Make the bed, adding your finished quilt, and stand back to admire your work!

QNM Editors

❖ Pillow Talk ❖

A quilted pillow makes a perfect accessory for a quilt. And if you're stumped about what to give family or friends for special occasions, a handmade pillow is always a welcome gift. The process of making a pillow is easy and quick, and the results can be spectacular. Here are the basics of pillowmaking; review these, then let your creativity take over.

The Step-by-Step for a Basic Pillow

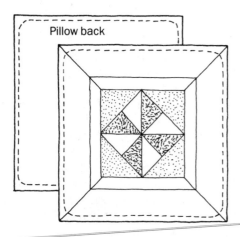

Step 1: *After you've quilted a block from which you want to make a pillow, add one or more solid borders to create whatever size pillow you like. Then use a pencil to round off the corners (it's easier to construct a pillow with softly rounded corners than with square ones). Cut a piece of backing fabric to match the pillow front.*

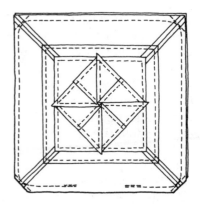

Step 2: *Make a simple, knife-edge finish by placing the pillow top face down on the right side of the backing and sewing the edges together by machine. Begin sewing a few inches before one of the rounded corners and end a few inches past the final corner, backstitching at each end of the seam. The opening in the seam line should be large enough to insert your hand, which makes it easy to turn the pillow right side out. It's helpful to sew a diagonal line at each corner to add strength and durability to the pillow. Trim the corners just outside the diagonal seams, but leave the remainder of the seam around the pillow untrimmed, creating firmer edges.*

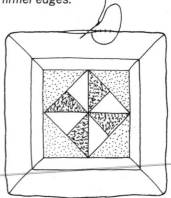

Step 3: *Turn the pillow right side out and stuff it with a purchased pillow form or polyester fiberfill. Sew the unstitched portion of the seam with a blind stitch.*

QNM Editors

❖ Accent with Cording ❖

Cording gives a professional, almost tailored appearance to any pillow. And it's one of those techniques that looks a lot harder to do than it actually is. Give it a try, following the three steps listed below, and discover how easy and how much fun it is to add this accent to your quilted pillows:

1. Cut enough 1½- or 2-inch-wide bias strips to go around the outside edges of the pillow. When sewing two or more bias strips together, use diagonal seams, trimming off the points and pressing the seams open.

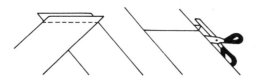

2. Cut a piece of cable cord that's several inches longer than the distance around the pillow. Fold the bias strip around the cable cord so that the right sides are out and the raw edges are even. Using a zipper foot, sew close to the cable cord, encasing it in the bias strip.

3. Pin the covered cording to the right side of the pillow top, with the raw edges of the bias strip toward the outside of the pillow. Align the stitching on the covered cording with the seam line at the edges of the pillow top. If the pillow has square corners, clip the seam allowance of the cov-

ered cording at each corner to fan out the bias fabric and make it lie flat. Overlap the ends of the bias strip at the middle of one edge of the pillow top.

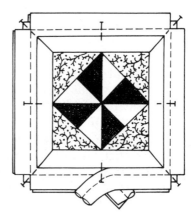

4. Place the pillow right sides together with the backing and sew them together, using the zipper foot to sew as closely as possible to the cording. Leave an opening in the seam large enough to insert your hand and use it to turn the pillow right side out. Stuff the pillow with a purchased pillow form or polyester fiberfill and blind-stitch the unstitched portion of the seam.

QNM Editors

❖ Ruffles and Flourishes ❖

Nothing dresses up a pillow faster than the flounce of a full ruffle. Make one out of fabric leftover from the quilt block that forms the pillow front, or pull in a different fabric to complement the colors already in the pillow.

1. Make the ruffle twice as long as the distance around the outside edges of the pillow. To determine the width to cut the fabric strips for the ruffle, decide how wide you want the finished ruffle, multiply by 2, and add 1 inch for the seam allowances. For example, to make a 2½-inch-wide ruffle for a pillow that is 11 inches square, the strips of fabric should be 6 inches wide × 88 inches long.

2. Sew the right sides of the short ends of the fabric strips together to make one continuous loop. Press the seams open and then press the entire ruffle in half lengthwise, with wrong sides together. Use pins to mark four equal segments in the ruffle. Set the sewing machine at 6 stitches per inch and place a row of gathering stitches ¼ inch from the raw edges of the ruffle in each of the four segments, starting and stopping a new line of stitching with each segment. Be sure to leave long tails of thread for gathering. Sew another row of gathering stitches ⅛ inch from each of these rows.

3. Pull up the rows of gathering stitches and pin each segment of the ruffle to the midpoint of one side of the pillow top, adjusting the gathers evenly in each segment.

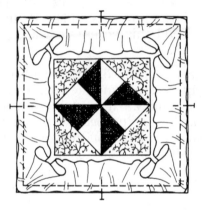

4. Place the pillow top right sides together with the backing and sew them together with a ½-inch seam, leaving an opening large enough to insert your hand. Turn the pillow right side out and stuff it with a purchased pillow form or polyester fiberfill. Sew the opening closed with a blind stitch.

QNM Editors

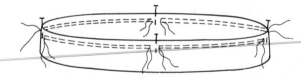

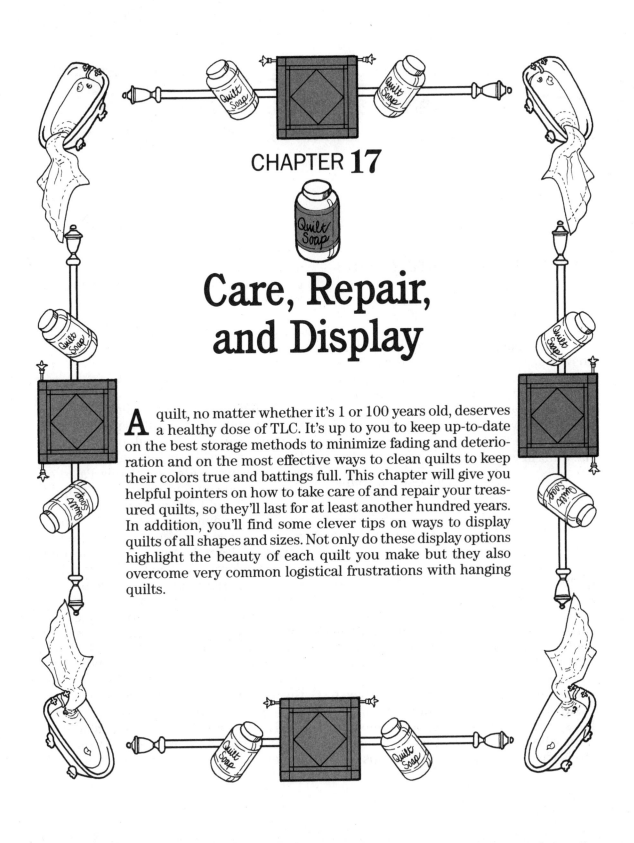

CHAPTER **17**

Care, Repair, and Display

A quilt, no matter whether it's 1 or 100 years old, deserves a healthy dose of TLC. It's up to you to keep up-to-date on the best storage methods to minimize fading and deterioration and on the most effective ways to clean quilts to keep their colors true and battings full. This chapter will give you helpful pointers on how to take care of and repair your treasured quilts, so they'll last for at least another hundred years. In addition, you'll find some clever tips on ways to display quilts of all shapes and sizes. Not only do these display options highlight the beauty of each quilt you make but they also overcome very common logistical frustrations with hanging quilts.

Essentials of Quilt Care

Laundering and Storing Quilts

❖ A Dry Subject ❖

Quilts that are displayed for long periods can accumulate more dust than actual soil. I've found it very effective to put a quilt into a dryer about every two to three weeks on low heat, which removes the dust. That way, I can wait a full year or more before having to actually launder the quilt in water and soap.

Lynn Lewis Young

❖ Safe Suds ❖

I like to use Orvis Paste for washing quilts in a washing machine. One or two tablespoons is enough to wash a quilt in cold water in a heavy-duty, large-capacity washing machine. Regular laundry detergents contain whiteners, brighteners, and other ingredients designed to remove soil from clothing, but those same ingredients can make the cotton fabrics in a quilt bleed easily. I have yet to encounter any problems with fabric dyes seeping out of a quilt when I used Orvis Paste to wash it. Orvis Paste is available at quilt shops and often at other fabric shops, as well as at farm supply stores (where it's sold in bulk for washing horses).

Liz Porter

❖ Rub-a-Dub-Dub ❖

The bathtub is my preferred place to launder quilts. If the quilt is really dirty, I start by soaking it in a tub of cold water for a couple of hours. Then I wash the quilt in warm water and Orvis Paste or Ensure (you can find these in most quilt shops and quilt supply catalogs), occasionally working soap through the fibers with my fingers. If the water in the tub darkens, I drain the tub, pushing the quilt to the back and patting it to let as much water as possible drain out. Then I run another tubful of water and let the quilt continue to soak until the soil is gone from the surface of the quilt. It can take several water changes to remove the soil from a quilt that's very old and dirty. When it's clean, I rinse it thoroughly. First I drain the water from the tub and pat the quilt to get out as much water as possible. Then I refill the tub and let it drain again, repeating the process as many as eight times to remove all traces of soap. There's no quick and easy way to wash a quilt effectively—it can be a daylong operation. But every minute you invest is worth it when your goal is a safely laundered quilt.

Lynn Lewis Young

❖ Squeeze-Dried Quilts ❖

Once you've washed a quilt in the bathtub, the big question is what to do with that heavy, dripping wet armful of fabric and batting. To dry a quilt inside the house, find a place where there's enough space to spread the quilt out flat, not a lot of foot traffic, and ideally, windows or a ceiling fan to provide moving air. Put a plastic drop cloth or tarp down to protect the carpet or flooring. Start to

remove the quilt from the bathtub, gently and gradually squeezing the water out without actually wringing the quilt out of shape. When you've removed enough of the water to lift the quilt out of the bathtub, wrap a beach towel around it and carry it over to the tarp. Spread the quilt out flat and cover it with a layer of clean, old faded towels, which won't bleed color onto the quilt. Roll up the quilt, letting the towels absorb the moisture, then unroll it and remove the towels. Repeat this process to remove even more water from the quilt. Allow the quilt to air dry, or even better, use a ceiling fan to speed up the drying process.

Lynn Lewis Young

❖ Comfort Zones for Quilts ❖

Cotton fabrics and battings survive best at the same temperatures and humidity as people do, so it's a good idea to store your quilts in a space where you'd feel comfortable yourself. Use these guidelines for deciding how and where to store your quilts so they stay in top condition:

◆ Avoid cold, damp spots like attics, garages, and basements, which can lead to mildew and odors in quilts. Look for a storage place in your home that is away from light, moderate in temperature, well ventilated, dry, and clean.

◆ Avoid using plastic bags as containers for quilts, because they can trap moisture and pests, causing mildew and other damage. Instead, wrap quilts in clean cotton sheets or pillowcases, or store them in acid-free boxes, which are often available at quilt shops and museums.

♦ Fold a quilt so that the right side is in, with the fewest number of folds possible. Crumple up some pieces of acid-free paper into long rolls and tuck them into the folds of the quilt, to keep creases from forming and becoming permanent. Taking a quilt out every few months and refolding it will also help to minimize damage during storage.

♦ Store quilts in individual boxes, or stack them only two deep in any single storage area. Storing several quilts on top of one another can create a great deal of stress on the quilts on the bottom of the stack.

QNM Editors

TLC for Older Quilts

❖ Caution Is Best ❖

One good thing to remember in repairing or restoring antique quilts is to avoid making changes to the quilt in any way, if possible. Changes to an antique are usually noticeable, and they can affect the value of the quilt. If the fabric in the quilt is torn in places, try to mend it rather than replace the patch with another fabric. If the binding on an antique quilt is tattered, try to darn the deteriorated areas carefully with matching thread rather than apply a new binding to the entire quilt.

Think about placing a piece of bridal veiling over a damaged patch and couching it down with matching thread.

Lynn Lewis Young

❖ Force-Fading ❖

Replacing patches in an old quilt can be difficult if the quilt is faded. You can sometimes simulate the look of age in a new fabric by using the wrong side of the fabric, which appears a bit "softer" than the right side. You can also fade new fabrics by placing them in a sunny window for several days, to make them match the look of an old quilt.

QNM Editors

❖ Sew First, Soak Last ❖

If you have a quilt that needs to be repaired, it's a good idea to make all repairs before you launder the quilt, to prevent holes, rips, tears, or other damaged spots from becoming larger and harder to mend.

Lynn Lewis Young

❖ Call on a Conservator ❖

Whenever you wash an antique quilt that's in very delicate condition, there is always a risk that it might become damaged or even destroyed. Rather than wash an old quilt that's very valuable, I prefer to send it to a quilt conservator for cleaning or to avoid laundering it altogether. To find a conservator, contact a museum with a good quilt collection and speak to someone in the textiles department who is knowledgeable about antique quilts.

Nancy J. Martin

❖ Quilt Before You Clean ❖

It's tempting to launder an old quilt top that smells musty, especially if you plan to quilt it. A lot of antique quilts have seam allowances of only ⅛ inch, or even ¹⁄₁₆ inch, which can make the seams fray very easily. I think it's best to quilt and bind an antique quilt top before you do laundering of any kind. That way, the backing, batting, quilting, and binding will give it added strength, making the seams less likely to fray.

Nancy J. Martin

❖ "Top" Antiques ❖

Reading a list of the pros and cons of quilting antique tops can make you stop and wonder what other options are available for using these tops. If you own some older quilt tops that haven't been quilted, think about some of these ideas for using them in your home:

◆ Fold a quilt top to hide the raw edges and display it draped over an end table in a family room. If the quilt top is very old, try to keep it out of direct sunlight, if possible.

◆ Sew a sleeve to the back of a quilt top and hang it on a rod or dowel, just as

you would a finished quilt. Using cotton fabric and thread, use single- or double-fold binding and bind the raw edges by hand.

◆ Mount a piece of backing fabric to an old quilt top before you hang it, to give it added strength. Baste the edges of the quilt top to the backing fabric with stitches that are about ¼ inch long on the right side of the quilt and about 1 inch long on the backing side. Then bring the backing fabric to the front of the quilt top to cover the raw edges and hand tack it to the top with as few stitches as possible.

◆ If you have an antique quilt top that's in very good condition, but you wouldn't enjoy displaying it unquilted, think about donating it to a museum that has a good textile collection. Curators are often interested in older quilt tops, because they offer wonderful opportunities for gaining insight into fabric printing and quilt construction techniques of earlier times.

Barbara Brackman

❖ Something Old, ❖ Something New

I think it's valid to combine an antique quilt top with new fabrics to create a finished quilt. I often see lovely quilts that were made during the 1930s using blocks from the 1880s or 1890s. I think it is better to complete a quilt and enjoy it than to simply keep an incomplete top or a set of individual blocks. And quilts often are treated more respectfully if they're finished in some way, rather than left incomplete. If you decide to complete an old quilt, it's a good idea to use cotton fabrics in combination with antique tops and blocks. I recommend not updating the style of an old quilt, but combining the old with the new to create a finished quilt that will give you enjoyment.

Judy Mathieson

Displaying Quilts

❖ Doweling Mastery ❖

When you want to use a wooden dowel for hanging a quilt, I think it's a good idea to make a muslin "sleeve" to cover the dowel. Cut a strip of muslin wide and long enough to cover the dowel completely and stitch it into a tube with a ¼-inch seam. You can then slide this "slipcovered" dowel into the sleeve on the back of the quilt. Covering the dowel will keep the tannic acids in the wood from coming into contact with the backing on the quilt.

Judy Mathieson

❖ Just Hanging Around ❖

It can be very handy to have an adjustable fabric sleeve on the back of your quilt that can expand to fit a thicker dowel or rod. Cut a piece of fabric that's as long as the top edge of the quilt and wide enough to hold a dowel or rod when folded in half and stitched with a ¼-inch seam into a tube. Make the sleeve adjustable by basting a ⅛- or ¼-inch pleat along the middle of the sleeve before sewing the tube. When you sew the sleeve to the quilt, position the pleat so that it lies away from the quilt. If you want to use a narrow dowel to hang the quilt, the pleat doesn't need to be removed, but if you decide later to use a stronger, thicker dowel, you can release the pleat to create a larger space for the dowel.

Liz Porter

❖ Put the Pieces Together ❖

I like to make pieced sleeves from fabrics I've used in my quilt. That way, the fabrics in the sleeve wear at the same rate as those in the quilt, so the perfect fabrics for repairing the quilt are always at hand, if they're ever needed.

Nancy J. Martin

❖ Hot Rods ❖

If you have quilts you want to display, don't miss out on the wonderful world of curtain and closet rods. They provide you with fast, fun, and easy ways to hang quilts—with a minimum of effort. All you need to install them is a screwdriver! To prepare a quilt for hanging on a rod, attach a fabric sleeve, which allows the weight of the quilt to be distributed evenly along the rod, minimizing stress on the quilt. (Lots of tips for easy and creative fabric sleeves can be found in this section.)

Tips for Using Curtain and Closet Rods

Curtain rods are available in many styles and sizes, and they're adjustable up to a length of approximately 86 inches. They have brackets with screws, which are easy to mount on a wall at whatever width you need for displaying a quilt. The depths of curtain rods can vary by type; some will hold a quilt flat against a wall, which can be helpful for making an uneven quilt hang more smoothly.

Some styles of rods hold a quilt several inches out from a wall, providing greater circulation of air, which can be valuable, especially in humid climates.

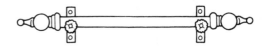

Some rods have decorative finials that add a nice finishing touch to your quilt display.

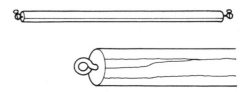

Wooden closet rods are very sturdy, which means they're often the best choice for hanging a very large, heavy quilt. If you choose a wooden rod, it's a good idea to seal the wood with polyurethane and put screw eyes at each end. Use nails or hooks on the wall to hold the rod.

QNM Editors

Shopping Savvy

A GREAT QUILT HANG-UP

Hanging a large quilt can be difficult, especially if you're working by yourself. I've developed a pulley system for displaying quilts in my home that's easy to make and inexpensive. All it takes is a quick trip to the hardware store and a total cost of less than $20! Best of all, it makes hanging a quilt almost effortless. Here's a list of things you'll need to make a quilt "hang-up" of your own:

* 2 small pulleys (½-inch roller) or eyebolts
* Kitchen cup hook
* Approximately 20 feet of traverse rod cord
* 2 café curtain rings with eyelets (or knot loops in the cord)
* ¾-inch × 6-foot metal café curtain rod with end caps

Follow these steps for making a pulley system and use the diagram at right for guidance as you place each piece of the system on a wall.

1. Attach the two pulleys or eyebolts to the ceiling, approximately 5 or 6 feet apart. If this placement seems too far apart or too close together, adjust it according to the size quilt you want to hang.
2. Screw the kitchen cup hook into the wall at eye level, at the midpoint between the pulleys.
3. Cut the traverse rod cord in half, to allow the same length for supporting each side of the quilt.
4. Thread the end of each cord through one of the pulleys or eyebolts.
5. Tie a café curtain ring, or knot a loop, at the end of each cord.

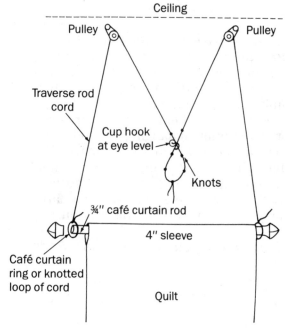

6. Remove one end cap from the café curtain rod and insert that end of the rod through the curtain ring or loop on one of the cords. Replace the end cap.
7. Remove the other end cap and insert this free end of the curtain rod through the sleeve on the back of the quilt. Put the other curtain ring or cord loop over the rod and replace the end cap.
8. Pull the quilt up to the height you desire. Standing behind the quilt, knot the ends of the cord and slide the knots over the cup hook. (You may end up making several knots before you get the height exactly right.) If the cup hook seems to protrude and distorts the quilt, you can bend and flatten out the hook to make the knotted cords lie close to the wall.

❖ Judy Mathieson

DISPLAYING ENJOYMENT

I am a firm believer that quilts should be visible, not tucked away out of view. I try to keep as many on display as I can in my home. Here are some of the ways I enjoy adding quilts to my decor.

✳ A closet door that opens out into a corner where there isn't much traffic is the perfect spot to display a quilt. Just fold up one of your quilts and drape it over the top of the door, so it's visible to anyone coming into the room.

✳ Baskets are beautiful with rolled or folded quilts in them. Hang the baskets from hooks in the wall, with quilts and in-progress projects spilling exuberantly out of them. Baskets are great for keeping quilts and your projects out of the way yet accessible, while allowing other people to enjoy viewing them at the same time.

✳ Antique furniture and accessories offer loads of creative options for displaying quilts. For instance, in my home an antique tobacco-drying rack holds up to three quilts at a time, and an old copper washstand looks great with a quilt draped over it. I also have an antique Amish cupboard, which looks wonderful with a quilt over one of the doors.

✳ Backs of chairs are perfect places for showing off beautiful quilts, especially if the chair is a decorative one or an antique that's not often used.

✳ The back of an upholstered chair is just the place for highlighting a small or miniature quilt—look around your home for areas that used to be reserved for crocheted doilies in earlier times.

❖ Sharyn Squier Craig

❖ Loops, Stays, and Rings ❖

Special circumstances require special solutions. It's easy to hang straight quilts, but any quilt that has an unusually shaped top edge is a candidate for one of these creative hanging methods.

Creative Ways to Hang Quilts

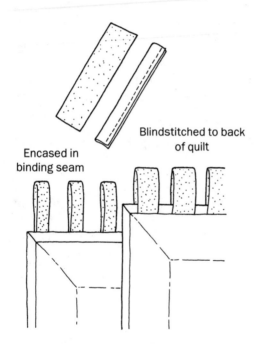

Encased in binding seam

Blindstitched to back of quilt

Use fabric "loops" to hang a quilt that has an uneven top or bottom edge. One method for sewing a loop is to cut a strip of fabric that's whatever length you need and twice as wide as you want the finished loop to be, plus ½ inch for seam allowances. Fold the strip in half lengthwise, right sides together, and sew it into a tube with a ¼-inch seam allowance. Turn it right side out and press it flat, turning the unfinished ends in. Blindstitch the ends of the loop by hand to the back of the finished quilt, or encase them in the seam when you attach the binding to the quilt.

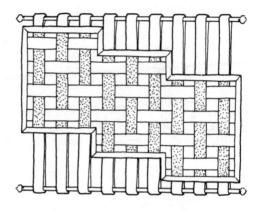

Try placing fabric loops at the bottom of a quilt to "mirror" the ones at the top edge, and use dowels or rods in both areas.

Stuff narrow fabric tubes to create three-dimensional loops that you can tie into bows or braid to acheive different lengths, as needed.

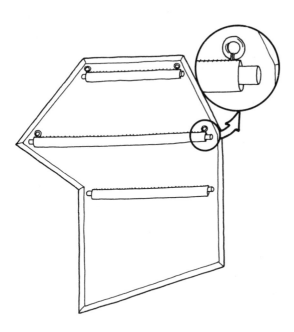

Stabilize an irregularly shaped quilt with narrow rods or "stays" inserted through closely fitted sleeves and placed at varying intervals on the back of the quilt. Measure the quilt and the rods you plan to use and then sew sleeves in whatever sizes you need. Plan the placement of each rod to accommodate the shape of the quilt. When you've stitched the sleeves on the back of the quilt, sew plastic or metal rings on the sleeves. Place nails or picture hooks on the wall at the same intervals at which you've placed the rings.

QNM Editors

❖ Casing the Place ❖

All quilts look best when they hang evenly, with no telltale "pooches" outlining the shape of a dowel. When it comes to hanging a quilt that has curved or unusually shaped edges, there are several creative options. Try some of these ideas for making your quilts hang straight and true, with no drooped or curled edges:

◆ Small bias sleeves make "casing" contours a breeze. Just cut a 3½- or 4-inch-wide strip across the width of a piece of muslin and cut the strip into several segments of whatever width you like for each casing. Turn the side edges under ¼ inch and machine stitch them in place. Then cut a 2- or 3-inch-wide piece of plexiglass or masonite that fits the curved edge of the quilt and center it on the backing about ¾ inch from that edge. Position the short casings over the curved plexiglass and pin them in place. Remove the plexiglass to blindstitch the casings in place.

◆ A wooden armature may be just the thing for hanging a quilt with a complex shape. Cut a piece of plywood about 2 or 3 inches wide and in the same shape as the top of the quilt. If the quilt is a very large one, you may need to cut the wooden strip even wider to support the weight of the quilt. Glue or staple a few pieces of Velcro to the armature and sew the other half of each Velcro piece in the proper position on the back of the quilt. Rest the armature on hooks or nails in the wall and press the quilt onto it until the Velcro "locks."

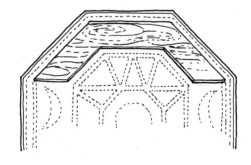

Sarah Doolan Gobes, Mickey Lawler, Sheila Meyer, and Judy Robbins

Acknowledgments

Quilter's Newsletter Magazine

Bonnie Leman's name is familiar to quilt lovers around the world. She has been the editor of *Quilter's Newsletter Magazine (QNM)* since its 1969 beginning. Bonnie's love of quilting goes back to her youth and fond memories of the colorful quilts set up in her Aunt Mae's quilt frames. Bonnie started a mail-order business for quilt patterns in 1969. The business began to grow very quickly, and on September 21, 1969, the first issue of *QNM* was published. Bonnie typed each issue of *QNM* on her Royal typewriter, and she wrote answers to mail, contributions, and suggestions sent to her by eager readers. From the very first issue, *QNM* was a family venture, with the magazine being produced in the Leman home. After school, Bonnie's daughter Mary helped with drawings, while Megan filled pattern orders. Emilie and Georgianne helped, too, keeping the office tidy, and sons David, Andrew, and baby Matt were enthusiastic supporters. Bonnie's husband, George, handled the printing and mailing, and in 1972 he joined the staff on a full-time basis. In September 1973 the Lemans opened the doors of their store, Quilts and Other Comforts. Bonnie feels that in opening the store, they were exposed to quilters' comments and suggestions that enhanced the magazine. In 1982 Bonnie started another magazine, *Quiltmaker*. Bonnie and the members of the *QNM* staff have continued to expand the horizons of quiltmaking, and the magazine is today the major forum for the quilts and quiltmaking expertise of the best quiltmakers all over the world.

Mary Leman Austin was 13 years old when she started doing artwork for *Quilter's Newsletter Magazine* in 1969. In the mid-1970s she began experimenting with traditional quilt blocks, changing and expanding them to create new designs. She very much enjoys thinking of new twists on traditional pieced designs. Her work in producing quilt drawings and other art in color has long been a major factor in the growth of *QNM*. Since 1984 she has been art and production director for Leman Publications, working in all phases of production on both *QNM* and *Quiltmaker* magazine, in the marketing department, and on all new projects, including recent books such as *The Quilter's How-To Dictionary* and *Family Keepsake Quilts*. Her personal hobby is designing and making one-of-a-kind pieces of jewelry. She also enjoys working on her computer, finding new ways to create quilt illustrations.

Carol Crowley learned to embroider and hand piece quilt blocks as a child, stitching, ripping, and stitching again under the watchful eyes of her mother and grandmother. She completed her first hand-quilted patchwork quilt in 1960. She was general editor and book reviewer for *Quilter's Newsletter Magazine* for eight years, and in 1987 she became managing editor of *Quiltmaker* magazine. She has enjoyed seeing *Quiltmaker* grow from a twice yearly to a quarterly to a bimonthly magazine.

Theresa Eisinger has been sewing for more than 20 years and has been a quiltmaker for the past 10 years. She has been a member of the Leman Publications staff for 8 years, and she is now senior design associate at *Quiltmaker* magazine. She likes machine piecing and machine quilting because they allow her to make more quilts during busy days as the mother of four children.

Caroline Reardon joined the staff of Leman Publications in 1988, after 13 years as a middle-school language arts teacher. She has been special projects editor and editor for *Quilter's*

Newsletter Magazine and is currently project editor for *Quiltmaker* magazine. She enjoys designing quilts, and her work has appeared in both magazines, as well as in shows at the Botanic Gardens and the state capitol in Denver, Colorado; the American Quilter's Society show in Paducah, Kentucky; the American International Quilt Association show in Houston, Texas; and the Quilts show in Louisville, Kentucky in 1993. Her art-oriented family includes a sculptor/art teacher husband and two daughters who are doing graduate work in theater and creative writing.

Vivian Ritter has been an editor on the staff of *Quilter's Newsletter Magazine* since 1983. She began making quilts in the early 1970s and has taught classes in quiltmaking for the past 15 years. She has written many of *QNM*'s "Easy Lessons." Her love of making quilts for family members resulted in her authorship of the book *Family Keepsake Quilts*, published in 1992. She lives in the foothills of the Rockies.

Marie Shirer learned to sew when she was four years old, making dolls and doll clothes. By the age of ten, she was making her own clothing. In 1972 she made her first quilt from the Garden of Eden pattern, using white broadcloth, red gingham, and blue chambray fabrics. She chose cotton batting and elected to tie the quilt rather than quilt it by hand. After the quilt made one trip through the washing machine, the batt separated into clumps. She still has the quilt but never allowed anyone else to see it. Marie earned a bachelor of science degree in textiles and clothing from Kansas State University in 1974, and for the next nine years, she owned and operated The Crewel Cupboard, a needlework and quilt shop in Lawrence, Kansas. In 1982 she sold the business to join the staff of *Quilter's Newsletter Magazine*. She is coauthor with Barbara Brackman of *Creature Comforts*, published by Wallace-Homestead in 1986. She also wrote *Quilt Settings: A Workbook*, published by Moon Over the Mountain in 1989, and *The Quilter's How-To Dictionary*, published by Leman Publications in 1991.

Jeannie Spears has been a quilter since 1974, and she is now a teacher, judge, writer, and publisher in the field of quilting. She was a charter member of the Minnesota Quilters and served on the board of the National Quilting Association, Inc., as chairwoman of the Teacher Certification Committee, the Master Quilter's Guild Committee, and the Show Judges Committee. She enjoys all parts of the quiltmaking process, especially hand quilting. Jeannie left Minnesota in 1992 to become managing editor of *Quilter's Newsletter Magazine*, which she considers a dream job for a quilter because it provides opportunities to view at close hand the wonderful quilts that are photographed for *QNM*, to talk to marvelously creative quilters around the world, and to be continually inspired by new products and ideas.

Marla Stefanelli was born in Beirut, Lebanon, and now lives in Arvada, Colorado. She began to learn needlecrafts when she was five years old, and her interests include embroidery, knitting, crochet, and sewing, as well as quilting. Marla has always felt the need for artistic expression, enjoying drawing and painting from her earliest years. Her first "real" job was as a costume designer. She is now a graphic artist at Leman Publications, which offers her the opportunity to combine her love of both sewing and art. She has illustrated eight quilt books and enjoys designing quilts. Her other interests include soft sculpture, cooking, camping, gardening, walking, running, reading, and travel.

Louise Townsend started making quilts in 1972, after ending a career in teaching Spanish, English, and history at the junior high school level and at the University of Kansas. She started working at Leman Publications in 1978 and was managing editor of *Quilter's Newsletter Magazine* for six years. She wrote *QNM*'s "Easy Lessons" column for nine years and also was on the staff of *Quiltmaker* magazine. Currently she is a book editor with C & T Publishing in Martinez, California.

Kathryn Wright's mother taught her to sew clothing when she was 11 years old. Her mother also taught her to hand quilt, and Kath began her first quilt at the age of 16 or 17. In October 1987 she joined the Leman Publications staff as an artist and currently is senior art director for *Quilter's Newsletter Magazine*. She enjoys both handwork and machine work, and she prefers piecing over appliqué. She feels that her job is the ideal combination of her interests, from design to sewing to quilting to working with fabric and color.

Other Contributors

Margaret Lydic Balitas is the executive editor of Home and Garden Books at Rodale Press. She has an extensive background in fashion sewing, particularly in pieced contemporary fashions. She is experienced in tailoring techniques and making garment alterations and has an ongoing passion for the art of hand appliqué.

Peggy Beals has had a long-standing interest in quilting, with a background both as a teacher and as a free-lance writer whose articles appear in quilt publications such as *Quilter's Newsletter Magazine*. She loves making appliqué quilts, especially with heart motifs and lots of rich color. She makes wallhangings, crib quilts, and bed-size quilts, and her other interests include rug hooking and gardening.

Jeanne Benson began making quilts in 1978 and has exhibited her work in international juried quilt shows since 1987. She presents workshops and classes regularly through the Smithsonian Resident Associate Program, as well as for guilds and quilt shops. Her book *The Art and Technique of Appliqué* was published in 1991 by EPM Publications of McLean, Virginia.

Kathy Berschneider has a lifelong background in quiltmaking, sewing, and crafts of all kinds.

She designed, constructed, and contributed projects to the book *America's Best Quilting Projects*, published in 1993 by Rodale Press. She has participated in cooperative craft bazaars. She has also designed and constructed display samples for Quilter's Cupboard in Rockford, Illinois, where she has taught a variety of quilting classes. She specializes in teaching children's quiltmaking classes.

Jinny Beyer began quiltmaking in 1972 when she and her family lived in the Orient. It's her feeling that this Eastern exposure has been a great influence in her work. She is the author of six quilt books: *Patchwork Patterns, The Quilter's Album of Blocks and Borders, Medallion Quilts, The Scrap Look, Patchwork Portfolio,* and *Color Confidence for Quilters.* She has produced three videos—"Mastering Patchwork," "Palettes for Patchwork," and "Color Confidence!"—and she designs for RJR Fashion Fabrics, coordinating cotton prints especially for quilters. Jinny teaches and lectures throughout the United States and in many foreign countries. She conducts her own seminar each year on Hilton Head Island, South Carolina. She was born in Colorado, grew up and was educated in California, and received a master of arts degree in special education from Boston University.

Barbara Brackman is a free-lance writer, lecturer, teacher, and museum curator specializing in folk art, especially quilts. Her book *The Encyclopedia of Pieced Quilt Patterns* was published by the American Quilter's Society of Paducah, Kentucky. She is also working on *The Encyclopedia of Appliqué Patterns,* to be published by EPM Publications of McLean, Virginia. Barbara is a contributing editor to *Quilter's Newsletter Magazine.*

Eleanor Burns began to develop her quick, simple approach to sewing and quiltmaking in the 1970s, publishing her first book, *Make a Quilt in a Day (Log Cabin),* to help people learn to produce quiltmaking results quickly and easily. At her Quilt in a Day Center in San Marcos,

California, she has seen her business grow from 50 bolts of fabric to 5,000. In addition to the fabric business, the center houses a teaching program for shop owners and teachers-in-training, video facilities, and the art department where her books are designed and written.

Anne Colvin is a member of the Quilter's Guild of Dallas, and she works and teaches at a local quilt shop. Since 1988 she has published clothing patterns under the name A Quilter's Wardrobe, and her work has been published in *Quilter's Newsletter Magazine* and *Quilting Today*. Her garments have been shown in competitive fashion shows and galleries, and she has won awards from the American Quilter's Society and Silver Dollar City. In 1987 she created a coat and dress that toured internationally with the Fairfield Fashion Show.

Janice G. Cooke became a quilter in 1974, starting to take classes in 1978. Quilting became a full-time profession when she and Rob Benker-Ritchie began Bellwether Enterprises in 1987. They wrote two articles about template appliqué that appeared in *Quilter's Newsletter Magazine* and *American Quilter* magazine. Since Bellwether dissolved in 1990, Janice has taught classes in template appliqué techniques in 15 states, as well as for the American Quilter's Society (AQS) national show and the North Carolina Quilt Symposium. AQS also produced a video in 1989 showcasing template appliqué techniques.

Sharyn Squier Craig holds a bachelor of arts degree in home economics from San Diego State University. She has been a quilter since 1978 and a teacher throughout the United States and internationally since 1980. In 1985 the *Professional Quilter Magazine* named her the Quilt Teacher of the Year in an international competition. She was the president of her local quilt guild for three years and served as the vice president of finance for the American International Quilt Association from 1990 to 1991. Her first book, *Designing New Tradi-*

tions in Quilts, was published by Chitra Publications in 1991.

June Culvey was 11 years old when she took her first quilting stitches with her grandmother. She became a full-fledged quilter in 1978 when she began to make quilts for her children's room. She started making quilts by machine and doing channel quilting. Her interest in appliqué came from seeing a floral appliqué quilt, made by Arlene Statz, in a quilt show held in Sun Prairie, Wisconsin. Her "Tribute to Hallmark" quilt won Best of Show at Sun Prairie, and it is now included in the archives of Hallmark. Her "Tranquil Violets" quilt won Second Place at the American Quilter's Society (AQS) show in 1985 and was named her Master Quilt by the National Quilter's Association (NQA) in 1991. Her "Amish Nod" quilt won First Place at the AQS show in 1986, and "Colored Nectar" won Second Place at the AQS show in 1989. "Golden Camelot" won the Workmanship and First Place awards at the Quilter's Heritage Celebration in Lancaster, Pennsylvania, in 1992; Best of Show at the NQA show in Ohio in 1992; and Third Place at the AQS show in 1992. It also won Best of Show at Dollywood Quilter's Showcase in Pigeon Forge, Tennessee, in 1993.

Rita Denenberg is a contributing editor to *Quilter's Newsletter Magazine*.

Mimi Dietrich enjoys sewing and needlework projects and has been quilting since 1974. She has a degree in American studies from the University of Maryland, Baltimore County. Her career as a high school teacher was short-lived after she discovered the joys of teaching sewing, needlework, appliqué, and quilting. She now teaches Baltimore Album quilt classes in Maryland. She is one of the founders of the Village Quilters in Catonsville, Maryland, and is a member of the Baltimore Heritage Quilters' Guild. Mimi is the author of *Happy Endings: Finishing the Edges of Your Quilt, Handmade Quilts,* and *Baltimore Bouquets,* published by That Patchwork Place, Inc.

Carol Doak is an award-winning quiltmaker and teacher. Her quilts have been exhibited and have received recognition at national shows such as the American Quilter's Society, the National Quilter's Association, the American International Quilter's Association, the Vermont Quilt Festival, and The Quilter's Gathering. Carol's award-winning quilt, "Quilt of Quilts," was featured on the cover of *Quilter's Newsletter Magazine*, and her quilts have also been highlighted in publications such as *Lady's Circle Patchwork Quilts, Traditional Quilter,* and *Quilt World* magazines.

Judy Duerstock has been sewing since the age of 4, and she has made all of her own clothing since she was 11 years old. She has been quilting since 1970 and has taught quilting classes since 1979. She has been a contributing editor to *Quilter's Newsletter Magazine,* specializing in developing quilting techniques. Judy is a native of Miami and has been married for 26 years, with two sons, ages 20 and 12. Her younger son quilts and loves to clean her sewing machine, and her older son helps her install quilt-related software programs on her computer.

Janet Elwin started quilting in 1973 and almost immediately began teaching quilting classes in a night-school adult education program in Arlington, Massachusetts. She is one of the founding members and a past president of the New England Quilter's Guild, and she helped to establish the New England Quilt Museum in 1987. She teaches quilting classes nationally and internationally in Australia, the United Kingdom, and Japan. She constantly revises the content of her classes and creates new techniques. She is the author of the books *Hexagon Magic,* published by EPM Publications in 1987, and *Ode to Grandmother* and *The Celebration Quilt,* which she self-published in 1985 and 1987. Her book *Creative Triangles for Quilters* will be published by Chilton. Janet has developed a line of patterns for sophisticated patchwork skirts, which have at least two or three variations in each pattern. For more information on Janet's patterns, contact Prentiss Cove, HCR #64, Box 012, Damariscotta, ME 04543. She is a contributing editor to *Quilter's Newsletter Magazine.*

Caryl Bryer Fallert is known internationally for her award-winning art quilts, which are distinguished by their scintillating colors and multilevel illusions of movement and light. Most of her current work is made from cotton fabrics, which she hand dyes, paints, and then pieces, appliqués, embroiders, and quilts by machine. Her work has been exhibited extensively throughout the United States, Europe, and Japan, as well as in Singapore and Australia. Her work has also appeared in many national and international publications and in a number of private, corporate, public, and museum collections. Her goal in leading workshops is to provide an atmosphere in which each student can find his or her inner creative potential.

John Flynn became interested in designing a quilt frame in 1981 for his wife, Brooke, who was already a quilter. In the process of designing the frame, he became "hooked" on hand quilting. In 1986 he developed his own trapunto techniques, and in 1989 he started a business to promote his quilt frames and trapunto rods. He began to teach classes in his techniques for making Double Wedding Ring quilts, and he wrote the volume *Double Wedding Ring Step-by-Step Workbook* in 1990. His *Step-by-Step Braided Border* was published in 1991, and in 1992 he published *John Flynn's Step-by-Step Trapunto and Stippling.* His most recent book is *Feathered Sun Quilts,* published in 1993. John travels and lectures nationally and internationally in Holland, England, Australia, and Canada. He continues to refine quilting methods and tools.

Marianne Fons became interested in quilting at the time of the American Bicentennial, when she took her first quilting class. There she met Liz Porter, and the two became friends and began to team-teach quilting classes. Marianne is one of the founders of Heritage Quilters Club. In 1982 she and Liz wrote *Classic Quilted Vests*, and in 1984 they coauthored *Classic Basket Patterns*, both published by Yours Truly, Inc. In 1991 the basket-pattern book was republished by the American Quilter's Society as *Classic Basket Quilts*. Marianne wrote *Fine Feathers* in 1987 and *Let's Make Waves* in 1989, both published by C & T Publishing. Marianne and Liz's first hardcover book, *The Quilter's Complete Guide*, was published by Oxmoor House in 1993. Their second hardcover book, *Quilts from America's Heartland*, was published by Rodale Press in 1994.

Sarah Doolan Gobes was inspired to make her first quilt by the birth of a friend's daughter, who is now in college. During the intervening years, quiltmaking has provided her much joy and satisfaction. Some highlights have been teaching quiltmaking in several states, selling quilts to specialty shops, and participating in juried shows. Most exciting was coauthoring a book, *Not Just Another Quilt*, with three fellow quiltmakers and kindred souls. Sarah later went on to complete her college degree. Five original quilts, which interpreted areas of academic interest, fulfilled her senior project requirements. Her quilts are now even more personal, as she stitches them for grandchildren whom she hopes will inherit her passion for quilting. Sarah is a contributing editor to *Quilter's Newsletter Magazine*.

Tina Gravatt began making miniature quilts in 1985 when she made a doll bed from a kit for her daughter. From there, her enthusiasm for miniatures developed into an ongoing interest and involvement in re-creating American quilts through historically accurate miniatures. While her quilts are diminutive, they contain all the elements of their larger counterparts, from the focal point of the design, to border interests, to quilting in the appropriate style and scale. She exhibits her miniature quilts on doll beds befit-

ting the time periods of the quilts. Tina is a self-taught quilter, a lecturer, a teacher, and the author of two books on miniature quilts, *Heirloom Miniatures* and *Old Favorites in Miniature*, both published by the American Quilter's Society in Paducah, Kentucky.

Mary Green is senior associate editor of Quilt Books at Rodale Press. She has been an avid quilter since 1989 and is a member of a quilt group at her church. She has a background in fashion sewing, and her other interests in needlework range from designing and making original cloth dolls to crocheting and knitting sweaters. She specializes in making patchwork quilts from her own and her husband Stan's original designs.

Stan Green is a graduate of the University of Oregon in the areas of fine arts and design. He was art director for *Backpacker* magazine for four years, photography director for *Bicycling Magazine* for two years, and is currently associate art director for Health and Fitness Books at Rodale Press. He feels that his design experience, coupled with his twenty-year background as a free-lance photographer, has helped him to relate his study of color, shape, and light to the world of quilt design. He has designed more than 70 quilt blocks based primarily on traditional shapes, which have translated into literally hundreds of original quilt designs.

Harriet Hargrave has been involved in quiltmaking in one form or another all her life. She has a degree in textiles and clothing from Colorado State University and began teaching machine arts and quilting for adult education in 1978. In 1980 she and her mother opened their quilt shop, Harriet's Treadle Arts. Since the 1986 publication of her first book, *Heirloom Machine Quilting*, Harriet has been traveling and teaching internationally. Her latest book, *Mastering Machine Appliqué*, has brought quilters complete instructions for both satin stitch and invisible appliqué by machine. She specializes in textiles and batting and has become actively involved in creating new batting for Hobbs Bonded Fibers.

Cyndi Hershey became interested in quilting in 1978 when her daughter was born. She taught herself to quilt using a pattern for a Pennsylvania Dutch Tulip pillow from *Family Circle Magazine*. She still has her first project and shows it to students in her quilting classes today. In 1987 Cyndi began to teach adult education classes in quilting, and in 1989 she became the owner of the Country Quilt Shop, 3303 Limekiln Pike, Chalfont, PA 18914. She has a strong background in design and loves to teach both design and color for quilters. She lectures widely throughout Pennsylvania, New Jersey, and New York.

Roberta Horton of Berkeley, California, holds a bachelor of science degree in home economics from the University of California at Berkeley. She began teaching quiltmaking in 1972 in the San Francisco Bay Area and now spends a good part of each year traveling across the United States to lecture and teach at quilt guilds, museums, and symposia. She has also taught in Canada, Japan, New Zealand, Australia, South Africa, the Netherlands, Denmark, and Germany. Her book *An Amish Adventure: A Workbook for Color in Quilts* was published in 1983, and in 1984 her next book, *Calico and Beyond: The Use of Patterned Fabric in Quilts*, appeared. In 1988 Roberta began to design plaid and striped fabrics for Fabric Sales Company (FASCO) of Seattle, Washington; her creations include the Lines Collection, inspired by the wonderful plaids and stripes in antique quilts, and the Mood Indigo Collection, inspired by antique Japanese textiles. In 1990 she authored *Plaids and Stripes: The Use of Directional Fabric in Quilts*.

Marjorie Kerr has been a quiltmaker since 1955. In 1973 she began to teach patchwork, appliqué, and quilting, and in 1978, after seeing her first Hawaiian quilt, she began to teach that subject, as well. (Deborah Kakalia of Honolulu, Hawaii, is responsible for Marjorie's commitment to teaching Hawaiian quilting as it has been done in the Hawaiian Islands for more than 100 years.) In 1982 she had an appliquéd sampler quilt and block patterns published in *Better Homes and Gardens Treasury of Needlecraft*. Most of her quilt articles deal with Hawaiian quilting, and her "Kaiulani's Fan and Crown" quilt appeared on the cover of the July/August 1986 issue of *Quilter's Newsletter Magazine*. This quilt was also published in *Textiles as Art*, by Lawrence Korwin, in 1990. Her contemporary memory quilt, "Erin's Quilt," was published in *Memory Quilts*, by Nancy Smith and Lynda Milligan, in 1991.

Jeana Kimball pieced her first quilt top at the age of 12 while learning how to use a sewing machine. By 1981 she was teaching quilting classes at a local quilt shop, and in 1984 she designed her first appliqué quilt. Her appliqué publications include *Reflections of Baltimore, Red and Green: An Appliqué Tradition* and *Appliqué Borders: An Added Grace*. As a continuation of the quiltmaking process, she wrote about the process of hand quilting in her book *Loving Stitches: A Guide to Hand Quilting*. Today she travels and teaches extensively throughout the United States, Europe, and Australia. All of her books, as well as patterns for many of her designs, needles, and other sewing supplies, are available from her company, Foxglove Cottage, P.O. Box 18294, Salt Lake City, UT 84118.

Mickey Lawler has been a contributing editor to *Quilter's Newsletter Magazine* and specializes in hand painting fabrics and selling them through her own business, called Skydyes.

Gwen Marston is a professional quiltmaker, author, and teacher who has written three books, coauthored seven books, and produced eight videos on quiltmaking. She has been a regular columnist for *Lady's Circle Patchwork*

Quilts magazine for seven years and is currently writing a series on drafting quilting designs for that publication. Her books, *Amish Quilting Patterns* and *70 Classic Quilting Patterns*, were published by Dover, and the American Quilter's Society published her book on drafting quilting designs, *Quilting with Style*, in 1993. For ten years Gwen has offered quilting retreats at her Beaver Island home on Lake Michigan. Her quilts have been shown in many exhibits throughout the United States, and a selection from her collection of more than 150 small quilts has been exhibited by seven museums over the past several years. Her work is represented by the Tamarack Craftsman Gallery in Omena, Michigan.

Judy Martin has been a quilter for 24 years. She is the author of nine quilt books, including *Yes You Can! Make Stunning Quilts from Simple Patterns*, published by Crosley-Griffiths Corporation. She was an editor at both *Quilter's Newsletter Magazine* and *Quiltmaker* magazine for eight years. She has had a long-standing interest in scrap quilts, and her most recent work involves adapting quick techniques to make scrap quilts of uncompromising beauty.

Nancy J. Martin, talented author, teacher, and quiltmaker, has written more than 20 books on quiltmaking. The ever-popular *Pieces of the Past* explores quilting history. *A Dozen Variables, Back to Square One*, and *Ocean Waves*, coauthored by Marsha McCloskey, were written with the development of the Bias Square cutting ruler and technique. *Rotary Riot* and *Rotary Roundup*, two best-sellers on quick cutting, have earned Nancy and coauthor Judy Hopkins the title "Queens of Rotary Cutting." Nancy, president of That Patchwork Place, Inc., still makes time in her busy schedule for teaching, something she has been enjoying for more than 18 years.

Mary Mashuta has a love of fabric and color that began during her childhood and led to two degrees in home economics. She has been an active member of the San Francisco Bay Area quilt community since the early 1970s, and in 1985 she began to work full-time on quilt-related interests, including teaching, writing, and designing. She has taught nationally and internationally in Canada, South Africa, and Japan. She is the author of the book *Wearable Art for Real People* and has participated in the Fairfield Fashion Show. Her garments have won awards in the American Quilter's Society Annual Fashion Show. Her articles on studios, wearables, and quilts have appeared in *Quilter's Newsletter Magazine, American Quilter, Lady's Circle Patchwork Quilts*, and *Threads* magazines. She has also been featured in Japanese, French, and South African magazines. The author of *Story Quilts: Telling Your Tale in Fabric*, Mary is currently working on a book about creating optical patterns with stripes in quilts.

Judy Mathieson became interested in quiltmaking in 1973 while completing a bachelor of science degree in home economics-textiles and clothing at California State University, Northridge. She began teaching quiltmaking in 1977, and today she teaches regularly at local Los Angeles fabric shops, as well as lectures and conducts workshops throughout the United States for quilt guilds and conferences. She has also taught internationally in Canada and Japan. The National Quilting Association has given her a certificate in Judging and an award as a teacher of Basic Quiltmaking. Selected for the Quilt National juried show in Athens, Ohio, in 1979, 1981, and 1987, Judy's quilts are shown on Quilt National's poster and in the catalogs *The New American Quilt* and *Fiber Expressions*. She has been interviewed on Georgia Bonesteel's public television program "Lap Quilting," and her work is frequently featured in *Quilter's Newsletter Magazine*. Judy's book *Mariner's Compass: An American Quilt Classic* was published in 1987 by C & T Publishing of Martinez, California.

Marsha McCloskey has been quilting since 1969. A graphic arts major in college, she turned from printmaking to quiltmaking because motherhood and family responsibilities made the messier medium impractical. Marsha's designs concentrate on the use of multiple fabrics, rotary-cutting methods, and machine piecing, and her quilts can be made by the average quilter. She started teaching in 1975 and teaches nationally as well as internationally in Australia, Belgium, and Holland. Her first pattern book, *Small Quilts*, was published in 1982 by That Patchwork Place, Inc., and her other titles include *Wall Quilts* (re-released by Dover in 1983), *20 Projects for Blocks and Borders* (1985), *Christmas Quilts* (re-released by Dover in 1985), *Feathered Star Quilts* (1987, out of print), *Stars and Stepping Stones* (1989), *Lessons in Machine Piecing* (1990), and *On to Square Two* (1992). With Nancy J. Martin, she coauthored *A Dozen Variables* in 1987 and *Back to Square One* in 1988. Her new book, *100 Pieced Patterns for 8" Quilt Blocks*, was published in 1993.

Diana McClun was handed her first needle, thread, and piece of fabric at the age of seven, and since then her love of quilts has flourished and grown to become a full-time career. She earned a degree in clothing and textiles from the University of Idaho and San Francisco State University and studied art at San Jose State University. Her first one-woman quilt show was held at Diablo Valley College in 1980, just before she opened her quilt shop, Empty Spools, in Alamo, California. Diana searched for the finest teachers and held shows of both students' and guest artists' quilts in her shop. The 1983 Made in America show featured handmade quilts, decorative clothing, needlework, and crafts, ranging from French handsewn layettes to elaborate appliquéd heirloom quilts—all created by Empty Spools teachers and staff members. Diana soon began to hold five-day quilting seminars in which students could study with quilt artists from around the world, and

her seminar business continues to grow. With Laura Nownes, she wrote *Quilts, Quilts, Quilts!* and *Quilts Galore*.

Susan McKelvey is a quilt artist, teacher, and author of the books *A Treasury of Quilt Labels*, *Color for Quilters*, *The Color Workbook*, *Light and Shadows*, *Friendship's Offering*, and *Scrolls and Banners to Trace*. She earned a bachelor of arts degree in English and drama from Cornell College and a master of arts degree in English and education from the University of Chicago. Her great love in quilting is color and helping quilters to use color effectively in their work. Susan has been a quilter since 1977, and her work has appeared in museums, galleries, and quilt shows throughout the United States, as well as in magazines and books. She formed her own company, Wallflower Designs, in 1987 to design and produce supplies and patterns for quilters who want to write on quilts.

Sheila Meyer started making quilts in 1970 and taught classes in quilting for West Hartford Continuing Education from 1977 to 1988. From 1990 to 1992 she coordinated a program called Project Comfort, which involved making quilts for people at a homeless shelter. Her quilts have been exhibited in a one-woman show in Simsbury, Connecticut, in 1983; in the Quilts Today exhibit at the University of Connecticut library in Storrs, Connecticut, in 1984; and the Emerging Quiltmakers exhibit at the Columbus, Ohio, Cultural Arts Center in 1984. She is coauthor, with Mickey Lawler, Judy Robbins, and Sarah Gobes, of *Not Just Another Quilt*, published in 1982 by Van Nostrand Reinhold. She is a contributing editor to *Quilter's Newsletter Magazine*.

Margaret Miller is a studio quilter who travels widely, lectures, and holds workshops on color and design to encourage students to "reach for the unexpected" in contemporary quiltmaking. Margaret learned to appliqué and quilt in 1978 while she was on the faculty of the home economics department at California Polytechnic

State University, San Luis Obispo, teaching a class in creative textiles. She later moved to San Diego, where she started a pattern business, Tanglethread Junction, featuring appliqué and stained glass designs. In 1982 she sold the business and made the commitment to become a full-time quiltmaker. Many of her quilts are displayed and sold through galleries and art consultants. Her teaching schedule has taken her on travels throughout the United States, as well as to New Zealand, Australia, and South Africa.

Debbie Mumm is a quilt designer and illustrator with her own pattern company, Mumm's the Word. She has a loyal and devoted following for her creative country-style designs, and she has earned a reputation for writing accurate and reliable pattern instructions. Since attending the International Quilt Market in 1986, her business has grown to include a support staff of six employees, and her pattern line now consists of 80 quilt and craft patterns and 22 stationery items. Her first book, *Quick Country Quilting*, was published in 1991 by Rodale Press. Her projects feature a combination of quick-cutting and sewing techniques that appeal to quilters of all skill levels. She is currently working on several new projects, including a sequel to her first book.

Suzanne Nelson is senior editor of Rodale Quilt Books. A firm believer that quiltmaking is one of the best forms of therapy available, she has spent the past five years "in therapy," stitching pieced and appliquéd quilts to cover all the beds, walls, and practically any other available surface in her house. She is working hard to pass the joy of quilting on to her two young daughters, each of whom began a fabric collection at the tender age of two.

Anne Oliver became interested in quilting in the mid-1970s when she saw a quilt show in a bank in California. She looked at the quilts and said to herself, "I could do better than that,"

and then taught herself to make quilts. She has an early background in sewing garments and feels that a sewing background promotes the discipline necessary to complete a quilt, whether by machine or by hand. Her "Four Seasons" Album quilt, made in 1980, is a portrayal of her life, with each block representing a nice memory in simple appliqué. Her trademark is to put a great deal of quilting in each of her quilts. Her 1989 "Painted Metal Ceiling" quilt is the third quilt in a series and is an example of architectural ceiling plates taken from old tin ceilings of the early 1900s. "Mama's Garden," made in 1991, was taken from a Mennonite pattern for a whitework quilt. It won Best of Show at the 1992 American Quilter's Society show and is a permanent part of the Museum of the American Quilter's Society in Paducah, Kentucky. It also won Best of Show at the Quilter's Heritage Celebration in Lancaster, Pennsylvania, in 1992. Anne feels that her purpose in the world of quilting is to help average quilters gain the confidence and the ability to finish their quilts and be proud of their own work.

Nancy Pearson was trained at the American Academy of Art and the School of the Art Institute of Chicago. She worked as a graphic artist for 9 years before becoming a quiltmaker. Her design background and her quest for quality craftsmanship have brought her numerous awards for her appliqué quilts and designs. Nancy's most notable quilts are "Techny Chimes" and "Nancy's Garden," both multiribbon winners that have been featured in the pages of *Quilter's Newsletter Magazine*. She has been teaching quiltmaking for 11 years, both nationally and internationally.

Mary Coyne Penders began teaching quiltmaking in 1975 in the Washington, D.C., area. Since then she has taught at major conferences, symposia, guilds, museums, embassies, and shops throughout the United States, as well as in Australia, Canada, Denmark, England, Holland, Germany, New Zealand, and Norway. Described as an "ambassador of quilting," Mary uses her interest in women's textile and social traditions to infuse her workshops and lectures with cross-cultural enrichment. In 1982 she wrote *Quilts in the Classroom: A Guide to Successful Teaching*, which became a widely respected textbook for planning classes and managing a quilt-teaching business. Her book *Color and Cloth* was published by The Quilt Digest Press in 1989, and her three-book series *Quilts from Simple Shapes* appeared in 1991. Mary's traveling and teaching schedule keeps her involved in research on the state of quilt-making around the world, and her writing appears frequently in *Quilter's Newsletter Magazine, American Quilter, Lady's Circle Patchwork Quilts,* and *The Professional Quilter.*

Liz Porter has been quilting since 1975 and is a self-taught, third-generation quilter. Her association with Marianne Fons began in 1976, when they began to team-teach classes in basic quilting. Their first book, *Classic Quilted Vests,* was published in 1982 and was followed in 1984 by *Classic Basket Patterns,* both published by Yours Truly, Inc. The latter book is now available as a revised edition called *Classic Basket Quilts,* published by the American Quilter's Society. Liz has been a contributing editor on a regular basis to *American Quilter* magazine and also maintains a schedule of national and international lectures and classes. She and Marianne have designed a line of fabrics especially for quilters, based on authentic designs from the late 1800s, for Piney Woods Prints.

Mary Reddick is a fourth-generation quilter on both sides of the family. One of her family quilts was shown in the Texas Sesquicentennial Exhibit in 1986. She has been the treasurer, the quilt show chairwoman, and the newsletter editor for the American International Quilt Association. For one year she was the executive director of the Texas Sesquicentennial Association. She has been teaching at Great Expectations quilt shop in Houston for the past seven years and has also lectured and conducted workshops in the greater Houston area. Her articles have been published in *Quilter's Newsletter Magazine, Quilt Talks, Quilt, Country Quilts,* and *The Professional Quilter* magazines. Mary was the first person to actually write about working with children and quilting, in her article "Quilting Goes to School" in *QNM.*

Rob Benker-Ritchie is a podiatrist practicing in Massachusetts. He developed the technique for template appliqué in December 1981 while watching a Bruins hockey game. The first project on which he tried it was a full-size Dresden Plate quilt. The technique worked so well, he took the quilt into a quilt store, where he met Janice G. Cooke. They discussed the merits of template appliqué, but did nothing more with developing the technique until 1985, when they coauthored an article that was later published by the American Quilter's Society magazine. Eventually they formed a business called Bellwether Enterprises to promote the technique and sell supplies.

Judy Robbins is a Connecticut quiltmaker, writer, and counselor. From the time her children were born in the early 1970s until they were in their teens, she taught quiltmaking and wrote about quilts. She recently completed a master's degree and now works as a psychotherapist.

Sue Rodgers is a native of St. Louis, Missouri. She taught herself to quilt by making crib quilts for her children in the 1960s. Her love of hand quilting led her to trapunto, and her work in this style has won numerous awards. She has written and published extensively, including a book, *Trapunto: The Handbook of Stuffed Quilting,* published in 1990 by Moon Over the

Mountain. Her quilt "Shalom" placed second in Quilts: Vision of the World, The First International Quilt Competition, held in Salzburg, Austria, in 1988. Sue teaches trapunto, appliqué, and hand quilting, and she sells her work through exhibitions and on commission. Her quilts are in private collections and that of the Port Authority of New York and New Jersey. She recently moved to a new home in Princeton, New Jersey, where she is designing her first real quilt studio/teaching space.

Helen Whitson Rose is a native of Birmingham, Alabama, and has been interested in quiltmaking since 1975. Her first book, *Quilting with Strips and Strings*, was published by Dover in 1983, and her second book, *Quick and Easy Strip Quilting*, appeared in 1989. Her articles and patterns have appeared in magazines such as *Decorating and Craft Ideas*, *Quilt World*, *Stitch 'n Sew Quilts*, *Quick and Easy Quilting*, and *Crafts 'n Things*. Her original design "Pink Dogwood," a pieced flower, appeared in the book *A Garden of Quilts*, by Mary Elizabeth Johnson. Helen feels that she is a "process person" because of her interests in designing quilts, working with color, and figuring out construction processes, and she manages to have a quilt in the making at all times.

Mary Klett Ryan is a designer, teacher, and judge whose award-winning work has been featured in magazines and on the cover of *Quilter's Newsletter Magazine*. She has been a board member of local, state, New England, and American International Quilt Association guilds. She is a member of the Board of Trustees of the Vermont Quilt Festival, and she is cofounder with Jan Snelling of the Vermont Classic Weekend Seminars for Quilters. She also is owner of and designer for a line of patterns called Mary K. Ryan Designs, which include pieced star designs such as Mariner's Compass, Persian Star, Feathered Star, Carolina Lily, Paramount Stars, and several others. For more information,

contact Mary K. Ryan Designs, 23 Grandview Terrace, Rutland, VT 05701; (802) 773-6563.

Elly Sienkiewicz has combined her love of history, religion, art, and needlework with her expertise on the Baltimore Album quilts of the nineteenth century. In her eight-volume *Baltimore Beauties* series, published by C & T Publishing, Elly uses her connoisseur's enthusiasm to probe the artistic, technical, historic, and philosophical depths of these antebellum appliqué Albums. Her other books include the phenomenally popular *Appliqué 12 Easy Ways! Charming Quilts, Giftable Projects, and Timeless Techniques* and the upcoming *Appliqué a Paper Greeting! 50 Inexpensive, Easy-to-Make Cards and Gifts for Crafters of All Ages*, which reflects her fondness for the Victorian decorative mode and warmth of written expression. Degrees from Wellesley College and the University of Pennsylvania led Elly to a teaching career in history, social studies, and English. After her children were born, she pursued a number of entrepreneurial endeavors from home, teaching quiltmaking and running a mail-order quilt supply business for seven years. She is in great demand as a teacher, writer, designer, and lecturer. With the exception of her first, self-published book, all of Elly's books are available from C & T Publishing, P.O. Box 1456, Martinez, CA 94549.

Doreen Speckmann started making quilts in 1977, after years of knitting, crocheting, cross-stitching, spinning, Hardanger, and needlepoint. She is noted for her innovative adaptations of traditional patterns and her use of "Peaky and Spike" to create the illusion of curves from straight pieces. Doreen is becoming increasingly well known for her sense of humor and often offbeat perspective on quilting. She travels and teaches extensively nationally and internationally in Australia and Canada. Each year she leads quilters' cruises to the Caribbean and Alaska, as well as tours to England, Norway, and Australia. Her book *Patternplay* was published in 1993 by C & T Publishing. For information about her teaching schedule, contact Doreen Speckmann, 3118 Cross Street, Madison, WI 53711.

Kay Steinmetz owns Quilter's Cupboard, 4614 E. State Street, Rockford, IL 61108. She has had a lifelong interest in needle arts. Since discovering quilting in 1978, she has devoted all of her time and effort to promoting this medium. She has taken classes from experts such as Jinny Beyer, Eleanor Burns, Sharyn Squier Craig, Mary Ellen Hopkins, Judith Montano, Elly Sienkiewicz, and Doreen Speckmann. She purchased Quilter's Cupboard in 1990 and has lectured and taught extensively throughout northern Illinois and southern Wisconsin since that time.

Jane Townswick has been interested in quiltmaking since 1983. She owned Quilter's Cupboard quilt shop in Rockford, Illinois, and taught classes in quilting and appliqué from 1987 to 1990, when she began a career in editing at Chitra Publications' *Traditional Quiltworks* magazine. She is currently a senior associate editor in needlecrafts at Rodale Press.

Debra Wagner has been a machine embroiderer for more than 20 years and calls herself a traditionalist in design if not in technique. Her main interest is in developing machine methods that duplicate hand techniques. She is a three-time First Place winner and a one-time Second Place winner at the American Quilter's Society show, and in 1990 she also won the Viewer's Choice Award. Her quilt "Rail through the Rockies" won the Masters Guild Award of the National Quilting Association in 1992, and her work appears on the cover of the Singer Reference Library book *Machine Quilting*. Debra does commissioned work for corporations, as well as individuals, and her work has been displayed in the United States, Europe, and Japan. She teaches on both the national and international levels, and she is

the author of *Teach Yourself Machine Piecing and Quilting*, published by Chilton, and *Striplate Piecing*, published by the American Quilter's Society.

Valda Whitman has been a judge at the Marin County Quilt and Needlework Show and has been teaching quilting for more than ten years. She also has been a contributing editor to *Quilter's Newsletter Magazine*. Her "From Darkness into Light" quilt was accepted into a quilt show in Holland in 1990 and was subsequently published in a book called *Quilter's Feelings* in Holland. She loves making a wide variety of quilts and has won ribbons for both her appliqué and pieced quilts. She enjoys taking a traditional pattern and "bending" it to create something new.

Joen Wolfrom enjoys creating both traditional quilts and contemporary textile art. In the past ten years, she has devoted much of her time to commissioned landscape quilts and abstract curved designs, while at the same time making an extensive study of color in nature. She teaches and lectures nationally and internationally on landscape design, color, curved designs and techniques, abstract design, innovative designs for traditional quilts, and creativity. Joen is the author of *Landscapes and Illusions* and *The Magical Effects of Color*, published by C & T Publishing. For information on her lectures and workshops, write to Joen at 104 Bon Bluff, Fox Island, WA 98333.

Lynn Lewis Young is involved professionally in many aspects of quiltmaking. She travels, teaches, and lectures extensively on all facets of quilting, including technique, design, fabric dyeing, surface design, and the appreciation of antique quilts. She writes for quilt publications, has worked for the International Quilt Festival and Quilt Market, and has served on the boards of many quilt organizations. Currently she edits the newsletter of the Studio Art Quilt Associates. Lynn holds a bachelor of arts degree in biology and chemistry from the University of Texas in

Austin. She also pursued graduate studies in biomedical research, earning a master of science degree from the University of Texas Health Science Center. She received her art training at the Glassell School of Art, Museum of Fine Art, in Houston, where she is completing a certificate with a concentration in jewelry. She has studied quiltmaking with such artists as Virginia Avery, Nancy Crow, Nancy Halpern, Michael James, Ruth McDowell, Jan Myers-Newbury, and Yvonne Porcella. Lynn has been included in the Fairfield Fashion Show for three years and has participated in the American Quilter's Society Fashion Show for five years, winning an honorable mention in 1991. Her quilts have been included in juried and judged shows in the United States, Europe, and Japan.

Cindy Zlotnik Oravecz teaches and writes about quiltmaking for many quilting publications. She specializes in three-dimensional flowers for appliqué album quilts and uses her own realistic flowers. She teaches her own simplified methods of flower making, "Flowers by the Strip," and welcomes workshop inquiries at 137 Winter Lane, Cortland, OH 44410.

Index

Note: Page references in *italic* indicate tables.